WAR AS AN INSTRUMENT OF NATIONAL POLICY

AND ITS RENUNCIATION IN THE PACT OF PARIS

By

JAMES T. SHOTWELL

Writing both as historian and philosopher, James T. Shotwell has developed in this book an original and profound study of the whole history and nature of war. He shows the vital part it has played in human affairs and makes clear why it has been impossible to end it, or even do without it, in the past. He also makes clear why all reality today is working with those who have now set themselves the task of bringing war at last to an end. He lays down the strategy by which the civilized nations must, can, and gradually will, bring peace to the world.

The book also recites the story of the Pact of Paris (the recently signed Kellogg treaty), and submits that great anti-war treaty to an analysis and exposition that is so detailed and penetrating that it may be accepted by students as final and authoritative. This agreement to renounce war as an instrument of national policy in which fifty nations are participating, has often been associated, especially in the mind of Europe, with the work which Mr. Shotwell has done as technical expert in this field; and the present volume sums up his views on the whole negotiation.

James T. Shotwell, Professor of History at Columbia University, has had an unrivalled opportunity in the last ten years to study war and peace. He was the first Chairman of the National Board of Historical Service; he was a member of the American Commission at the Paris Peace Conference; he is a present director of the Carnegie Endowment *Economic and Social History of the World War*. Since the war, he has lived much in Europe and has been in closest contact with the statesmen engaged in the task of reconstruction and international affairs.

Harcourt, Brace and Company
383 MADISON AVENUE, NEW YORK

WAR AS AN INSTRUMENT
OF NATIONAL POLICY
AND ITS RENUNCIATION
IN THE PACT OF PARIS

WAR AS AN INSTRUMENT
OF NATIONAL POLICY

AND ITS RENUNCIATION
IN THE PACT OF PARIS

BY JAMES T. SHOTWELL

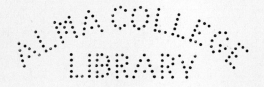

HARCOURT, BRACE AND COMPANY

NEW YORK

PREFACE

THE generation that has endured the World War has at last come to grips with the problem of war itself. The movement to eliminate it from international dealings is not based upon sentiment nor emotion, although they may fortify its purpose; it is gaining rather than losing in strength as the poignant memories of the war grow fainter, because it embodies the major lesson of the whole vast tragic experience, that as between the highly civilized nations war has become a futile instrument incapable of direction and therefore criminal in use. A new attitude is forcing its way in international politics,—as it also is revealing itself in the world of business and internal economics,—one which seeks to substitute for ruthless competition some measure of coöperation, so that each member of the community of nations may have a larger share in an increasing common good. This change in attitude is itself a fact of history.

The renunciation of war, however, even if only as the instrument of national policy, establishes a new basis for international law. It strikes at that anarchy of nations which permitted under the pretext of national interest the old predatory world of conquest and violence. That era is now passing; governments repudiate it because the peoples whom they represent insist upon its repudiation. The instruments of international justice are not yet perfected, and the Pact of Paris leaves this problem unsolved, but henceforth, with the arbitrament of war no longer permitted and all disputes referred to settlement "by pacific means," those means will be developed through the practical experience of the coming years. Whether or not the new structure of international affairs is to be imbedded in a code of laws or in the uncodified practice of peaceful dealings,

v

is a speculation which lies beyond the horizon at this moment; but it is clear to any but one blinded by legalistic tradition that the realm of international law will gain in both extent and authority in proportion as the anarchy of nations gives way to conceptions of a community of interest, and the extravagant assertion of absolute sovereignty no longer blocks the path of ultimate justice.

Patriotism, too, is throwing off those tribal prejudices which carried into the modern world the barbarian attitude toward foreigners. It is becoming a more civilized thing, but none the less effective. There is no need to fear that patriotism will be lessened if based upon intelligence instead of merely upon emotion; intelligence alone can supply the ideals which furnish the inspiration to the citizen in a world so constantly changing as that which has been brought into being by the inventions of modern science. The old-time patriotism that repeated without analysis the prejudices of the past was suitable as a guide only to those nations whose present problems were also simply repetitions of their past. But that is no longer the situation in the civilized world. The age which has achieved a mastery over time and space has no parallel anywhere in the human past. Problems of the present and future are, it is true, rooted in history, but their solution does not lie in a repetition of its experiences. The new and uncharted course upon which we have embarked calls for intelligence in patriotism, and intelligence in turn calls for the relinquishment of the unintelligent procedure which is war.

The history which follows is largely documentary. But where the documents are so few, as in this case, the student of history must read between the lines, or rather between the documents. For instance, from April 6, when M. Briand made his initial statement, to the twentieth of June, when he submitted his formal draft of a treaty to the American Government, there

were other things going on. This was even more true of the six
months' interval which elapsed before the American Government replied. In the pages which follow, reference is made
from time to time to the efforts on the part of private citizens
which finally secured government action, but it is impossible to
review here all of this story of unofficial effort. It is, however,
the opinion of those who watched it develop, that the rising tide
of public opinion, voiced in Congress by the Resolutions of
Senator Capper and Senator Borah, and others in the House
of Representatives, is directly responsible for the negotiations
which led to the Pact of Paris.

It was not only in the United States but in France and Great
Britain as well, and also in Germany, that public opinion showed
itself in advance of the action of governments. The impatience
of the British press over the slow decisions of the Foreign
Office, which delayed a month and more before replying, found
expression in all but the most conservative press. On the Continent and in Japan, public opinion played a similar rôle. In the
case of Japan this was of peculiar significance, as matters so
vital as these had previously been left in the hands of the Elder
Statesmen, and the discussion of them subdued to the dominant
note of authority.

The conclusion to be drawn from this short page of history
is that the World War has, after all, taught its full lesson to
the generation that has suffered from it. The will to peace is
paramount in the civilized world; and it is in this fact that the
strength of the Pact of Paris resides. But at the same time a
world that has been disillusioned so often in the effort to realize
its ideals will demand, in some form or other, either now or
in the future, that the test of history and experience be applied
to the proposed reform itself. There is all but universal agreement on the need for war-renunciation by the civilized Powers,
but the tragic failures of the past—I speak of the period prior
to the World War—have left a doubt as to whether the reform

can actually be achieved or not. The question is therefore not any longer a moral issue, since there is practical agreement as to what should be done; it is almost wholly a matter of ways and means, examined cautiously but fairly, and in the light of the ultimate purpose to be attained. The Pact of Paris must be judged, not merely as an expression of international morals, as some of its friends have tried to interpret it, but as the effective embodiment of political realities; unless it has some practical value, it has little value at all. The present study is an attempt to apply these tests of practicality in terms of both history and contemporary politics. It is not intended to be either an apologia for or a defense of the treaty, but an analysis of it and the diplomatic history which it involved, so that the judgments passed upon it may have the corrective of the historical outlook.

Acknowledgments are due to the New York *Times,* the New York *Herald Tribune,* the New York *World, The Century* and *Foreign Affairs,* for permission to use portions of articles previously published.

JAMES T. SHOTWELL.

New York,
October 14, 1928.

CONTENTS

APPENDICES

PART ONE

HISTORICAL PERSPECTIVES

CHAPTER I

THE PROBLEM

On the twenty-seventh of August, 1928, a historic event took place in the hall of the Foreign Office in Paris. The governments of fifteen nations signed on that day a treaty by which they renounced the right to use war as an instrument of their national policies, and invited all the other nations of the world to give their adherence to the same great act of renunciation. The whole world watched the ceremony, as the Foreign Ministers of France and Germany, in the presence of the representatives of the other Powers, subscribed to this far-reaching principle of international peace. But although the act itself was as simple as the terms of the renunciation, the world that watched it saw it through different eyes. In every country comment ranged all the way from denunciation of it as hypocritical demagoguery to the enthusiastic endorsement of it as the realization of the supreme ideals of morals and religion. Between these extremes of those whose minds were already made up beforehand, lay the great body of public opinion, rejecting alike the cynic and the ultra-pacifist, insisting upon the acceptance of the act but haunted by doubts as to its effectiveness in a wicked world and not less troubled as to its exact meaning. These elements of hesitation were not strong enough to check the movement of assent; but the questions which were raised in the great debate have not yet been solved. The debate itself has somewhat subsided in the succeeding weeks and months, for the world must go about its everyday affairs, affairs still fraught here and there with the danger of war; but this only means that the question has been thrown back now from diplomacy to

3

legislatures, and that when they take up the question of ratification the peoples represented by these governments will once more have to come to conclusions with this unprecedented proposal.

One thing is clear; the generation that has endured the realities of the World War will demand that the strategy of peace shall be real also. This is not only true of the generation as a whole, but it is true of the different countries in proportion as they have suffered and endured. Humanity cannot afford to trust its wistful hopes to anything, however promising, that may betray it in the hour of crisis; nor is it likely that the instrument of war so bravely denounced will be actually discarded if nations still believe that the use of this instrument is essential to them. The meaning of the Pact of Paris is, therefore, to be found not solely or even mostly in the text itself but rather in the study of the history of civilization and a survey of the practical politics of the immediate present. If war has been with us since the beginning of time, it will only yield to forces stronger than itself; whether these really exist in the world today or not is as much the subject of this inquiry as the story of the Pact itself.

The full treatment of this subject would carry us very far afield indeed; for it would call for nothing less than an analysis of civilization itself, civilization with war in it and a hypothetical future with war no longer functioning as it has throughout all the centuries of history. It would involve something more than the actual history of war, for the place of war in history is a much larger one than that of actual conflict. War has been in the background of most policies of state down to our own day, so much so that its constant menace has been taken for granted by historians as a commonplace of politics and thus has escaped attention and analysis. It has never yet been dealt with by students of either history or political science. No one knows, and perhaps no one will ever know, the full extent of the influences upon civilization exerted by the fact that the decisions of international politics have been so largely reached through the arbitrament of the sword. We cannot go so far afield in this short survey as these problems would lead; but there is no solving the problem before us unless we keep in mind these historical elements which still persist within and then test their continuing strength by an analysis of those other forces in the modern world which seem to be giving to the movement of international peace a reality and power still more effective than that which has lain behind the instrument of war.

It is, after all, this last element of the problem which is of supreme importance, how to measure the movements of our own day. Unfortunately, there are no such tests to apply here as history supplies when events have already yielded up their ultimate meaning. The peace movement has not yet revealed its full possibilities and is only now gathering momentum in the field of practical politics. But it will become clear from what follows that we are passing from the theoretic beginnings to the practical and definite application of a great reform, and that in spite of all the pressure of accumulated experience, which tends to drag the world back to the routine of the past, the outlines of a new community of nations are emerging before our eyes and the formulation of its principles have passed from the stage of academic discussion to that of political reality.

It may take a generation yet, or even more, before the civilized nations can be sure that they have really turned the corner in this great enterprise; for if it takes a century for nations like France and Britain to assure themselves the gains of an internal revolution, it will undoubtedly take longer for the whole world to appropriate to itself this revolution, which reaches to the very base of international relationships.

In fact, it is by no means clear that the whole world is ready for the proposal to renounce war as an instrument of national policy. Where a people is in a semi-barbarous state, force, either

applied or held in reserve, is the very condition of peace itself.
International peace is applicable only to responsible governments that are able to comply with the conditions of the new
régime. It is a wholly false conception of international peace
that makes it merely synonymous with a renunciation of war.
The new régime of pacific relations is not of this negative
character. It does not lessen our international obligations, but
on the contrary it is in proportion as the isolation of states is
given up that the renunciation of war becomes a factor in real
politics.

The movement to rid the world of war is therefore one of
those major changes in human affairs which in the very nature
of the case can never be fully embodied in any one slight document, however much that document may stimulate the imagination or contribute to the basic ideals of a new world structure.
Even the Covenant of the League of Nations is only a single
chapter in the transformation now under way. Similarly, the
Pact of Paris is only a part of a larger whole. Even if it be all
that can be claimed for it, it still remains far short of a complete
embodiment of reform. No historical analysis is needed but
merely common sense to withhold assent from those who would
hail the Pact of Paris as marking that single point of time in
which the world turns from darkness to light.

The paeans of triumph which have found expression in
certain quarters tend to make one hesitate to grant even a just
measure of appreciation to the treaty. The statement that this
is the natal day of peace—meaning the day of the American
proposal—is just the kind of expression that tends to turn
any serious student in history toward more conservative ap-
praisals. The realization of international peace is a very different thing from the formulation of a denunciation of war;
nations which live under the shadow of possible and impending
war know only too well the difference between the general
statement of their ideals and the practical application in forms

that will safeguard them against the bitter disillusionment of all their hopes in the hour of crisis. But while withholding our superlatives with reference to any specific proposal, the fact remains that the world is in the midst of a revolution in international affairs which, if it is destined to succeed, is even farther reaching in its consequences than the revolutions that established self-government within the states themselves. The issues which it presents cannot be solved by any rapid legerdemain of cleverness in diplomacy or by that simple idealism that blinks realities.

But although the Pact of Paris is in itself only the embodiment of a single phase of the movement to eliminate international war, it has so challenged the imagination of the world as to become—for the day at least—a sort of symbol of the larger movement. One does not learn the meaning of a symbol by regarding it alone. Therefore, before we take up the story of the negotiations and discuss the documents themselves, we shall pause for a moment to get our bearings by an examination of both the rôle of war in history and those new facts which tend to make it henceforth an anachronism.

CHAPTER II

WAR IN HISTORY·

THOSE who talk in a light-hearted way of the easy task of eliminating war from the state system of the world have little idea
of the extent to which that institution has been woven into the
fabric of our civilization. The red thread dominates in the pattern of every age, but by the time the design has revealed its
form, the passing feet of a work-a-day world have worn both
warp and woof until history can only faintly trace their weav-
ing; or else mere distance tones the tragic note into those har-
monies which we call romance, those

> Old, unhappy, far-off things,
> And battles long ago

which under the color of heroic deeds have lost the crude reality
that lies in the sufferings of the inarticulate. From the dim
beginnings of society, and beyond, down to this very hour, war
has been used without question and almost without interval;
and upon the vicarious sacrifice of its countless victims rests
the structure of our peace. The state system of today was built
up by a process in which the Christian virtues of charity and
self-effacement have had little part; it is a misleading figure
of speech to speak of the unfolding of the flower of modern
civilization. Nations are not natural units like the tribe or clan,
for the science of politics begins when blood relationships are
left behind and ways must be found for fitting in the resident
stranger along with primitive kinship. This artificial process
is one which has been reluctantly entered upon by every
privileged member of the ancient group, and the new institu-

8

tions which embody the enlarged community have almost everywhere been hammered into shape on the forge of war. Blood and iron have been not only the historical instruments of every state for the assertion of its will among its neighbors, but they have been as well the instruments within the state by which political institutions have come into life and maintained themselves throughout the centuries.

The argument of the militarist that "man is by nature a fighting animal" is supported by the overwhelming evidence of anthropology. The natural man is a savage; and savages attack and kill each other with such complete success that, where no other influences enter in to tame the appetite for war, they remain today where mankind was when the ice sheets receded and the cave shelters of Europe lured the wandering huntsman of the neolithic age. The hunt, itself, of beast or man was the chief and only honorable occupation. Valor gave rank and standing in the social group; there was only one other thing that could measure with it in importance and that was the mastery of those mystic terrors that lay in the taboo. The warrior and the priest rose to control, each in his place, by the exercise of the variant terrors which he could command. There were those who could kill by strength or strategy and those who could kill by fear. Where these two elements are unchecked by any other influences, savagery and superstition preside alike over the twilight of human intelligence and that of the gods themselves. Fortunately, also, from those early days more benign influences were at work; otherwise there would have been no civilization. The masters of the taboo were also the priests of the beginnings of religion, and the warrior huntsman was a protector of his home as well as the destroyer of others.

This early stage of society, however, has the ethics of the pack; it is predatory by nature, robbing either the labor of others or the laborers themselves, a fact which is inherent in

the nature of warlike societies. The killers are also the en-
slavers; the economic as well as the social structure of primitive
society is merciless to the victim, except as the profit from the
victim's work wins him some slight security from violence.
Slavery marked in this regard an advance upon absolute
savagery. The earliest decisive advance in civilization seems to
have come in those communities which learned to keep their
victims working and so through slave industry built up that
accumulated wealth of goods which made the owners turn at
times from their predatory occupations to defend their possessions from the onslaught of their neighbors. For the very increase of their wealth made them all the greater temptation
to the invader. With these changing preoccupations and the
growth of settled life, superstition, too, dropped its cruder
forms, and religion learned to give expression to new ideals
in the splendors of creative art. Thus civilization began to disguise its predatory activities and sometimes even to forget them
in the enjoyment of enlarging comforts, to carve out for itself
areas of security either behind city walls or the frontiers of
mountain and desert, and in the routine of settled life to
develop the industries of peace.

Practically all the centers of antique society had some such
beginnings. If the intervals of peace were long enough and the
slave labor sufficiently abundant, they could accumulate the
leisure necessary for the development of the arts and those
early speculations which precede the sciences. But it should not
be forgotten that the splendor of the Parthenon not less than
the monuments of Egypt rested upon a predatory economics
which, in the last analysis, was but the disguised perpetuation
of the savage raid. Tribute from the conquered or from those
held in subjection was an advance upon slavery, as slavery had
been an advance upon mere wars of extermination; but it rested
equally with slavery upon the superior power—mostly brute
strength—of those who imposed it. There was, of course, free

labor in the ancient world, but it was not given the chance to develop healthfully owing to the competition of the slaves or the forced contributions from conquered territories. Thus the war system was doubly injurious to the arts of peace, both in the robbery of enemies and in crushing out by wholesale competition the honest industries at home. This was the fundamental weakness of antique society, and ultimately was responsible, more than any other factor, for its downfall.

The peace movement of today can, therefore, learn as much from the downfall of antiquity as from any other single fact in history. The antique peoples had solved practically all other problems but one, that of the just appreciation of the day's work. This could never happen until that work was done by those who were themselves free to choose.

The warrior state was able to measure all other values, in art and literature and life itself, but it never guessed that the marching legions which protected it from attack were the symbol of a destructive economics which had vaster forces at its command than all the armies of an organized world,—forces which slowly but steadily mined the walls and overthrew the defenses of all antique civilization. The ancient world was not so much overthrown by invaders as devastated from within by the effects of its own war system, which had destroyed the vitality of both agricultural and industrial pursuits. Dependence upon the subjected, outlying territories ultimately extended into the army itself, and so even the machinery of war became dependent upon the barbarian. Thus the resources of a world that was built upon predatory economics failed to maintain the organization necessary for that one industry of war, to which it had, by a false inversion, made the industries of peace subservient. The strength of Rome, which its citizens had thought eternal, died out, as the strength of other empires had before, because it was not repaired from within. Its last defenders were themselves chiefly drawn from among the barbarians, and when these gave way before their fellow warriors of the north, the frontiers were open, and history closed its page upon the antique world.

The fall of Rome was not due to a decline in morals, as the Christian philosophers have led the world to imagine. For, in spite of Tacitus, the morals of the barbarian invaders were on a far inferior plane to those of the Romans of the provinces whose society is mirrored for us in the writings of the silver age. Stoic courage and Christian virtue were altogether on the side of the empire, but the structure of society had rested on a false basis and there was no strength left to repel the invasion.

But the major lesson was never learned. The conquerors repeated again the story of antiquity; for another thousand years and more Europe suffered the anarchy of war, and carried on most of its economic life by the oppression of those who were held to the day's task by slavery or serfdom. Feudalism at its height was simply this anarchy erected into a system. The profession of arms was the only honorable one; the knight was a *miles*, or soldier, and his home was a fortress, a *castellum*. On almost every commanding hilltop, by river fords or behind protecting swamps, these castles which have left their ruins all over western Europe are reminders of local tyrannies and an age of plunder and rapine. But, throughout all except the darkest age of anarchy there were other forces becoming visible, which were destined, after centuries of growth, to supplant and overthrow the feudal lordships. There were traditions, even among the villeins, of a freer day, kept alive by customary law, and finding, in due time, their support in a kingship which was itself both the product and the enemy of feudalism. There were artisans as well in the communities which nestled beneath the castle walls, or by the monastery gates, and which, ultimately, by bargain or happy chance, gained charters of emancipation from the exactions of the overlord. Communes became cities, and the supply of the mere needs of life passed more and more out of the grasp of the warrior class. Commerce played its part in this, as markets arose and guilds developed.

There was, moreover, another modifying influence, one which reached back through all the history of the Middle Ages, in the civilizing influence of the Christian church. It is a strange fact that while the religion which it taught centered its ideals in the world to come, its missionaries gave the first example that the West had seen of the dignity of human labor. The monks of the Middle Ages were economic missionaries as well, and the Christian equivalent of the primitive taboo—in ecclesiastical law—protected the product of their industry. Slowly and imperceptibly the processes of independent economic life wore their way through the war structure of feudalism, and all sections of society found in royalty the protection necessary for these peace-time developments.

Then began the political formation of the national state, with territorial instead of merely personal allegiance. The institutions of justice in the king's name were safeguarded from violence by a stronger force than any local chieftain could muster, and the war machine became an instrument for the policing of the realm—and an instrument of national policy. By the thirteenth century this new embodiment of mutual aid was reducing tyranny to terms of contract; and so once more the world was ready for law and order, to embody them this time in the institutions of free government. From the thirteenth century to the twentieth the long transformation was slowly matured by which within the state not only war but arbitrary power was forced out of existence and at last, through revolutions in every country, the conception of justice for all men and equality before the law became a reality, or became the fundamental principle and ideal of politics itself, in the self-governing state.

But there still remained one problem not only unsolved

but practically untouched until the World War presented it to this generation in unescapable form. Although war had been suppressed within the state itself, it remained a free prerogative of nations in their dealings with each other. To eliminate this ancient privilege at any earlier stage of political development might have endangered the whole process of internal evolution, for liberty within the state, so slowly and so hardly won, had still to be maintained against possible external foes. Thus, as the state developed, it grew, if anything, more jealous of its rights and asserted the claims of sovereignty in the most absolute terms. The theory of divine right passed from the apologists of kings to those of the nation. There is little practical difference between the theory that the king as the head of the state can do no wrong and that which holds that no power exists higher than the state itself and that its own will is final justice. The temporal powers had become something more than the inheritors of the claims of the medieval church. But whereas there had been one church there were several nations, and because each nation was supreme, there was no other arbiter to settle their disputes than war. Thus the more that the national state gained by the reduction of war and disorder within, the more it accentuated the international anarchy without. This meant an added, not a lessened, importance for the nation's army and navy. The war system was necessary as an effective instrument of policy in dealing with other nations.

The power to declare war was therefore the admitted right of any sovereign state; indeed it was proof and token of sovereignty itself. This fact was a recognized principle of international law; witness any handbook written in the eighteenth or nineteenth centuries. Perhaps it was never more effectively set forth than in the manual which was most generally in use during the latter part of the eighteenth century, Vattel's *Law of Nations*. There one will find the full elaboration of the theory that the state is in time of war as in time of peace the sole judge of its own actions. From this it also follows that the state is entirely free to strike at any adversary or to work its will by force and to accept no curb upon its power save only such as it may agree to in the exercise of its very sovereignty. The one sure measure of the rights of a state, or at least the one recognized by its neighbors, was the strength of its armed forces. Sheltered behind them, its diplomats met diplomats of other states and used them as the pawns in the game of diplomacy. In the parlance of diplomacy, a nation was a "power."

War, then, has been the instrument by which most of the great facts of political national history have been established and maintained. It has played a dominant rôle in nearly all political crises; it has been used to achieve liberty, to secure democracy, and to attempt to make it secure against the menace of its use by other hands. The map of the world today has been largely determined upon the battlefield. The maintenance of civilization itself has been, and still continues to be, underwritten by the insurance of army and navy ready to strike at any time where danger threatens. Thus, even in peace, the war system has to a large degree determined not only international relationships but the character and history of the nations themselves.

The proposal to renounce international war reaches, therefore, into the heart of a very complex problem; for war has been used as an instrument against criminal aggression as much as it has been the instrument of aggression itself. It has played a beneficent rôle in history as well as a criminal one. Where would this nation be now, or for that matter any other civilized nation, if it had not met oppression with force and asserted its determination to maintain as against the world those institutions which embody its political career? If, therefore, we are to achieve the real principles of the reform which proposes to eliminate violence from the calculations of statesmen, and if we are to secure conditions upon which lasting peace can be founded, we must recognize this complex nature of the problem. Are we of this generation to take the strange position that, after having made thorough use of the war tool to establish liberty, to secure democracy and to create our modern states, we are now to deny ourselves these uses? It is no wonder that thoughtful men and women, sharing to the full the highest ideals of social welfare, should pause and hesitate upon the brink of such an action. We draw the contrast between war and law; yet the soldier has created many of the very conditions which the law preserves.

Naturally, the rôle which war has played has varied in different parts of the world, and the reality of the proposed reform will vary equally according to the past experience of nations or their present needs. There is no more persistent error in the calculations of reformers than the attempt to reduce a complex situation to a single formula and then to apply that formula in its absolute fullness to varying conditions and stages of culture. We shall revert to this point later on, but it would be a superficial reading of history which would put all the emphasis upon the similar experiences of peoples and cause us to forget their fundamental differences.

If the peace problem has been stated in different terms in the United States than in Europe, or at least with a different emphasis upon its terms, that is because the problem of war has also been different in the history and outlook of the old world and the new. International war is less real to those countries which are removed from the menace of attack by distance or rest behind protecting frontiers of mountain or morass. It is least real to a land which has oceans for frontiers and has never known the horrors of hostile invasion. It is most real to those countries which have had to create for their security the arti-

ficial equivalents of distance and physical barriers, equivalents
which are the lives of their citizens and the protecting armaments. Nations like Great Britain—especially the Britain of
the pre-airplane days—and the United States do not come upon
this problem of war and peace with the same degree of realism
as the countries of continental Europe, where throughout all
history potential enemies are at the doors of every nation.

Although war has played its part in American history, still
it has not been a continuing preoccupation of American politics.
Our historic task, at least our chief one, has been the conquest
of a continent, and although we speak of this in terms of militant achievement, the conquest after all has been in the realm
of industry and economics rather than of the forcible displacement of other nations in our path. The Indian was not using
his vast heritage, and his displacement was only a preliminary
skirmish to the great advance which conquered the forest and
the prairie with the implements of peace.

We, therefore, do not fully appreciate the continuing
emphasis upon this age-long implement of war, which other
nations continued to employ because they have had to, or at
least because they have known no other way to secure their
rights in the conflicting current of nationalities. Although we,
too, had to use the sword on more than one occasion, it was
chiefly for the settlement of our own internal problems. But
the great trend of American history is that which has to do
with the day's work rather than with those relatively few dis-
turbing elements which, while they have taught us what war
is, have nevertheless left us free from its constant threat.

This glance at American history and its contrast to most of
that of other nations furnishes the first clew to the understanding of the present proposal, as indeed it supplies the clew to
the still greater proposals that will be forever associated with
the name of Wilson.

We have the advantage of a perspective far enough removed

from the phenomenon of war to see it less disturbed by the immediate preoccupations of statesmanship than is possible in Europe. But this clarity of vision as to the ultimate end to be achieved is gained at a cost of practical knowledge or even concern as to the immediate effects which such a reform would cause in the existing state system of the civilized world. This is a dangerous privilege for any nation. To view an imperfect world from a safe distance tends to develop an unreal criticism of the frailties of others. It permits us to expound the principles of morality without much danger of being held down closely to their application. It is by no mere chance that the two nations which have most enjoyed natural security and so have been safeguarded from the dangers which confront the rest, are accused by their less fortunate neighbors of the national fault of hypocrisy. National hypocrisy may be, after all, little more than the cherishing of high ideals without sufficient knowledge of the difficulty of their achievement. Because neither war nor security has been an American preoccupation, much of the peace movement in America has been pacifist in character and impatient of European devices. We need imagination, therefore, if we are to read history aright, that kind of imagination which enables us to penetrate at least the difficulties of the ordinary life of ordinary people in other lands.

Take, for instance, this problem of security. It is at bottom only a state of mind, for no country can be absolutely secure against every danger. But there is a world of difference between the American outlook and that of modern France. No sensible American expects this country ever to be invaded. The farmer of Indiana does not know what it means to be afraid of any foreign army. Whoever thought of the Lincoln Highway as a military road along which the hosts of a neighboring empire might march as the Germans marched along the turnpike roads of France and Belgium from Liége to the suburbs of Paris!

Yet down to the coming of the automobile, all the great

roadways of Europe had been planned for military strategy, from the time of the Caesars when the legions tramped along them—from the wilds of Rumania to the forests of Scotland —to that of the engineers of Louis XIV and Napoleon. The link along the Riviera which binds France and Italy together was built to hold the latter in subjection a thousand years after it first pierced those hillsides. The Storm King Highway of the Hudson River would, if it ran along the Rhine, be guarded by forts at every widening of the river valley against the successors of Turenne. The chief provisions for the coming and going of people throughout the ages have been for attack or defense. With a society that was so largely predatory the first condition of peace was adequate defense. Compared with this insistent reality, defense is with us a theoretic problem, although no less a fundamental one. This is perhaps one reason why the subject of defense was not mentioned in the text of the Pact of Paris, and why there were such constant reminders of it in the replies of the European Powers.

If each reader in the quiet of a rural town or countryside were to lay down this page at this point, and look out to the familiar landscape and then try to imagine that the countless dead of Verdun are still lying along hillsides like those of New England or Pennsylvania, that every gentle rise of land along the central plain of New York State or southern Ohio had been held as a long glacis for the machine guns of a Hindenburg line, and that the lower banks along the river-basins where the cattle pastures run had held the heavy guns for the destruction of the cities that stretch from Pittsburgh to New York, he would have some sense of the realities which the problems of the Pact of Paris hold for those whose theories of peace have been tried in the tragedy of modern war.

If, however, war—that is, international war—has meant less in the history of the United States than in the Old World, there

was one other institution presenting a partial analogy with that
of the history of war which entered into American history
more fully than into that of European countries in modern
times. Slavery is practically as old as war; its origins go back
to the beginnings of social life, and it has seemed perhaps
even more inevitable to past ages because it literally has kept
humanity alive. Yet, in our own day, this world-old institution,
upon which the antique civilization rested, has been abolished.
Antiquity would have regarded this step as utterly impossible
and equally unimaginable. Its poets, thinkers, and philosophers,
the great creators of art, and the initiators of science accepted
slavery as an essential element in the social structure. Plato
with his dreams of the future; Aristotle, with his world views
of life and civilization; Seneca, a slave himself, or the imperial
Aurelius, and the Fathers of the Church who followed them
to weave into their questionings of the meaning of life the
hopes and aspirations of Christianity,—all alike accepted
slavery as the inevitable background of culture and concentrated
their efforts upon the amelioration of the condition of the
individual slave. The Church of the Middle Ages set itself
not against the institution of slavery but against the conditions
under which it was carried on. It is true that from time to time
there appeared priests or prophets who saw in slavery itself a
thing to shock the human conscience, but until the eighteenth
century no real effort was made to abolish it. And not until our
own time was it completely brought to an end.

What was it that did finally abolish slavery? If one looks into
the matter closely in its historical setting, one sees that in the
eighteenth and nineteenth centuries, when the slave trade was
suppressed, there was a movement developing in the world
which was born not of religion but of science. A movement of
liberation came in the technique of the daily work of the common man. We had begun to master the forces of nature and

make them work for us. Without at first seeing the reason for it, we had found that slavery on the one hand and modern industrialism on the other could not survive in common. The democracy of labor is a product of that victory of the intelligence which has remade the conditions of the day's work. Now no one today in the civilized world believes that slavery is still necessary,—I speak of legal slavery, not of other kinds. Yet slavery was, if anything, more deeply interwoven in the fabric of civilization than war; for by it was performed the world's daily labor, while war was at least intermittent.

This historical parallel holds good even in details. War, like slavery, was accepted as inevitable until the growth of modern science so changed human relationships as to make new conditions for both the day's work and the policies of nations. Moreover, just as practical science brought substitutes for labor, so its destructive inventions brought substitutes for the ancient ways of waging war. We are therefore at a point in human development in which science, having given the world a substitute for slavery, is challenging society to find the substitute for war. Whether this challenge can be met or not is a question which cannot be answered without examining in some detail the change which has come over human affairs through inventions of science. The lesson of history would seem to be that there is a single problem behind the policies of peace and war, the fundamental problem of intelligent control of social forces— forces not less blind and elusive than those with which the natural sciences grapple in their assertion of mastery over time and space, but whose harmonious adjustment is not only peace but justice. The scientific attitude of mind may, after all, turn out to be a much more humanizing element than any one would suppose who thought of it only in terms of the battle with the forces of nature. Triumph in that struggle brings us now to seek as well the elimination of that primitive barbarism which has remained with us from the period when life was a crude and often losing struggle with these forces now within our control. The answer to our question, therefore, lies chiefly in the nature of science itself.

CHAPTER III

THE NEW WORLD OF SCIENCE

IF the history of past ages were a sure guide for the present and the future, there would be no doubt as to the answer to a proposal to rid the world of war. It could not be done. All through the centuries men of good faith have cherished the ideals of peace only to see them yield in the time of crises to the policies of iron—and blood. This is the recurring theme of the human tragedy; dreams of a world at peace in the midst of a world at war; Christianity unable to establish even its human ideals of good will among men; and Oriental philosophy and religion equally futile in this regard. The real and the ideal have seemed forever irreconcilable. Now, has anything happened in the history of our own days which is not in the history of the past that changes this world-old antithesis?

In Carlyle's essay on Voltaire, there is a striking passage which deals with the relative importance of events in history. It points out how the truly great events are most often those which are almost unnoticed by the generation living at the time when they occur. About the time when Tamerlane was moving his armies across Asia, laying waste empires and destroying civilizations, a little boy may have been playing in the streets of Mainz, in Germany, who, when he later changed his ninepins for movable type and so made possible the invention of the printing press, did more to transform human history than all the Tamerlanes, whose chronicles his types were later to record. So, says Carlyle, the quiet movement of creative thought transcends in importance the dramatic and the temporary.

The Tartar Khan, with his shaggy demons of the wilderness, "passed away like a whirlwind," to be forgotten forever; and that German artisan has wrought a benefit, which is yet immeasurably expanding itself, and will continue to expand itself through all countries and through all times. . . . Truly, it is a mortifying thing for your Conqueror to reflect, how perishable is the metal which he hammers with such violence: how the kind earth will soon shroud-up his bloody footprints; and all that he achieved and skilfully piled together will be but like his own "canvas city" of a camp,—this evening loud with life, tomorrow all struck and vanished, "a few earth-pits and heaps of straw!"

There is but one enduring power "of more than imperial authority" and that is in the quiet realm of ideas, where solitary workers evolve the magic formulas of thought.

It is in a setting like this that one must judge the relative importance, not only of past events but of those of our own day. The traditional perspectives of history are so filled with the figures of a passing show that the obscure but enduring elements escape attention. There are two things more important than all others to the human race, work and thought; the day's labor and the inquiring mind. Until our own time these two never met—or never met to know their common task which is the amelioration and enlightenment of life itself. Their meeting, in the inventions and discoveries of the scientific age, has caused the greatest of all revolutions in history. From the ice age down there is nothing to compare with it. It is not a revolution of the old-fashioned kind. It does not proclaim itself by spectacular events, mob violence, or any of those "revolutionary phenomena" by which historians have recognized revolutions in the past. There are no national uprisings, no armies, no Napoleons. Nevertheless, this revolution has struck more at the heart of existing political systems—and all other systems—than any other single change since politics began.

War may determine the direction of the current of history, it may check it or clear away the barriers which impede it, but the current itself is fed by the springs of peace-time industry. The real meaning of human affairs lies in our commonplace activities. The conditions of policy and also of war have been largely fixed by the primal fact that somehow or other mankind must extract a living from the crude material world around. This has been the fundamental problem underlying all others, whether it was the individual as savage, as artisan, or as industrial worker; or whether it was the labor of slaves working under private owners or for the state,—that greatest of all chapters of the history of work. At the base of all human activity lay the elemental struggle with nature.

From the beginning of settled life, beyond which the conditions are too rudimentary for us to notice here—the work of man and woman has been done under conditions which are remarkably similar everywhere. In the old pre-modern stretch of history the day's work was done under very narrow limitations of both space and time. Most people lived in isolated communities, cut off from any but immediate neighbors; and within these communities they kept on doing the same things over and over again, year after year, generation after generation, century after century. In the agricultural life, which dominates, the recurring seasons held mankind—in this pre-scientific era—to the iron law of its recurring activities. Cities and commercial peoples escape only in part, for their supplies are mainly local and depend upon the countryside. The apparent exceptions in the modern-like business of the chief cities of the antique world and of states in the Middle Ages like Venice, are but episodes which anticipate in part the modern age. But the chief characteristic of the life of the people before our day— and perhaps still the chief characteristic in spite of the change which is setting in—is repetition. One must sow and reap each year at the same time; one must repeat yearly and daily what was done before; for life depends upon it. The farmer's calendar of Hesiod is valid still, although it comes to us from the

dim beginnings of history and records the home life of those
who were among the first to listen to the poems of Homer. The
isolated groups of farming-folk clustered around shelters or
local markets, to whom the outside world supplied only superfluities—if luxuries were superfluities—were almost as much
conditioned by nature as the soil they cultivated.

Now the effect of this upon men's minds is prodigious. It
makes conservatives of all who must submit to the recurring
routine. The weight of this tendency to repeat is perhaps the
strongest single tendency in the pre-modern era. There are
stone spindle-whorls in the prehistoric remains of the caves
near Mentone, which were twirled by women whose eyes looked
out upon the Mediterranean five or perhaps ten thousand years
ago; and the present women of those hills are still twirling
their spindles now as those once did before there was a Greece or
Rome. All through the centuries those fingers have been at
work doing the same task the same way. The power of the law
of repetition, of which the calendar is only a visible if outstanding symbol, extends over all the recurring needs of life.

So it was in the pre-scientific era, so it is wherever human life
depends upon a close relationship with the processes of
nature. And so humanity would have gone on for untold ages
more, had it not been for the revolution caused in this process
of routine by the interjection into it of science and attendant
discovery. When face to face with this homely chronicle of
the past, one sees by way of contrast the significance of that
new technique which implies the conquest of time and space.
The routine of nature still continues to play its ancient rôle, but,
so far as the scientific worker is concerned, it is only a rhythm in
the growing orchestration of life, not the dominant theme.
The conquest of time brings the southern summer to the north
in the speedy shipment of its products, and spins the threads of
a lifetime in the moment's work of the thousand spindles of

the mill. Spatially, communities move together as the time for travel lessens.

But greater than all the achievements of science is the difference in the *nature* of its processes from those of the pre-scientific world. For as the law of the pre-scientific era was repetition, that of the scientific era is change. This is what we mean by the dynamic character of our age. The rhythm still repeats as we have just admitted, but it repeats in ever-varied tones. The past and future were once alike, now they are eternally different. For every discovery, every invention, causes a displacement in society that calls for new discoveries and inventions. The process is almost one of geometric progression.

The result is that we are making another map of the world than that of land and water; rivers, plains, mountains and the like are still the physical framework for it, but the relations of peoples are no longer indicated wholly by this visible map. Our American cotton States move over towards and then away from Manchester, with the movements of the market; nitrate factories of Saxony may affect the workers of Chile and the farmers of Iowa, and therefore are a part of their economy. A new invention of tomorrow may change the center of industry from one land to another, as in the case of that English invention which made possible the iron and steel works of the Ruhr. And the drift of these shifting activities is not charted by any old-time calculation of the seasons; its chart is in the financial sheets that record the prices of the money-market. Infinitely complicated is this web of finance, and almost infinitely far-reaching. It is the mysterious index of the dynamic forces let loose in the world by the Industrial Revolution. Commerce is no longer an interchange of the margin of production, it is more and more an interchange of necessities. This means that a world community is emerging, based upon the solid ground of joint and common interests. But it is only just emerging, and is still in the early stages of development. I should be sadly misreading current history if I implied that it is strong enough to have a political form of its own. It is merely a function of existing politics. We are still living in a world of nations, and not under any international super-state. Fortunately the creators of the League of Nations conceived of that organization in this sense, not as a super-state but as an instrument of existing nations.

Although the world-community is not yet realized, nevertheless we can already state with confidence, not only that it is coming, but the nature of its dominant historical characteristic, that which will mark it off from the pre-scientific era.

In a word, the two fundamental conditions of social and political life are time and space, and science has largely mastered these. The isolation of communities a century ago is now as far away as that of the city state. George Washington at Mount Vernon was closer to Aristotle, who used the word "economics" to describe the Mount Vernons of ancient Greece, than we are to the household economy of an estate of Colonial days. This change has been brought about not by designing politicians forsaking the precepts of the fathers of the country but by the inventions of science which produced the industrial world of today. We forget that there never were factories in the world before! Then came the financial revolution, banks (there were none of the modern type when Louis XIV was King), national and international debts and bonds, both domestic and foreign. We need to reconsider our relationship to "abroad" when we recall that since 1914 we have invested there the equivalent of approximately the entire wealth of all New England, excluding Massachusetts; or of the empire of Texas, Arizona and New Mexico; or of five or six States of the Rocky Mountain region. This covers the equivalent of farms, cities, railroads, factories, public utilities, everything but credits and money in the bank. Other countries are doing the same. Few of the smaller countries have financial capitals of their own. The other great Powers, recovering rapidly from the war, are doing just as we are doing. In a world of interlacing credits such as these, with the prosperity of our own homes involved in the prosperity of other lands, and this in turn dependent upon the promise of settled conditions and continued security, the problem of international peace has now become real and its solution urgent.

As long as nations lived by themselves alone, their contacts with each other were chiefly those of conflict; a fact which is registered in the history of European diplomacy, and finds its peace-time expression in the sinister formula, "the weight of armaments," an expression almost synonymous with the influence which one nation has exercised upon another in obtaining recognition of its claims. It is only as the isolation has been broken, through the development of industry and finance and the recognition of common interests in this new world without a frontier, that diplomacy has emerged from its iron framework and grappled with the problems of reciprocal rights and duties in all the varied activities of a nation's life.

The era of international peace coincides with this new extension of national interests and its success depends on having something more powerful still than the weight of armaments behind it. That there is a more powerful instrument is the major fact behind the whole movement. We are not eliminating power from the affairs of nations when we renounce war, as liberals of the tentative mind have feared. We are only bringing into play more pertinent powers than those of the old barbaric and destructive sort, powers that are inherent in the constructive rather than the destructive energy of civilization.

It surely ought not to be any mystery what this new force is; for the one new fact in the world, completely new and without parallel in any past, is the process of industrialization now under way.

In the opening days of this new economy it was still seen in terms of conflict and rivalry, but in 1776 Adam Smith proclaimed the principle of economic coöperation, based upon the theory that the wealth of his own nation depended upon the increase in the wealth of others, thus dissociating the theory of commerce from the predatory conception that had hitherto prevailed and that is inherent in the war system of international relations. Of the two documents published in that same year, history may yet attribute to the liberating conception of Adam Smith as great a place or greater yet than that which gave expression to the political liberties of a single nation.

But the economic history of the nineteenth century, and especially of the post-war period, shows how extremely difficult and slow is the application of these theoretic truths. The political doctrine of international peace is a parallel to the economic doctrine of Adam Smith, for it rests similarly upon a recognition of common and reciprocal material interests, which extend beyond national frontiers. The political, however, has this advantage over the economic doctrine, that we grapple with the problem internationally from the beginning, and embody it in treaty obligations instead of in internal legislation.

In short, as we shall see below, the movement for international peace owes its validity, which is real, to the fact that a new civilization has arisen which rests upon the interdependence of nations, and that the prosperity of the present depends upon the buying power of the future. The world of credit is essentially a world of peace. The activities of business now decide most of the major relationships within and between societies which formerly were left in the last resort to the instrument of war. If we are to have world peace, it is because the world has turned that corner in history when civilized societies need peace for their continued existence and find the instrument of war no longer pertinent. This much will become clear from what follows; but to determine just where these conditions do exist is another question. Not all the world is civilized, not even all that claims to be.

CHAPTER IV

WAR IN THE NEW ERA

Now it is time to see the bearing of this analysis upon the problem before us. War, too, has shared in the change which has come over social and political relationships. In the pre-scientific era—in which we are still rather deeply rooted, and in which some nations are still living—war partook of the nature of other industries; there were new inventions in it, as in the industries of peace, but it was conservative and localized, even more so than they. Thus, throughout most of European history, wars have been fought within fixed limits between the armed forces of two or more states, while the rest of mankind—even within the belligerent nations—looked on with more or less neutral indifference. Under such conditions war was controllable or relatively so. It was employed to conquer or defend this or that territory or to reduce or to aggrandize commerce. By land and sea the enemies were clearly discernible: there was no need to mistake either the aim of war or the limits of its operations. In the old isolated economy of nations, war was primarily a question of man-power. A nation which went to war simply called upon its citizens—or rather a monarch called upon his subjects—and each one came with his own arms and accouterments. The advancing armies lived off the supplies of the countryside through which they marched. It was a straightforward operation, limited strictly to those engaged in it. A nation which did not wish to fight could remain aloof from the conflict by simply keeping its armies from the field.

Under these conditions the place of war in political theory was well defined. It was a legitimate exercise of sovereignty,

32

the final argument, the *ultima ratio,* of governments. It established or enforced policies of state, and was therefore a usable instrument with calculable results. In such a world the only hope of peace was to use this final argument to impose a universal will; a hope like that which inspired the dreams of Dante. A superior power should coerce the anarchic and warring elements of civilization into a single empire. The restoration of the *pax Romana* proved impossible, however; and the modern states, hewn in every case out of this anarchy by war, continued to depend for their security upon the instrument which had been used for their creation.

Had war remained what it was in Dante's day, it is probable that the problem of international peace would still have to be stated in Dante's terms. But in the industrial and financial era of today, the nature of war has utterly changed from the simple strategy of man-power of earlier days. Not only does war involve the entire economic structure of the belligerent nations, but it spreads like a contagion throughout all those other countries whose economic life has become involved with that of the nations at war; which means more or less all the industrialized nations of the civilized world. As the armies advance in one direction, the ships go out in another for the raw materials of war, and the more the conflagration grows the more the belligerent becomes dependent on ever new supplies, and so, when the war is over, finds that the territory covered by the advance of its armies is perhaps of far less value to it than the wealth which it has sacrificed to win the victory. In other words, the direction of war in the modern world of industry and finance does not wholly follow that of military strategy; it follows rather that of economic needs satisfied only at the ruinous cost of war-time prices.

The World War offered an unparalleled opportunity for the study of these phenomena. This was seen early in the war by Professor John Bates Clark, who was then Director of the

Division of Economics and History of the Carnegie Endowment for International Peace. From his suggestion has grown
the *Economic and Social History of the World War*, to the
preparation of which I have devoted nine years. Some two
hundred contributors, among them thirty-five cabinet ministers
of various governments, are contributing to its hundred and
fifty volumes. The subject of this survey is what I have just
indicated as the very heart of our problem. It avoids political
controversy, leaves entirely aside such vexed questions as that
of war-guilt, and deals with the World War from the angle
of its displacement in the normal processes of civilization.

Viewing the World War from the historical standpoint just
indicated, it becomes growingly clear—and subsequent discussions on national security bear this out—that during the years
1914 to 1918, the industry of destruction, which is war,
definitely passed into the industrial phase of economic history.
This fact is disguised by the long deadlock of armies in the
field, which gave many indications of a return to the war-
economy of an earlier day. But when one deals with modern
war, one is dealing with something larger than military facts.
The survey covers—or may cover—every activity of those
at war, in finance, industry, agriculture, housekeeping, engineer-
ing, even scientific research. For all these activities were more
or less at war. Germany was the first to realize this. In all the
literature of the war, there is nothing more striking than the
little memoir in which Dr. Walther Rathenau describes the
vision which he realized in the creation of the Division of
Raw Materials of the War Office (*Rohstoffsabteilung*). When,
in the early days of the war, the attention of the world was
fastened upon the armies in the field, he saw in imagination
the mobilization of factories and the belching furnaces instead of guns alone. It was because others did not have this
vision that, when the war began, almost every one—including

economists—said that it could not last more than a few months, because of the exhaustion of resources as well as of men.

Science falsified this prophecy. Medicine kept up the supply of lives for the front by reducing the death rate, by hygiene and surgery. Had the science of medicine been as primitive in 1914 as it was in 1870, or with us in the Spanish War of 1898, a war that cost a nation a million dead upon the field of battle would have cost it anywhere from ten to twenty times as many. The importance of this phase of the social and economic history of the war has not been fully appreciated. As for the parallel exhaustion of economic resources, similar surprises were sprung, too familiar to all of us now, however, to be described here. One need only recall the unrecognizable England of 1916 to 1918, in which almost every principle of its economic past was violated, as it has to be when a country becomes an arsenal; or the case of the United States, where still stranger transformations took place.

But the important point for us is that this economy of war followed the law of dynamics, change producing changes in geometric progression—with the whole process speeded up by the fact that the competition of war must follow a faster pace than that of peace, since in war the delay in adjustment may be fatal.

It is not so significant that the war involved so many peoples as that it involved them so completely. There was no keeping events within bounds, as in the simple economy of the past. The shifting map of economic interests was invaded to a far greater degree than the march of armies invaded any country on the geographic map, as the blockade and the financial dislocation of the war both clearly showed. Not only this, but sometimes the losses inflicted upon an enemy turned out to be one's own.

In its economy, therefore, the industry of war combines two

techniques, both of them dynamic: the technique of peace which supplies war with its resources, and the technique of destruction. Now, since both of these are progressively modified by every new development, war is as uncertain in its direction as in its intensity, or its spread. It is no longer a safe instrument for statesmanship under such circumstances; it is too dangerous to employ. It is no longer an *ultima ratio*, for it has lost its *raison d'être*. Victor and victim may suffer a common disaster. Its effects reach even into the unformed future, and rob the savings of generations yet unborn. Time, as well as space, levels its barriers to the march of destruction. This new dynamic world, the creation of human intelligence, containing as it does the most precious things in our heritage, has no other defense against it, once it is loosed, than that which endangers it as well. Such are the phenomena of war as revealed by a study of the tragic years 1914 to 1918. Moreover, it is equally clear from this analysis, that these phenomena are not merely incidental and temporary. They are typical and more and more true as civilization develops.

In short, war which was once a directable instrument of policy has now changed its nature with the nature of modern society and ceases to be controllable and directable in the hands of statesmen. By reason of its all-embracing needs, it becomes a contagion among the nations; and one cannot safely use a contagion as an instrument.

This was the supreme lesson of the World War. The fact was at last made clear that war had been industrialized,—war, that is, between the highly civilized nations. This means not only the complications of financial and industrial involvements, but it means something far more significant, that science has conquered nature not only for the welfare of civilization but also for its possible destruction. We talk about disarmament; but as long as war exists we must face the fact that the implements of war are also those of peace. We may limit our battleships in a Washington Conference, but there is no ratio of 5-5-3 or any other number in the capacities of chemistry or organized industry. These will vary with the vitality of the scientific or industrial development of nations and no arithmetic of limitations can set their bounds. There are, for instance, factories now in existence which can extract nitrate of ammonia from the air in thousands of tons each day to fertilize the farm land of their own country and of others; but these same factories can likewise produce high explosives in quantities no less enormous because the constituents of fertilizer and explosive are practically the same. The nitrate of the air is the base upon which both build. It needs no imagination but mere common sense to realize that this most essential industry for the maintenance of human life could produce and distribute *daily*, even with commercial airplanes, the material which could destroy entire cities. If there is to be another war between the highly civilized Powers, the laboratories of the universities and the workshops of towns and cities would be the arsenals of destruction and it would be a war of mutual extermination, since whatever nation is attacked would be compelled to make use of the same kind of chemical warfare in its own defense.

Can we prevent the use of such methods in war? Can we block the progress of science? No. Those same scientific processes which make life richer for us and supply bread in abundance for those who would otherwise be in need, processes particularly necessary in a world left with such misery as ours today, these processes are the very ones, with but minor changes in their apparatus, that are the modern equivalents for the armies of Caesar or Tamerlane. The same scientists, with the same formulae, can make both things—the life-saving and the life-destroying—in one and the same laboratory. I remember, for example, visiting an establishment where, during the war, poison gases were made, and found that other chemists working in that same laboratory had, at the same time, discovered the cure for sleeping sickness, by which it was hoped that at least as many lives might be saved as were lost through the instrument of death upon which their colleagues were working. Two laboratories side by side, men of science working in them in the same spirit of scientific inquiry,—so long as war is legitimate their services to society rest upon even terms. We have reached a place in history where we must choose between the dangers of the destruction of civilization in its entirety, and the possibility of making secure the happiness and well-being of nations by the abolition of war as the instrument of their policy.

PART TWO

DIPLOMATIC HISTORY

CHAPTER V

THE BRIAND OFFER

On the sixth of April, 1927, on the occasion of the tenth anniversary of the entry of the United States into the World War, Monsieur Briand, Foreign Minister of France, issued a statement which has now become the opening of a new chapter in the world's history.

After a glance backward over those tragic and critical years when it seemed as though the very structure of civilization were in danger of destruction, M. Briand turned from these memories of the past to the duties of the present and the hopes of the future with a call to American idealism in words which have reached further into the heart of this generation than any others since the war messages of President Wilson. In a statement given to the Associated Press and addressed to the American people, he formally and openly proposed that France and the United States should definitely renounce war as an instrument of national policy and so at once proceed to give reality to the fundamental ideals of these two republican democracies. The full text of the vitally important paragraph in M. Briand's statement reads as follows:

> For those whose lives are devoted to securing this living reality of a policy of peace the United States and France already appear before the world as morally in full agreement. If there were need for those two great democracies to give high testimony to their desire for peace and to furnish to other peoples an example more solemn still, France would be willing to subscribe publicly with the United States to any mutual engagement tending to outlaw war, to use an American expression, as between these two countries. The renunciation of war as an instrument of national policy is a conception already familiar to the

signatories of the Covenant of the League of Nations and of the Treaties of Locarno. Every engagement entered into in this spirit by the United States toward another nation such as France would contribute greatly in the eyes of the world to broaden and strengthen the foundations on which the international policy of peace is being erected. These two great friendly nations, equally devoted to the cause of peace, would furnish to the world the best illustration of the truth that the immediate end to be attained is not so much disarmament as the practical application of peace itself.

Strangely enough, the importance of this utterance by the Foreign Minister of France escaped notice both in America and in Europe. The newspapers which printed it did not even give it the journalistic distinction of a place on the front page. No headlines in any paper called attention to the significance of the statement, no editorials were devoted to it. For a fortnight after its publication it seemed as though the proposal had entirely failed to draw even the casual attention of those to whom the statement was addressed.

Then finally on the twenty-fifth of April, the New York *Times* published a letter from Dr. Nicholas Murray Butler which was the real starting point, in the United States at least, of what was ultimately to become a proposal for a world-wide treaty.

Dr. Butler not only republished the offer of M. Briand, but he reminded the readers of the *Times* that no such statement as that could have been made by a cabinet member of the French Government unless he had previously gained the full support of the Cabinet of which he was a member. No pronouncement upon any important question of public policy is ever made by a Minister of France until that pronouncement has been accepted by the Government of the day, and therefore when M. Briand stated that France was willing to sign a treaty with the United States, it meant that the Government of France, and not M. Briand alone, was speaking. Having thus established the importance of the offer from the standpoint of France, Dr. Butler turned to the American side of the question, and in a few pertinent paragraphs challenged the public opinion of the United States to take up and answer the offer of France. He pointed out that the fact that the statement was addressed to the American public instead of to the Government in Washington, increased rather than lessened its importance, for M. Briand had addressed his question in a way not only fitting and proper in these democratic days, but one which would elicit whether or not the will to peace really exists among the peoples of the two republics so that those moral forces might speak out which, when roused, not only stir and compel governmental action but are the guarantee of a permanence of policy.

The closing paragraphs of Dr. Butler's letter may well be quoted along with those of M. Briand, for it was this ringing challenge which brought the offer of France to the mind and conscience of the American people.

The question [said Dr. Butler] is now squarely before the people of the United States. If those moral forces to which M. Briand makes appeal do not really exist among us, or, if existing, they cannot secure such direction of our policies as shall realize these ideals, then in international relations we shall have reached a stage which no American who understands his country's traditions and who realizes his country's ideals can look upon without shame and sorrow.

M. Briand's mind is thoroughly practical. He does not ask the Government of the United States to accept the Covenant of the League of Nations; he does not ask the Government of the United States to accept the principles of the pact of Locarno; he does not ask the Government of the United States to adhere to the protocol for the establishment of a Permanent Court of International Justice. All that he asks is that the people of the United States shall take their own way to express the fact that in no case will they employ war to enforce their policies with reference to France.

We have been celebrating, and justly celebrating, the tenth anniversary of the entry of the United States into the World War. Where and how could we find a more fitting tribute to the memory of those whose lives were given in that stupendous struggle than by making a solemn compact with that nation most severely stricken by that war, for the formal and definite renunciation of war itself as an instrument of policy?

M. Briand, speaking the voice and expressing the soul of France, has called out to us across the ocean. What answer is he to hear? What evidence is he to have that these noble words have been heard and understood?

The answer which he was to hear was one which surprised even America itself. M. Briand had addressed himself not to the Government of the United States, but to the country at large, and it is not in any way detracting from the unique significance of his offer to say that the response which it received in the succeeding months from the plain people of the United States was still more significant and important, because it revealed that very will to peace in the moral fiber of the nation upon which must rest the hopes, not only for the great experiment of war renunciation, but for the permanent adjustment of national policies to the new era which it would inaugurate. The first indication of the attitude and interest of America was the news value which the journalists suddenly discovered in the French offer when revived by Dr. Butler's letter. By all rules that govern in the newspaper world, the French offer had ceased to have any real news value after its initial failure to attract attention. Dr. Butler's letter was not news in the strict sense of the word; it was at best but a subject for editorials; the news editors could still remain oblivious of either offer or comment; the item might still remain dead for them. But this is not what happened. The offer of France and the challenge of Dr. Butler passed once more to the news columns, not only of the metropolitan press but of the newspapers of the smaller towns and cities throughout the whole country. At last America heard, or at least was beginning to hear. Thoughtful and intelligent people began to ask that we make ready our answer and that the answer should be in the affirmative. The United States, it was claimed, could at least go as far as France in the ways of peace.

It is difficult now to recall the basis of this mixed and somewhat contradictory appreciation of the French proposal. Almost without our noticing it, the attitude towards France in the United States, and elsewhere in the world as well, has changed chiefly as a result of this very offer, for it has come with the emphasis of a climax to the long series of acts of pacification which are the outstanding achievements of the foreign policy of M. Briand. Now, at last, the charge could no longer stand that the France of the Third Republic was a militaristic nation. But this had been the general impression in the United States from the days of the discussion over the Treaty of Versailles, an impression strengthened if not justified by the policy of M. Poincaré in the invasion of the Ruhr. Those who knew France well enough knew that the charge of militarism was not justified, but they were relatively few; and so firmly had the other impression become fixed in the popular mind that any statement to the contrary was likely to be treated as if it were merely French propaganda. Moreover, the pacific basis of the French political life is one that lacks expression, at least in terms that can be understood outside of France, for it is the peasantry of a predominantly agricultural country. The World War had increased the anti-militarist tendencies of this farming class of France because they had borne by far the greater portion of the human sacrifice. While the industrial workers had been called back to the munition plants, the farmers' sons were left to bear the brunt of the attack in the trenches. None of this deepening intensity of the longing for peace was visible, however, in the stern policies of M. Poincaré, and as the measures taken against Germany were news, which the longing for peace was not, the criticism of France had almost become a dogma in some of the very countries which had been its allies and associates in the

World War. It is hard to recover from the attacks upon one's motives when our actions lend any color to the imputation. Mere protestation will not suffice. One needs to outbid the assailment of character by some outstanding and dramatic contradiction, as well as by a reversal of policy. This has been the task of M. Briand, the task which he has achieved to the honor of France so well that now even the secular enemy of France recognizes in him a sincere and almost a necessary guarantee of its own peace.

But American public opinion had never been deeply stirred by the earlier efforts of M. Briand; although it had praise for Locarno, the merit for that negotiation was divided and the British participation in the negotiations had had a much better press in the United States than had the French. The proposal of April 6 was the first definite step toward the complete revision of the attitude towards France. But that did not come at once and the existing suspicion for a while blocked the way to any effort at correcting the impression. M. Briand, himself, was well aware of the situation which might make it difficult for the United States to appreciate the genuineness of his offer. He had memories of the treatment accorded him during the Washington Conference on Naval Disarmament when the frank statement of the French technical difficulties in lessening the minor craft, which protect the Mediterranean route to France's African dominions, was taken as an additional proof of obvious militarist and imperialist designs. In conversation, he frankly stated that he did not know how to take American public opinion nor what to make of it. But this, it may be said in passing, is true of most European statesmen.

Just at this juncture, by a fortunate chance the inventor of the phrase "outlawry of war" arrived in Paris. This was Mr. S. O. Levinson, of Chicago, who had not only originated the phrase itself but had made it the center of an American movement for international peace. The support for this movement lay chiefly in that section of the Middle West which has inherited the New England tradition of morals and religion,—what the British term the "non-conformist conscience." Later in the summer a more direct exponent of this great body of opinion was to visit Europe as well, the Rev. Dr. Morrison, editor of the *Christian Century*. But Mr. Levinson arrived in Paris in the days immediately following M. Briand's declaration and quickly discerned the opportunity which it had opened up for interpreting to Europe the program of war-outlawry. As will be evident from later chapters in this book, the need for interpretation was real enough. Any student of literature or morals knows how far removed from Continental ways of thinking is that portion of England or America which maintains the Puritan outlook, or even that much larger portion which cherishes it in retrospect. In politics the distance to be bridged is greater still, because politics reflects not only the content of divergent pasts but the variant interests of the present as well; the differences in political attitudes are due to geographical as well as to historical factors. Moreover, each body of opinion, the continental European and the continental American, is so sure of itself as to be largely indifferent to the other. Now, when Briand called the attention of Europe to the "American expression 'to outlaw war,'" the author of the expression was happily at hand to convince his European listeners that it represented a real political force in the United States.[1]

There was real need of interpreters between America and Europe in more matters than this one, if M. Briand's proposal was to make headway. Transatlantic misunderstandings had been steadily growing in the years since the war. Even the traditional friendship of France and the United States had been troubled by two problems still unsettled between them. The question of naval disarmament was once more acute, and, again,

[1] On the movement for the outlawry of war, see Chapter X below.

France was pursuing a policy which lent color to the charge of militarism, for it had refused the invitation of President Coolidge to attend, or at least to participate fully in, the Geneva Conference on Naval Disarmament, which was just then taking shape. But there was an underlying basis of disagreement still more serious in the unsettled problem of war debts. Without in any way going into the issues of that controversy, the effect of it should be recalled here, for it was steadily developing a hostility to America on the part of nearly all European countries, the kind of hostility which has ugly possibilities, some of which were already beginning to show themselves. Even in Germany there were those who claimed that the intransigence of America was responsible for the retention of French troops in the Rhineland and that these might therefore in the last resort be regarded as the disguised and mercenary agents of the United States. Resentment in England was, if anything, deeper, because of the relatively harder terms of the debt settlement that Mr. Baldwin had initiated in Washington before he was Prime Minister. It is perhaps worth while recalling that on this occasion of the tenth anniversary of America's entry into the World War which produced the Briand offer, there was hardly a comment in London recalling what it had meant to the hard-pressed Allies in April, 1917. The British Government took no such formal notice of the event as was the case in France. The dislike of the situation in which the war had left the British financial world was a new and somewhat disquieting note in Anglo-American relations. Formerly, such hostilities as had developed had been chiefly on the part of the Western Power. Now, Britain was apparently a partner in the European solidarity directed against the United States.

These elements of international misunderstanding should not be taken too seriously nor too literally, but, at the same time, they should not be forgotten in appraising the change which has come over American-European relations in the last few months, and chiefly as a result of the Briand offer. The political aspect of the debt problem which had left its mark in an European antagonism to the United States naturally had led to a similar response in this country. The situation did not improve as time went on. M. Briand's offer came at a time when the transatlantic sky was, if not ominous of storm, at least darkened and obscure. At such a moment, for a Foreign Minister deliberately to seek the hidden star by which to pilot his ship of state was an act, not only of the imagination, but of courage as well. The charges made in a part of the conservative American press that M. Briand was merely playing with the formula of peace in order to secure better terms of debt settlement is not only unworthy but untrue. It should not be forgotten that the negotiations concerning the war debt do not fall to the Foreign Office of France any more than to the State Department. It was M. Poincaré who was responsible for the proposals concerning the debt and the subsequent history shows rather clearly how little this master of logic in the field of politics seemed to care for what was possibly—unless America made it otherwise—a mere gesture of sentiment. M. Briand's offer was an individual act in harmony with his pacific statesmanship, the sincerity of which is no longer questioned in any country in Europe, and it would be as mistaken as it is ungenerous to attribute other motives to him.

As a matter of fact the offer was more than a gesture, even if America had not responded. It dealt with the fundamental rights and privileges of nations and touched that inner and sacred sphere of politics, which bears the mysterious name of sovereignty. As has already been pointed out, the proposal to renounce war as an instrument of national policy meant that the sovereign state was no longer free to use the most ancient symbol of its sovereignty, that of the free right to go to war.

At once, therefore, objections began to be raised and, as is always the case with great reforms, comment upon the proposal shaped up in terms of an informal and far-reaching debate. On the one hand, there were those who regarded the offer as doubly dangerous in that it awakened hopes incapable of fulfillment, or if partially fulfilled, imperiling the security of those who build upon it their policies of peace. Honest convictions were behind this opposition as well as nationalist prejudice. People began to see that the elimination of war involved a good many other things, some of which they were reluctant to accept. For there must be alternatives for the age-long method of settlement of dispute, and these were not yet agreed upon. Then, over against the conservative objections, there were those equally convinced that the proposal should be accepted for the very reason that the conservatives rejected it, arguing that it would increase rather than lessen the security of nations because the menace of war would be removed if it were carried out. They looked to the growing strength of public opinion in the civilized world to ensure that it would be carried out. The convinced internationalist at once joined issue with the convinced nationalist over the proposal.

But the mass of a nation belongs to neither of these two extremes of opinion; no civilized country is at bottom either predominantly pacifist or predominantly militarist. Between these two opposing wings lies the sober opinion of the mass of citizens, anxious for peace but equally anxious for the maintenance of their national institutions, their liberties and their rights in the world, and aware that war has been the instrument by which most of these have been won and asserted in the past. How could these two great interests of the state, international peace and national sovereignty, be harmonized so that the peace should be permanent and the sovereignty inviolate?

The heart of the peace problem lies in the second of these two questions. There are no two opinions in the civilized world concerning peace itself; but there still remains a doubt as to whether it is a safe measure to renounce the possibility of using force in a world which has grown up under the régime of war, and whether those nations which carried out in good faith their promises in this regard might not find themselves the defenseless victims of their unscrupulous neighbors. Moreover, war has been used in the past not only to establish the power of the strongest but also to restore the balance of justice and to restrain tyranny. Would it not be an ill-advised or even a dangerous thing for any nation to join in the renunciation of war before it had at its disposal alternatives and substitutes by which it could assert its claims and secure its rights with other nations? Seen in this light, the problem of international peace is not simply one of moral attitude but of practical politics.

M. Briand's proposal was destined to bring these issues to the consciousness of the civilized world in a way which no other proposal had ever done before, not even the controversy over the League of Nations. But problems of this magnitude do not exist simply by themselves in a realm of theory. They are set in a very real world of previous limitations and national engagements. M. Briand himself had referred to this fact in the terms of the offer itself when he reminded the United States that France had already entered upon obligations similar to those which he now proposed to the United States; that he regarded the Covenant of the League and the Treaties of Locarno as already binding France to the renunciation of war as the free instrument of its national policy, and that, therefore, so far as his Government was concerned, there was no novelty of experiment in the proposal which he made to the United States. The United States was confronted with a different situation; it had rejected the obligations of the League and was not a party to the Treaties of Locarno by which peace had been guaranteed for the countries of Western Europe.

Nevertheless, the United States was not entirely free of obligations of this kind, for it had been a party to two sets of treaties with most of the Great Powers, one of which—the so-called Bryan Treaties—involved at least a suspension of war in times of crises, and the other—known popularly as the Root Treaties—provided arbitration for the settlement of international disputes. Discussion of the Briand proposal therefore had to proceed upon the basis of these definite facts and not simply upon the broad basis of general theory. It was in order to clarify this definite situation that the document was prepared which forms the second chapter in the history of this movement to renounce war as an instrument of national policy.

CHAPTER VI

AN UNOFFICIAL DRAFT TREATY

THE best way to test a theory is to attempt to write it down under the conditions set for it by the stern facts of the existing world.

During the month which followed the publication of M. Briand's offer, discussion upon it continued in those general terms which permitted the repetition of convictions and prejudices but furnished no further light upon the exact meaning which the proposal would have for the United States under its existing treaty obligations and in view of its political and historical traditions and interests. To bring the matter to a more definite focus, in the closing days of May, my colleague Professor J. P. Chamberlain and I undertook to state in the terms of a draft treaty just what seemed to be involved in the French proposal.[1] The treaty form was chosen so as to make the statement as clear and definite as possible; but it was never intended to be anything more than a clarification of the situation upon which policies might be built and treaties conceivably drawn up which would state in pertinent and varying terms the three or four great principles set forth in this document.

The choice of a treaty form of statement had the great dis-

[1] There were several other drafts of treaties which appeared in the United States as suggested answers to the Briand offer. The American Foundation, which had turned aside from its original interest in the League of Nations,—as administrator of the Bok prize,—to a vigorous campaign for the adherence of the United States to the World Court, prepared a text which interpreted the Briand offer in terms of membership of the Court, or at least made this act an essential of acceptance. Professor Sayre of Harvard also prepared a treaty with similar emphasis upon international arbitration. These texts are not discussed here because they did not enter into subsequent phases of the diplomatic history. The Kellogg proposal did not take up the problem of substitutes for war.

advantage of being technical and forbidding. It was a legal document in which the very conciseness of statement presented an obstacle to the general reader, for almost every phrase of this short text had a history of its own. But although the form of statement was forbidding and the accompanying comment kept almost wholly within the field of technicalities, yet once more the surprising thing happened. The Draft Treaty, a mere academic document, became an item of national and even international news. Like M. Briand's first offer and Dr. Butler's letter, it was copied from paper to paper and commented upon to an extent which showed a surprising and vital interest both in the proposal to renounce war and in the position in which the United States had found itself after the refusal to become a member of the League of Nations.

There were some half dozen papers of the more conservative tendencies which came out now in open opposition to the proposal and attempted to throw ridicule upon the Draft Treaty, but although these papers secured, or claimed to have secured, through their correspondents at Washington sufficient material of denunciation from anonymous but highly placed officials of the Government, the denunciation and the opposing articles were hardly ever copied on the pages of the small-town papers of the Middle West, even those which had opposed most bitterly the entry of the United States into the League of Nations. This silence of the potential opposition was a no less striking fact than the nation-wide comment which the Draft Treaty secured.

But this was not the full extent of the journalistic surprise. The news of M. Briand's offer, combined with the fact that a treaty could be drafted which apparently both met the offer and safeguarded America's vital interests proved to be something more than a momentary incident. Through the entire summer the debate upon it continued with a steady trend of opinion in its favor.

When one looks over this discussion as a whole, one realizes how a democracy deals with the technical aspects of policy. The proposal itself had stated in terms which every one could understand a purpose and an ideal of American foreign policy concerning which there was practically no difference of opinion. But still the doubt remained as to whether the ideal could be embodied in definite and workable terms. Politics of the popular sort had been so much the embodiment of hypocrisy that with the growth of popular education there was an increasing distaste for the assertion of ideals which no one really intended to carry out. Parenthetically, it may be said that the older politicians have not learned that there is this growing aversion to hypocrisy in politics, and that is one reason why they are now giving way to men of more realistic bent. However this may be, the Draft Treaty of Professor Chamberlain and myself seemed to offer an assurance that the proposal of M. Briand was not an idle, if magnificent, gesture. It was something real, for which there were definite precedents both in the history of Europe and in our own. The United States had already taken on obligations which reached a long way toward the Briand offer and France had bound herself to other stipulations which covered the remainder of the proposal. The Draft Treaty did not merely assert that this was the case; it actually was built up out of the texts of existing treaties and drew them together into a single and consistent whole, adding the Briand renunciation of war to the Root treaties of arbitration and the Bryan treaties of conciliation, and restating them to fit in with the great declaration of Locarno. Popular interest lay not so much in the exact way in which these elements were harmonized into a single text as in the fact that any such harmonizing was possible. The importance of the Draft Treaty therefore lay in this fact, that it definitely brought the proposal for the renunciation of war into the sphere of practical and not merely theoretic discussion.

The full text of the Draft Treaty will be found in the appendix to this volume. Fortunately for the reader it is not necessary to discuss it in any great detail in this narrative because in the course of negotiations the treaties of arbitration and conciliation were kept separate from the proposal to renounce war, and formed the subject of independent treaties. Our interest here, therefore, is limited to that part of the Draft Treaty which dealt with the renunciation of war, Part I, and as it presents the main proposal in almost the literal terms of the Treaty of Locarno, it may be worth our while to have the exact text before us at this point. It reads as follows:

ARTICLE 1. The United States of America and . . .[1] mutually undertake that they will in no case attack or invade each other or resort to war against each other.

ARTICLE 2. The stipulation in the above article shall not, however, apply in the case of—

a. The exercise of the right of legitimate defense, that is to say, resistance to a violation of the undertaking contained in the previous article,

provided that the attacked party shall at once offer to submit the dispute to peaceful settlement or to comply with an arbitral or judicial decision;

b. Action by the United States of America in pursuance of its traditional policy with reference to the American continents,

provided that the United States will use its best endeavors to secure the submission to arbitration or conciliation of a dispute between an American and a non-American Power.

The sweeping renunciation of war in Article 1 states the general principle which is to determine and govern the policy of the signatory nations in the future. It is in the exact language of Locarno and is therefore already embodied in the international law of Western Europe. There, however, it is not

---

[1] For example, the countries whose plenipotentiaries signed the Pact of Paris and comprise its original signatories are: Germany, the United States, Belgium, France, Great Britain, Canada, Australia, New Zealand, Union of South Africa, Irish Free State, India, Italy, Japan, Poland and the Czechoslovak Republic.

merely a statement of general principle; it has behind it the guarantee of Britain and other Powers that in case a signatory does resort to war or invade or attack another signatory, it will have to reckon with the police power of Britain. In the American Draft Treaty, as we shall see later on, this provision for the enforcement of the peace is lacking. Nevertheless, it was possible to state the general principle in the language of Locarno.

Article 2 attempts to fit the new principle embodied in Article 1 into the existing world of real politics, and here at once we come upon the chief difficulty which confronts any treaty maker who attempts to provide for the elimination of war. There is another principle of the life of nations still more fundamental than that of international peace. It is the right of legitimate defense. The renunciation of war must in no way endanger the free exercise of this most fundamental of the attributes inherent in national sovereignty. And yet the free right of national defense has meant, in terms of history, the free right of waging war, for there have been few wars of modern times, at least between the highly civilized nations, which have not been wars of defense in the eyes of those who waged them or have not been so camouflaged as to be presented to the world under the color of defense. It is not necessary for a nation to be invaded to fight a defensive war. Its interests, even its vital interests, may be attacked outside its own frontiers. If, therefore, wars of defense are to be permitted under a treaty which purports to renounce war and there is no way for reaching an agreement as to what constitutes defense, but on the contrary each belligerent is free to determine for itself whether the war it is waging is defensive or not, we have a situation in which the general principle is falsified in the application. If the right to go to war is to be renounced and the right of a nation to defend itself is to be retained, there must be an agreement among the signatory Powers as to what constitutes the right of defense, for otherwise the same act of renunciation will mean different things to the different signatories when tested in the hour of trial.

The Draft Treaty met this dilemma by stating that national defense was legitimate in case the attacked party offered to submit the dispute to pacific settlement or to comply with an arbitral or judicial decision. This definition of legitimate defense is the same as that which is guaranteed in the Treaty of Locarno, although that Treaty states the principle by defining the aggressor rather than the defendant; the aggressor being that state which goes to war in violation of its pledge to submit the matter of the dispute to peaceful settlement, having already agreed to do so.[1]

The definition of defense has been rejected in the negotiations which followed, as inadequate and misleading. It has been claimed that it is inadequate because diplomacy can dress up the claims of nations so that the one which is really the aggressor may have the better legal case. It has been claimed that the definition calls for compulsory arbitration in cases where national honor and vital interest are at stake, and makes that nation an aggressor which will not accept the judgment of a biased or hostile international tribune over whose decisions it would have no controlling influence. This is not the place to argue the question in detail because the subsequent negotiations cut the Gordian knot of this discussion by refusing to face it. Nevertheless, although it has been purposely eliminated from the multilateral treaty, the problem still remains a real one and it may be worth while here to say in passing that neither of the two objections raised against this definition holds. The statement that an aggressor nation may present a winning case is not to the point, for aggression and defense do not concern themselves with the substance of the claims which one

[1] As a matter of history, it may be noted in passing that the Locarno Treaty took this device from the American suggestion which was embodied in the Geneva Protocol of 1924. Cf. International Conciliation Pamphlet No. 201.

nation may hold against another; they deal with an entirely
different question, namely, how does the nation proceed to
realize its claims? If it is by force and violence, by the exercise
of that continuing barbarism which is war, then no matter what
a nation's claims may be, it proceeds to seek redress by the
method of aggression; for aggression already has been defined
for approximately half the civilized world in the Treaties of
Locarno as the employment of force in the attainment of national purpose or the assertion of national claims. Behind this
force lie all the complicated motives and diverse interests of
nations which have hitherto been free to reach their purposes
unhampered by any such restriction as to the use of force. The
definition of aggression and defense not only denies the free
assertion of sovereign will to use war as an instrument of policy, but it erects a formal and definite test by which genuine
defense may be retained while the aggressive use of force is
denied. That test is the refusal of the alternative to war, which
is some pertinent form of peaceful settlement. To put it in the
simplest terms, that nation is a legitimate defendant which de-
fends itself while on the way to court. For "court," however,
in the international world, we must substitute a variety of institutions. A full discussion of this will follow later on, but it
is important even here to warn against the idea that the only
alternative for war is court or even arbitration. There are other
alternatives which do not involve the acceptance of a judgment
or a sentence from an international tribunal. In questions of
national honor and vital interests—terms which have been in
recent disrepute but nevertheless come back to us in one disguise or another—nations seek something less final than the
judgment of a court and find it in the processes of conciliation
and conference which seek agreement but do not necessarily
insist upon the binding acceptance of any given set of forms.
Now when a nation signs a treaty renouncing war as an instrument of its national policy, this means the alternative accept-

ance of institutions of peaceful settlement, for the problems of international politics do not cease with the signing of any one treaty, however far reaching it may be. Disputes and crises are ahead of us just as definitely in the era of pacific settlement as they have been under the régime of war; therefore it follows that that nation which proceeds to use the methods of war, which are force and violence, for the maintenance of its case even when it believes that that case touches its vital interests or national honor, is violating in practice the renunciation of war, and any treaty which fails to hold in the hour of crisis in which its safeguards are especially intended to apply, is admittedly inadequate. It would seem, therefore, that in renouncing war and at the same time reserving the right of defense it was necessary to know just what the reservation meant so that we should at the same time know what was meant by the renunciation of war itself. We shall, however, revert to this matter in a later chapter.

From questions of defense the Draft Treaty then turned to another problem which has hitherto escaped definition, that of the Monroe Doctrine of the United States. The Draft Treaty simply stated that the renunciation of war should not apply to action by the United States arising out of this traditional policy with reference to the American continents. But again there was a proviso which, while not defining the Monroe Doctrine, nevertheless prescribed the terms of its application so as to strengthen the institutions of arbitration and conciliation. The United States would not be *bound* to use either of these implements of settlement, but it promised to *use its best endeavors* to that end. This is a forward-looking statement in harmony with the most enlightened of recent international treaties. As Dr. Butler has pointed out, "It does not affect relations between the United States and other American powers, but only relations between the United States and non-American powers with reference to other American states. Matters of domestic jurisdiction, such as immigration and citizenship, are cared for and cannot be forced into arbitration under the terms of the treaty. Such questions could only come within the scope of the treaty if at some future time they become part of international law and so pass into the field of international relations. No such far-reaching step can be taken without the consent of the United States." In the unofficial discussion on this Draft Treaty it was this article on the Monroe Doctrine which received more attention and approval than any other single phase. This fact should not escape the notice of those who are interested in the fate of the multilateral treaty. Approval of the express reservation of the Monroe Doctrine from the renunciation of war was by no means limited to the conservative press of the country. If one could judge from the underlying tone of the comments, there was a general feeling of relief that the proposal for war renunciation did not involve giving up the Monroe Doctrine. On the other hand, the more radical wing of the peace movement objected strenuously to this reservation, apparently not realizing that to reserve the Monroe Doctrine from the operation of a new treaty merely left matters where they had been in the past, a point which at first escaped the Japanese commentators on the plan until their attention was called to it. For as we shall shortly see, the discussion of these issues soon extended outside the United States.

The first article of the Draft Treaty, as stated above, provides the general principle of war renunciation. The second article defines the terms of its application, safeguarding and defining the right of defense and of the Monroe Doctrine. The third article covers the equally important field of peace enforcement. It provides for what should happen in case of a violation of the treaty; and the subsequent negotiations over the Kellogg multilateral treaty were to show that without some such provision, the governments of Europe would regard the rest of the proposal as a mere declaration of good intentions. If America would not supply the pacific nations with a guarantee of peace, by taking action against a violator, at least she should not supply the violator with that guarantee by covenanting to remain at peace with it in spite of its aggression.[1] If there was need for a definition of aggression, there was still more need for some kind of assurance of solidarity of action against an undoubted aggressor. On the other hand, the United States had made it sufficiently clear in the debates over membership in the League of Nations that this question of peace enforcement was one in which it would not enter into any general covenant which would affect its freedom of action if war actually were to break out between other nations. In all the differences which have arisen between the American and European points of view concerning the League of Nations this question of peace enforcement is the one outstanding problem and is still farther removed from settlement now than when the issue was first joined in the Senate debates. Europe tends more and more to put its emphasis upon the joint and coöperative action of peace enforcement, and America tends more and more to withdraw from any such method of joint action. Article 3 of the Draft Treaty attempts to bridge the gulf between these two divergent points of view. It makes provision for peace enforcement by denying to the aggressor, that is to say, the violator of this treaty, the assurance of continuing peace-time relations; but does not bind each signatory to apply any definite measures or become involved in an international police. Each signatory undertakes not to aid or abet the treaty-breaking Power, and in

[1] The first to call attention to the difficulty of peace-enforcement upon the part of the League of Nations, and more especially of Great Britain as League member, due to the possible insistence of the United States upon its rights as a neutral to trade with a Power which might be defying the League, was Mr. David Mitrany, in his short but compact volume, *The Problem of International Sanctions* (1925). Subsequently Mr. Wickham Steed pointed the same argument very effectively. See also below, especially in connection with Senator Capper's and Congressman Burton's Resolutions, in Chapter IX.

case the aggressor is one of the signatories of the treaty the other signatories recover liberty of action with reference to it. They are released from the obligation to remain at peace. Nevertheless, the treaty provides only a warning and a menace. It does not stipulate definite measures but provides that each government shall determine for itself and in the light of its own obligations how it will make good the moral duty not to further the designs of an aggressive government.

All of this was set forth in Article 3 of the Draft Treaty in terms which should have reassured those who feared that the Briand offer would tie our hands in case the other signatory went to war with some other Power. The text reads as follows:

For the furtherance of universal peace among nations, the High Contracting Parties agree:

that in the event of a breach of a treaty or covenant for the compulsory peaceful settlement of international disputes other than this covenant, each of them undertakes that it will not aid or abet the treaty-breaking Power. In the event that the treaty-breaking Power is one of the High Contracting Parties, the other Party recovers full liberty of action with reference to it.

The measures to be taken in this regard shall be determined in the case of the United States of America by the action of its own Government, in the case of . . .[1] in accordance with its existing treaty obligations.

The second paragraph of this Article was a reminder of practical politics. The provision that the American Government was to be its own judge of what it should or should not do was merely an emphatic insistence upon the existing state of affairs, to quiet any apprehension on that score. The United States has no treaty obligation applicable in such a case; but members of the League of Nations have. They are bound by the provisions of the Covenant, which, by its own terms

[1] France and each of the other signatories.

(Article 20), has precedence over any other treaty.[1] Thus, the reference to "existing treaty obligations" referred to either the Covenant or treaties in harmony with it. This ought to have been a clear reference, but it turned out not to be sufficiently explicit for European readers.

This declaration that a signatory to the treaty should recover liberty of action against an aggressor is after all implicit in the renunciation of war itself, a fact which was subsequently recognized in the final preamble of the multilateral treaty in the short but exceedingly important phrase, that "any signatory Power which shall hereafter seek to promote its national interests by resort to war should be denied the benefits furnished by this treaty." The significance of this form of statement will be discussed below.[2]

We need not delay here over Articles 4 and 5 of the Draft Treaty, one calling for the codification of international law on the basis of the renunciation of war as an instrument of national policy and the other providing for appropriate conferences to study the ways and means for the progressive reduction of armaments. Part II of the Draft Treaty, however, contains the two existing treaties with France for the peaceful settlement of disputes, the Arbitration Treaty and the Bryan Treaty, both of them readjusted to the new provisions of Part I.[3]

---

[1] "The Members of the League severally agree that this Covenant is accepted as abrogating all obligations or undertakings *inter se* which are inconsistent with the terms thereof, and solemnly undertake that they will not hereafter enter into any engagements inconsistent with the terms thereof.

"In case any Member of the League shall, before becoming a Member of the League, have undertaken any obligations inconsistent with the terms of this Covenant, it shall be the duty of such Member to take immediate steps to procure its release from such obligations."

This article of the Covenant should be kept in mind in all proposals for changes in the structure of international relations.

[2] Cf. Chapter XIX.

[3] First, as to the Arbitration Treaty which was due to expire at the end of a ten-year period, on February 27, 1928: it was the poor and emasculated text which Roosevelt denounced as being no arbitration treaty at all because, each

The Draft Treaty as a whole, therefore, covered the situation created by the Briand offer in terms of the existing treaties with France and showed as well the setting of such a proposal with reference to the League of Nations or the Locarno Treaties. It was clear from a study of this document that the proposal to renounce war as an instrument of national policy went far beyond the existing commitments of the United States, but equally clear that it was not beyond the commitments of Europe, if generously interpreted in the spirit in which they were conceived. Once more the United States was to be brought face to face with the realities of a changing world with which it had not kept pace and would be challenged to make good in practice the ideals of international peace which it had suggested in the past so often and so strongly. But it was also evident that the challenge of our idealism could be met without committing us to policies over which we should have no control or binding us to the fate of other countries. In short, the Briand offer could be met by the United States without other participation in international politics than was inherent in the peacetime intercourse of civilized nations. It was perhaps because this was seen to be the case that the Draft Treaty became the sub-

time a case arose, the United States Senate was to make a new and special treaty defining the matter in dispute. Besides that, it did not cover any question affecting the vital interests, the independence or the honor of the two contracting states or those involving the interests of third parties. In the unofficial text before us the arbitration treaty was left practically unchanged because it was prefaced by an all-inclusive clause that no matter whether the case went to arbitration or not, nevertheless the signatories would not go to war about it. There was no need for providing for compulsory arbitration if the signatories were deprived of war as an alternative. By mere necessity the scope of such a treaty as this would be exceeded in actual practice, for there would be no other way of nations dealing with each other than by extending and applying its peace provisions.

This was equally true of the second treaty embodied in the draft which was the Bryan Treaty of Conciliation. The text chosen here was also that already in force between the United States and France. There is a strange ignorance concerning these Bryan Treaties even in quarters where one might expect a familiarity with them. They are not treaties of arbitration; they simply provide that there shall be a neutral board of inquiry to examine the subject of dispute when two nations fail to reach agreement through the ordinary diplomatic channels, a ject of such extensive discussion in the summer and autumn of 1927.

The Draft Treaty was written from a distinctly American angle. Not only had the treaty obligations of the United States been kept in mind, but traditional American policies as well. One of these, the Monroe Doctrine, was mentioned in the text, but another not less fundamental principle of American foreign policy, the avoidance of anything resembling an alliance with other Powers, was responsible for a still more important change from the original Briand offer. M. Briand had not proposed a world-wide treaty, but that France and the United States should sign an act of friendship and mutual confidence which would give formal expression to the historical relationship of these two countries and would at the same time furnish an example to the rest of the world. He submitted his original offer somewhat in the light of a declaration of an established political principle limited to the two countries where it was already in operation. The formal statement of this principle would impress the public opinion of the world and thus contribute to the peace movement generally, but he did not draft his proposal so as to indicate that it should be extended to other signatories, at least in its original form.

board which has no power to reach a judgment or impose a sentence; all that it can do is to investigate the facts and set them forth, leaving the disputing nations to decide whether or not they can come to terms. After the report of the commission has been made, the signatories recover full liberty of action, which may very well mean the settlement of the quarrel by force of arms. The Bryan Treaty, therefore, interposed an interval of peace during which the contesting statesmen might have time to quiet and repress the war spirit arising from any provocative incident. But it is only an armistice that is secured. The Bryan Treaties imply a recognition of the right of war if the commission fails to bring the nations together. In the Draft Treaty the whole bearing of the text was changed by the addition of a single phrase: "The High Contracting Parties reserve full liberty as to the action to be taken on the report and recommendations for settlement of the Commission *subject to the provisions of Part I of the Draft Treaty.*" This means that the High Contracting Parties reserve full liberty of action except the right to go to war, for that right is denied them in the provisions of Part I. Thus the temporary armistice of the Bryan Treaty would become permanent and war ruled out as the arbiter of the dispute.

On the other hand, the authors of the Draft Treaty were fully convinced that anything resembling a merely rhetorical declaration of Franco-American friendship would be discounted even beyond its real merits by American public opinion, and therefore they reshaped the proposal for the renunciation of war as an instrument of national policy so that it might apply not only to France and the United States but to all other civilized nations. The press comment in the United States showed at once that this extension of the suggested plan truly reflected American opinion. There had been a quick suspicion that the original proposal might involve some sort of disguised alliance with France and might be used by it to further its own European policies. This was an unnecessary and a false interpretation of the Briand offer, but it emphasized the need of shaping America's reply in terms that could not possibly carry any such implication. The Draft Treaty, therefore, was drawn up in general terms, and not merely as a bilateral treaty between France and the United States. This, however, did not mean that it should be offered for signature to any and every government, for there are nations whose political development is so immature that they are unable to repress either war or revolution, and in the irresponsibility of their essential anarchy readily accept obligations which they have no serious intention of carrying out. It is a very serious question whether the highly civilized nations should make treaties of war renunciation with nations of this semi-barbarous stage of development even although they may present the outward forms of constitutional and settled government; the possible need of international police action in such countries presents a situation difficult to harmonize with the renunciation of war. The great experiment of war renunciation should at least be tested and worked out first by those nations to whom peace has become a definite ideal and a necessity. But among these there should be no distinctions. Therefore, the Draft Treaty was drawn up to apply to the great Powers of Europe and to Japan as signatories of the existing treaty of arbitration.

When the Draft Treaty was published in Europe, the widening of the proposal caused an entirely new turn in the discussion. In France it did not have a friendly press. As though responsive to some word of authority, the Paris papers withheld publication of the text but commented widely upon it in terms that showed both disappointment and concern, for although it was merely an academic document, the treaty form in which it had been drawn seemed to imply that it was based upon close attention to the conditions of American history and politics and that therefore the simple expression of Franco-American friendship in M. Briand's proposal would probably be taking another form. M. Briand himself fell ill, and his absence from the Quai d'Orsay added an element of confusion. When an inquiry was addressed to some members of the Foreign Office as to what was meant by the phrase "renunciation of war as an instrument of policy," the answer was that no one seemed to know exactly but that they feared the worst! It was evident that an attempt at the clarification of American opinion had had an opposite effect in France.

The situation there was not improved by the abundant signs of nation-wide interest in Germany concerning the proposal as restated in America. The papers of Berlin gave it far more space than those of Paris and one great liberal journal went so far as to have the entire text and lengthy comment cabled from New York, the kind of journalistic enterprise in which the Continental press seldom indulges without some official reason. German public opinion was quickly stirred and prompt to respond to the suggestion of the multilateral treaty. Attention was called to the fact that the suggestion of an "American Locarno" had been made in Berlin in the presence of the Chancellor and most members of the German Government at the inaugural lecture of the Carnegie professorship in the *Hochschule für Politik*, and that the conception had received wide publicity, although it was quite apparent at the time that it was then nothing more than an academic proposition.[1] A syndicate of German papers even cabled all over the world for the opinions of prominent statesmen and public men concerning the Draft Treaty. The answers yielded the rather doubtful result that some of the strongest assertions of approval came from the dictators of Fascist governments. It was already evident that the danger of demagoguery as well as of reaction lay in wait for any such proposal to renounce war as an instrument of national policy.

The favorable reaction in Germany did not improve matters in Paris, for it emphasized still more the contrast between a Franco-American agreement and one which would tie in with all the existing complications of European politics. Meanwhile, the British attitude towards the whole matter did not help the situation. There was an almost total indifference in England to both the initial offer of M. Briand and the American discussion as to the possibilities that it presented. There was the traditional British doubt as to whether a general proposal of this kind meant anything at all, and in the circumstances it apparently seemed best to the experienced British observers to let M. Briand find his own way out of the difficulties which he had apparently made for himself. There was nothing British in the method of approach to the question, establishing a general theory without a definite and clear idea of its application. Both officially and unofficially, therefore, Britain left the field to France and the United States and any other nations which cared to join in the study of international morals. There is a point at which the British attitude of mind can be more cynical

---

[1] The German text has been published by the *Hochschule für Politik*, an English text in the Year Book of the Carnegie Endowment for 1927, and a French text in *L'Esprit International*, October, 1927.

in practice than the French can be in theory. British interest in the proposal was distinctly lacking or suppressed until the American Government finally, some months later, threw back the initial challenge to Britain itself.

CHAPTER VII

THE BRIAND TREATY OFFER

On June 7 the Washington correspondent of the New York *Times* published the news that the French Government had approached the American Ambassador in Paris with a suggestion for the negotiation of a treaty between France and the United States for the elimination of war and the preservation of lasting peace between the two nations. The exact date of this earliest official move, judging from newspaper accounts, seems to have been June 3. The terms of the memorandum which M. Briand handed Ambassador Herrick on that occasion have not been published, but in the summary given out in Paris on June 9, it was stated that it proposed a treaty which would differ from any other treaty of the kind ever written. "Even Locarno had within it the element of threat and sanction in the case of aggression and war between any two of the parties. The League of Nations' Covenant, primarily framed for the preservation and development of peace, contained also the element of preparation against war. The Franco-American treaty would not contain, or in French opinion ought not to contain, any phrase or condition which could be in any way interpreted as indicating an alliance between France and the United States against any one or that it could become so. It should, in M. Briand's idea, be as simple as possible in phrasing and contain only the solemn declaration of the two countries that under no circumstances would they resort to war between themselves but would keep the peace always." The Paris correspondents again went on to state that "it was no secret that such a compact between the two great republics was regarded as

infinitely preferable for the moment to any other more grandiose scheme." That peace had existed for a century and a half
between France and the United States was the best augury that
it would continue. Similar ventures in other fields, however,
might prove riskier. France, for instance, had lived at peace
with her neighbor England for a full century, but it would be
going beyond what either country considered for the present a
natural and human relationship to extend the entente in such
a permanent peace.

In view of the subsequent events, the attitude of Washington
to this memorandum is somewhat puzzling. The only comment
from the State Department was that Secretary Kellogg would
be glad to discuss anything looking towards the preservation of
international peace and might answer M. Briand shortly;
which in the language of diplomacy is a somewhat definite hint
to let the matter drop. This hint was strengthened in the news
item which followed that "those whose views might be sought
by the Administration expressed the opinion that no such treaty
of peace was necessary between France and the United States
and, indeed, that it would not even be desirable." Opposition
was already taking shape, falling back upon the contention that
the Arbitration Treaty of 1908 was still in force as well as the
Bryan Treaty of 1914. The anonymous authority, quoted in the
Washington dispatches, went so far as to suggest that the Bryan
Treaty must have been overlooked by M. Briand, for no new
treaty would likely be any stronger in the provisions for preserving peace than those in the existing treaty. It was denied
that M. Briand's original proposal had met with anything like
nation-wide approval and, finally, it was contended that the
proposed treaty would bind the United States to come to the
aid of France in case the latter went to war with another European country. There was an additional discordant note which
was especially noticed in France, when, on the following day,

it was objected to the Briand offer that the French war debt should first be paid, before any such generous exchange of pacific ideals. Washington was reputed to have little interest in a peace note with France until the debt settlement was accepted by France. The French rejoinder to this, contained in dispatches from Paris, was a gentle reminder that this would imply that until its debts were paid in full the United States desired to keep free to break its long record of peace and friendship with France so as to be in the position of using a threat of war, however far removed, to collect its debts. The parallel with other debt-collecting operations with smaller states was hardly more than suggested, but enough was said to make the American student of the situation grateful that this kind of argument in Washington against the conclusion of the Briand Treaty was soon dropped.

There was one part of the Washington statement which called for and received attention from leaders of the peace movement in the United States. It was the reference to the Bryan Treaty. The Commission of Inquiry, for which that treaty provides, should be kept active and not allowed to lapse. The investigators discovered by inquiry at the State Department that of the score of treaties which had been negotiated, the only ones in full effect at the time were those with Denmark, Sweden and Portugal. No American commissioner had been appointed to the Franco-American Board since the death of Mr. Richard Olney, in the year following the ratification of the treaty; and the French member, the distinguished jurist, M. Louis Renauld, had also died during the war, and no new members had been appointed by either country. The Anglo-American Commission was similarly incomplete through the deaths of Lord Bryce and of the American member, Judge George Gray, and there never had been Bryan treaties with Japan or Germany, so that if the French proposal were to be enlarged in scope, as Washington intimated, the parallel of the Bryan treaties of investigation was still more inappropriate.[1] The plain truth was, as the New York *Times* pointed out, that to all intents and purposes the Bryan Treaties were no longer in force as between any of the Great Powers.

In view of what has happened since, it is necessary to insist on the fact that Washington did not at first readily accept and enthusiastically endorse the Briand proposal. On the contrary, it was cool to the point of discouragement and had not other unofficial events supplied the missing stimulus, it is doubtful if the proposal would ever have reached the terms of an official treaty. One of the most important events from the point of view of popular interest was the flight to Paris of Colonel Charles Lindbergh. It was not merely the heroic episode itself but the winning charm of personality and the sincerity of his friendly message which almost instantly dissipated the enmities which had been too long exploited in the daily press. Seldom has a private individual so stirred the pulse of two nations; and, at least in Paris, it seemed a fitting moment to give lasting expression to the new-found emotion. But one cannot build too much upon the passing interest of even such an outstanding event as this. It had to be taken up and consciously utilized or it would have marked no permanent turning of national attitudes. A temporary enthusiasm by cheering crowds is a vastly different thing from the formulation of policies of state.

Fortunately, just at this moment, Dr. Nicholas Murray Butler arrived in Paris and once more performed the service of unofficial *liaison* between American public opinion and that of France. Understanding both of these, and sensing the difficulties of a too complete statement of plans at that time, he restated the three main principles of the Franco-American

---

[1] It should be added that as a result of the light thrown upon the state of the Bryan Commissions, the Administration proceeded to fill the vacant places in a number of these Commissions during the following months.

proposal in three simple straightforward terms. These were, (1) the renunciation of war as an instrument of national policy, (2) the recognition of the legitimacy of national defense under definite and agreed conditions, and (3) the obligation not to aid or abet any nation going to war in violation of its given pledge to use pacific means of settlement. These three points were, in the words of M. Briand, already familiar to the signatories of the Covenant and of the Treaties of Locarno; indeed, it is doubtful if they go as far as those treaties to bind nations to policies of peace.[1] Dr. Butler's simplification of the proposal is almost as important for what was omitted as for what was retained. For one thing, there was no mention in it of the Monroe Doctrine. France could not easily become a party to any proposal likely to be unacceptable to Latin American states, if for no other reason than her possible need of their votes in the Assembly of the League of Nations. Even at the Peace Conference, the insistence of President Wilson that the Monroe Doctrine should be recognized formally in the Covenant of the League had shown how keen were the susceptibilities of other nations to the mere mention of the Monroe Doctrine. The record of that debate of the Paris Peace Conference shows as well how little the Monroe Doctrine was understood either in theory or in history.[2] In any case the formal offer of France could hardly include reference to a distinctly American doctrine.

Dr. Butler's three points as suggestions were, to be sure, not advanced to the Foreign Office but simply as a clarification of what America was thinking, or would be likely to think, of an offer of this kind. Nevertheless, his statement must have reassured those in France who had been somewhat disturbed by what they termed the "grandiose" character of the Draft Treaty and its complications.

[1] Speech before the American Club in Paris, June 16, 1927.
[2] Cf. David Hunter Miller's *History of the Covenant*, Vol. I, Chapter XXXII.

In the midst of these events, M. Briand was called to Geneva for the meeting of the Council of the League of Nations, and it is well known that the influence of Geneva worked strongly in support of the plan of the French Foreign Minister. Whatever discouragement he may have felt on leaving Paris for the city of the League of Nations, he had no sooner returned from the meeting of the League than he proceeded to take the first decisive step in the direction of an actual treaty. Some day America will learn the priceless value of the League of Nations, whose mere existence strengthens the ideals of governments and whose technical staff offers to them undistorted vision in international problems. In any case, without going too far beneath the surface of events, we find that on June 20 M. Briand offered to Mr. Herrick, the American Ambassador in Paris, the proposal for a treaty to embody his offer of April 6, the text of which was destined to outlast all the discussions of the year following and, finally, under another name to bear the brunt of world-wide scrutiny, as the two fundamental articles of Mr. Kellogg's multilateral treaty. There were just two articles of this treaty with the exception of the provisions for signature and ratification. They read as follows:

ARTICLE 1. The High Contracting Powers solemnly declare, in the name of the French people and the people of the United States of America, that they condemn recourse to war and renounce it respectively as an instrument of their national policy towards each other.

ARTICLE 2. The settlement or the solution of all disputes or conflicts, of whatever nature or of whatever origin they may be, which may arise between France and the United States of America, shall never be sought by either side except by pacific means.

This text was not given to the public at the time; it was not published until January 11, 1928, when Mr. Kellogg finally gave it out. Washington, upon the whole—that is to say, the State Department—maintained its air of mystery, and the existence of the offer of the French Government was both asserted and denied in the press. There was little to be gleaned by the newspaper correspondents, and Mr. Kellogg himself refrained from public comment of any kind.

In the interval of silence which followed, the forces of reaction received support from an unexpected quarter. The claim was made that the Constitution of the United States would not permit the acceptance of the Briand proposal because the Constitution bestowed upon Congress the right to declare war and this prerogative could not be nullified by treaty. There is no doubt about the Constitutional powers. Article 1, Section 8, of the Constitution [1] enumerates the powers of Congress and definitely places in its hands the right of declaring war. It was one of the safeguards of representative government which had been inserted in the Constitution by wise provision against a possible extension of autocratic or imperialist ambitions upon the part of the Executive. When the Constitution was written, the right to go to war was an unquestioned prerogative of sovereignty and its exercise had to be provided for in the Constitution. No one in the closing days of the eighteenth century could have foreseen that this very prerogative might some day pass away from the governments of all the civilized nations by a common act of self-renunciation, or even that the time would come when governments would agree to give up the practice of asserting a nation's cause by force of arms. Therefore, it at first seemed to many who read the legal argument that the Constitution of the United States would prevent acceptance of the Briand proposal.

It did not take long, however, for a contrary opinion to appear. It was pointed out that if Article 1, Section 8, of the Constitution were interpreted this way, we could hardly make any treaties at all, for the powers of Congress extended over most of the sphere of government covered by treaty provisions. For example, this same section of the Constitution stated that

[1] See Appendix II.

Congress was given authority "to provide for the common defense . . . ; to raise and support armies . . . ; and to provide and maintain a navy." This could not be taken to mean that the United States was disbarred from making disarmament agreements with other countries by treaty or conference, for at that very time President Coolidge had issued a call for just such a conference on the limitation of naval armaments. Moreover, the same section of the Constitution stated that Congress should have power "to regulate commerce with foreign nations." But this did not mean that the Government of the United States was prohibited from making tariff agreements with other countries or reciprocity treaties. In the very same sentence of the sub-section which granted to Congress the right to declare war, it was granted as well the right to authorize private warfare by the issuance of "letters of marque and reprisal." But this right of Congress belongs to an era which has passed away, for it would now be regarded as little else than the sanction of piracy. When the European Powers formally renounced it in the Treaty of Paris in 1856, the fact that the United States was not a co-signatory was not due to any argument that it could not do so on account of the provision in the Constitution. The American point of view was that the renunciation of lawlessness at sea did not go far enough, a fact realized still more in Lincoln's time, when the exercise of sea power was no longer an academic question to the Federal Government.[1] It would be a strange over-emphasis of conservative legalism to insist upon our retention of the right to equip

[1] President Pierce summed up the situation in his annual message of Dec. 2, 1856, by stating that the United States had declared itself willing to adhere to the clause of the Declaration of Paris abolishing privateering if it were agreed that at the same time the "public armed vessels" of belligerents should not seize non-contraband private property. The issue was purely one of policy. In April, 1861, Mr. Seward proposed to Europe the adherence of the United States to the Declaration abolishing privateering, *with or without* the above additional clause. The precedent of the Declaration of Paris is exactly pertinent to the Pact of Paris, because both are for all time. Cf. Moore's *Digest*, V, 561 ff.

privateers because that practice was permitted in the days when the Constitution was framed and therefore is embodied in our own instrument of government. Similarly, we may deny ourselves the exercise of the use of war "as an instrument of national policy," interpreting this clause in the Constitution in the sense in which it was first intended, namely, that this is a power which in no case should be exerted freely by the Executive without a legislative check upon its action. That check is now to be still further extended until the question at issue, the safeguard of liberty which this provides against our own internal dangers, is no longer a reality. If there is danger of tyranny through the undue exercise of war power on the part of the President—and the history of republics has many a sad reminder of this possibility—there is safety in the non-exercise of the right of war, and if that non-exercise is indefinitely extended by agreement with other states, it is but a still further fulfillment of the original purpose of this article.

Had the question of the Constitution not been raised in such authoritative quarters it would hardly be necessary to discuss it at length. The simple fact of the matter is that the objection raised concerning the Constitution does not hold. The United States has as complete liberty to participate by treaty in effecting measures for international peace as any other civilized Power.

This constitutional argument, however, does raise another question which is more far-reaching than the point which we have just been discussing. It is the relative scope and validity of treaties as over against domestic legislation. For example, take a subject like immigration. It is admitted everywhere that nations have, or should have, the right to determine who shall settle in their territory. The control of immigration, therefore, from this point of view, is a domestic matter. But immigration is also emigration, and here we come upon the international aspect of the problem. It has been wrongly asserted recently, in the Havana Conference, that in the United States the question of immigration falls wholly within the jurisdiction of domestic law. As a matter of fact a treaty negotiated under the Constitution of the United States has the force of law; it has the same validity as a statute, and where a treaty and a statute conflict, the latest controls. This may bring a clash between domestic law and treaty, and when they do clash, the civilized world has evolved no device to bring them back to harmony. The only hold that one nation has upon another in a question of this kind lies in its national honor. Among civilized nations the pledged word is the equivalent of law, and the more civilization develops, the stronger are these bonds of honor among nations. Nevertheless, the practical problems arising from the relation of domestic jurisdiction to treaties are not likely to be solved according to any single formula; for the very growth of the community of nations which forces the sovereign states to recognize rules of common obligation throughout the world is bound to extend the scope of international law in proportion as the dealings of nations with each other increase. At the same time, it would not be progress but a backward step for nations which have slowly but finally attained the goal of representative government and liberties guaranteed by constitutions to surrender these safeguards for anything that weakens or lessens them.

The problem which the Briand proposal raises is not merely one of peace and war but of the proper setting and orientation of internal and external government, the obligations that are self-imposed through domestic legislation and those accepted by mutual agreement with other free self-governing communities. International law and domestic law must find their harmony in working toward the same distant or immediate ends. The necessities of peace will increase the pace of this adjustment, but they will not immediately answer every question. The problem will perhaps never be fully answered, but just as justice itself has never yet been attained, though the striving for it is the highest aspiration of social life, so the upbuilding of international law in terms of the new conceptions of international morality will furnish not only the direction but the meaning as well to sound policies of state.

This slight digression on questions of sovereignty and constitutional law opens up a field too wide to be covered here. Fortunately, however, the steady pressure of public opinion has left the question behind for purely academic discussion. It is true that the United States cannot give an effective pledge that no future Congress will ever declare war; but neither can any other nation give such a pledge. Strictly speaking, no one Congress can bind future Congresses, nor can any one Administration bind future Administrations contrary to the vested powers of the Federal Government as stated in the Constitution. But the whole question of constitutionality can be avoided, and is avoided, in the present proposal, which does not deny the theory of sovereign powers vested in governments but only prescribes a direction for their use. The war power is not to be used as "an instrument of national policy." This, it is true, is a limitation of the exercise of that power, but it does not, in terms at least, deny the power itself. Moreover it applies only as between the signatories of the treaty in good standing. Outside the bounds of the treaty, war with non-signatory nations remains as valid an instrument of policy as in the past, and within the treaty whole fields are reserved in which it may still be resorted to. If, in these reserved areas, the United States were to go to war,—to assert its policies,—the declaration of that war would still be the prerogative of Congress. It ought to be self-evident that peoples living under constitutions which safeguard their liberties against their own executives' militaristic tendencies, can, in harmony with this provision, lessen still further the occasions in which those tendencies might be exploited. Democracy can direct its governments to choose only the ways of peace for the furtherance of its designs without divesting itself of its historic attributes of sovereignty.

Had there been a popular opposition to the Briand proposal, the legal argument would have made itself heard much more than was actually the case. The fact that it was not taken up widely nor strongly supported was an additional proof that the public opinion of the country remained favorable to the proposal.

CHAPTER VIII

THE GROWING POWER OF PUBLIC OPINION

IF the present proposals to rid the world of the menace of international war are destined to have any far-reaching measure of success, the ultimate credit for this achievement will belong not to any individual statesman, either to the imaginative foresight and courage and idealism of M. Briand, or to the coöperation and persistent diplomacy of Mr. Kellogg, as shown in the later phases of the negotiation. The ultimate credit belongs to the people themselves rather than to their governments; for, on both sides of the Atlantic, signs multiplied, as time went on, of the existence and the strength of that will to peace without which all the devices of statecraft and the formal promises of treaties are of slight value or endurance.

The real extent of popular support for the Briand proposal was doubly difficult to measure because of the natural tendency of people to state as more or less of a platitude their constant and enduring love of peace when they have given little thought as to whether they really mean it or not; and besides this, the news value which was ultimately discovered in M. Briand's words seemed to lie partly in the fact that it was the Foreign Minister of France who was speaking. It was not, therefore, easy to appraise at its full value the popular interest which showed itself in the early phases of the negotiations. But as the summer wore along and early autumn came, it was evident that the proposal was not likely to turn out an incident that could be passed by and forgotten, hidden away in that limbo for lost ideals which exists in the Foreign Offices of many countries. On both sides of the Atlantic popular support for it grew steadily. In America this was all the more surprising in view of the silence which was maintained at Washington. Nevertheless, slowly and practically unobserved by those who judge of public opinion through the great metropolitan press alone, the thought, or at least the hope, kept finding expression in the daily and weekly press of the small town papers that a way might yet be found by which the United States could, without unduly sacrificing its historical traditions, participate in the great work of world pacification. This expression of American opinion came from sections of the country which had seemed most remote from the influence of the outside world, the smaller towns of the Middle West beyond the Mississippi. It was becoming apparent that a new spirit was growing up within the United States, or at least had begun to show itself, which may yet register in terms of history the real and lasting impress left upon the country by the World War. Not all the great events of history, even in the field of politics, are those which find immediate expression through government action. The deeper currents of public opinion are those which gain their movement almost unobserved and with quiet but irresistible power sweep from their moorings the prejudices and time-worn conceptions of the past and carve out for themselves new channels as they go. This is what has been happening in the United States as a result of the World War, and while it is always unsafe to anticipate the judgments of history, we doubt if any other political effect of the World War has been of greater importance than that which has begun to transform the outlook of the common citizen of the United States with reference to international affairs.

What is referred to here is nothing less than the passing of parochial America. This is something more far-reaching than the issues involved in Washington's farewell address or Jefferson's first inaugural. Neither Washington nor Jefferson was parochial in outlook. The policy of abstention from the affairs

of other nations may be based upon a knowledge and understanding of them; it is only parochial when it is the expression
of self-satisfied ignorance. Parochial politics are those which,
ignoring the outside world, rely upon inherited prejudice for
the support of opinion and of policy. The distinctive mark of
parochialism is not so much aloofness from the world as a
certain distrust of it, a distrust which in its turn increases isolation by erecting barriers to the open understanding of the ways
and outlook of other peoples. This phase of a nation's development is often disguised even in its own eyes by the chauvinism
which boasts its strength while really confessing its political
immaturity. The United States was rapidly leaving this stage
of its development behind before 1917. The spread-eagleism of
the nineteenth century was no longer a dominant characteristic,
because the anticipation of power had already been realized.
The parochial outlook, however, was still there, for although
the idle or provocative assertions of national greatness were no
longer commonly to be heard, there was still but little interest
in the world outside our frontiers, and in those questions which
make up what is now called by the rather extravagant term,
"world politics." In the last ten years the national outlook has
largely changed in this respect and, while the inherent conservatism of American foreign policies has withstood the impact
of the new order of things which found expression in the
League of Nations, the gathering force of growing enlightenment in public opinion has at last begun to make its effect felt in
other ways. There was more than momentary significance in the
nation-wide popular demand for a cancellation or at least a
radical reduction of the navy-building program of last winter
and in the support given to the proposal for a multilateral
treaty to renounce war as an instrument of national policy.

It may seem like forcing a paradox to claim that the chief
political effect of the World War upon the United States has
been the passing of the parochial attitude of mind with

reference to world affairs when this has been the very period in which the United States has registered its strongest protest against direct participation in world politics in the refusal to become involved in the affairs of the League of Nations and to adhere to the Permanent Court of International Justice for the reason that the conditions attached seemed to be drawing us away from our traditional isolation. But the historian who looks for the clew to history in only outward and visible acts of policy is not likely to discover the real meaning of the events with which he deals. While there has been no lessening of the popular support of the traditional policy of non-entanglement in external affairs, there has been growing up an entirely different attitude towards other nations and their problems, and a new appreciation of the fact that any major event taking place in distant corners of the world, for which the United States has no initial responsibility whatever, is almost sure to involve this country sooner or later. The parallel existence of these two points of view is nothing new in politics; it is what lies behind the British maxim of "muddling through," and is valid because politics is no more logical than life itself. In the interplay of opposing tendencies, a nation's interest is stimulated to assume responsibilities. The United States is at the present day schooling itself in the best of all possible ways to take its place as a World Power. It is doubtful if any other nation, at least prior to the World War, ever took up the task of political self-education so earnestly and seriously as has been the case in the United States during the last ten years. It is only when one carefully examines the situation that one realizes the extent of the change which has been brought about primarily as an effect of the World War, not only in the formal education of school and college but still more in the vast process of adult education which through both the written and the spoken word affects the mass of the citizens of any alert democracy.

The change which has taken place in public interests during

the last decade cannot be measured by any statistical devices, but there are some visible signs of it in the number of new societies which have come into existence for the study of international relations. No one knows just how many of these there are in the country at the present time, but a survey made a year or so ago of those with a very considerable membership showed that there were something like twelve hundred organizations for the study of problems in international politics. In 1914 there could scarcely have been a tenth of that number. In addition to these new creations, the programs of existing societies which formerly had but little interest in international affairs now tend to give them a preferred place. This is true of such nation-wide organizations as the Federation of Women's Clubs with over five million membership, an organization which has apparently gained in strength as it has turned from literary and artistic discussions to those of the serious business of citizenship. It is also true, but in a less degree, of the programs of the business men's clubs, like the Rotary or Kiwanis. Naturally, much of this adult education is still in the primary grade, but even that is more than had been attempted in the past by some countries which have held a worldwide empire.

What is more, this interest is at bottom not academic but practical. There has been a simple feeling of dissatisfaction at the failure to make good the high promises of the early days of American participation in the War. Only a cynic can rest satisfied with his sneer at the results of "a war to end war," and public opinion, if it is sane and healthy, is not cynical at heart. The mass of the nation feels a sense of failure which it does not willingly accept, in fact does not propose to accept at all. President Eliot once put his finger upon a characteristic of America which has been too much ignored in the reactionary post-war era. It is the spirit of adventure called forth and nourished by conditions of frontier life. There has been a feeling throughout the country that somehow or other we are missing the greatest adventure of our day, which is the up-rooting of barbarism in the world of international relations. Many of those who were led by one reason or another to oppose America's entry into the League of Nations still felt the need of our participation in some such effort to organize international peace. But because no effective way could be found outside the very thing which had been rejected, the continuing reiteration of the high ideals without the ability to realize them led most other nations to regard our protests of international morality as nothing more or less than national hypocrisy; and national hypocrisy it has been in so far as hypocrisy is the cherishing of ideals without an adequate sense of the difficulties in the way of their achievement or a willing-ness to concentrate upon a means to the end instead of upon the end itself.

Viewing it upon this background, one can see how the pro-posal for a treaty to renounce war as an instrument of national policy and its popular acceptance in the United States might be regarded as perhaps the fundamental expression of America's reaction to the World War. Here was a proposal that looked to the end to be attained without becoming lost in the details of the machinery of attainment. There was no need to think out the alternatives for war nor the guarantees of peace, but a simple insistence upon those principles which had been the inspiration of the early crusading days of American participation in the World War, principles which had never been denied even in the discouraging days when the post-war settlements revealed how difficult they were of application. Professor Dewey is right in claiming that this simple method of asserting a great idea is distinctively and typically American. It meets, if it does not wholly satisfy, the demand for adventure. Clothed in such general terms as M. Briand first used, and interpreted here in still a wider sense than M. Briand had intended, the very breadth of the commitment made it all the more serious in its moral appeal so long as it was unhampered by the limitations of law and practice; and yet, just as the Constitution is superior to statutory law, so this declaration of war renunciation might be considered in the light of a fundamental reform in the principles of international law to which the United States could give its assent without becoming unduly involved in the guarantee of its enforcement, that kind of guarantee which it had refused in its rejection of the Covenant of the League.

Nothing in the papers of the time discussed these questions in detail, but the general comment was that evidently a way could still be found by which the United States could play its part and make good in the task which it had undertaken when it entered the war in 1917 to help "make the world safe for democracy." The phrase came back upon the pages of the papers this time with no cynical note, but as a reminder of something left undone.

Meanwhile, in Europe the proposition at which diplomats had looked askance was finding a voice in that great forum of the nations which is presented at the Assembly of the League in Geneva. The same forces which had encouraged M. Briand at the Council meeting in June were still at work. The technical staff of the League, containing as it does some of the ablest public servants of European governments, who, in turn, have learned to envisage their problem not in terms of national prestige but of the general good of the community of nations, placed its trained advice at the disposal of those statesmen who had framed and supported the Protocol of Geneva, a proposal which not only had proclaimed international war to be a crime, but had in addition bound the nations to its suppression. The Briand proposal furnished the inspiration once more to a declaration which should embody the concept of the "outlawry of war" as Europe had interpreted that doctrine. Without analyzing what lay behind it, for there were various influences at work, we may simply note that the Assembly finally adopted a motion proposed by the delegation of Poland, which restated in the form of a resolution the principles underlying the Protocol of 1924. It would probably have gone farther and attempted to revive the Protocol itself in some revised form had not Sir Austen Chamberlain declared once more, in strong and emphatic terms, the continued opposition of Great Britain to any such line of action. The Polish Resolution, therefore, remained merely an expression of the opinion of the Assembly, but the echoes which it awakened in the press of Continental Europe showed how firmly and persistently the will to peace was working among those very nations which the American reactionary press had pointed to as the reservoir of the war spirit. It was evident that there was no lack of agreement as to the end in view, but that the only difference of opinion lay in the method for its achievement.

The text of the Polish Resolution read as follows:

The Assembly,
Recognising the solidarity which unites the community of nations;
Being inspired by a firm desire for the maintenance of general peace;
Being convinced that a war of aggression can never serve as a means of settling international disputes and is, in consequence, an international crime;
Considering that a solemn renunciation of all wars of aggression would tend to create an atmosphere of general confidence calculated to facilitate the progress of the work undertaken with a view to disarmament:
Declares:
(1) That all wars of aggression are, and shall always be, prohibited.
(2) That every pacific means must be employed to settle disputes, of every description, which may arise between States.

The Assembly declares that the States Members of the League are under an obligation to conform to these principles.

For those to whom history is only the embodiment of completed acts and definitely achieved results, this Resolution may be discounted as something halfway between the protests of

demagoguery and the meaningless compliments of diplomacy.
It contained no binding obligations and therefore offered no
real guarantee. But the point to be insisted upon is that the
public opinion of Europe not only called for some such pronouncement, but supported it quite generally as an attempt to
state the real desires of the people behind the governments.
Few ventured to question but that it was a true expression of
the feeling of Europe, and this, in view of the recent failure of
the Disarmament Conference which had been held at Geneva,
although not under the auspices of the League, helped to reassure those who were still working for practical measures of
international peace at a time when such encouragement was
most needed.

Meanwhile, in the United States the various branches of the
peace movement, or most of them at least, decided to mobilize
their entire efforts upon the one immediate question of American acceptance of the Briand offer. This involved some temporary sacrifice upon the part of those who had supported other
movements in the past, such as the League of Nations or the
World Court, but the adherents of both League and Court
gave to the Briand proposal as generous and whole-hearted
support as the original members of the movement "to outlaw
war," who regarded the Briand offer as a definite step in the
fulfillment of their proposals. This concentration of effort was
not without its effect, but it would be wrong to record the increased indication of interest as a response to propaganda in the
ordinary sense of that term. All that it meant was that the
peace movement for the time being had ceased to confuse the
popular mind with conflicting claims and doctrinal discussions.
The peace movement had been largely futile in the United
States, not because of any general lack of support for the main
principles which it upheld, but because of its inability to decide
how peace was actually to be attained. Now that there was a

common agreement in support of the simple proposition that the United States should join in a renunciation of war as an instrument of policy, the peace forces gained rapidly in influence throughout the country at large. This became evident not only in the press but in public meetings which were held all over the country. The real attitude of the United States upon this fundamental question was at last becoming articulate in a way which could not fail to find expression in Congress.

Throughout the following months this general movement of American public opinion continued to gain in strength and find effective expression not only in Congress but outside it as well. This fact should not be forgotten as we turn to the proposals for actually embodying it, on the part of the Government of the United States.

CHAPTER IX

THE RESOLUTION OF SENATOR CAPPER

SHORTLY before the opening of Congress, in the first week in December, it became known that in both Houses resolutions would be presented in support of the Briand proposal and calling for action upon the part of the United States. The reference was still to the proposal of April 6 and not to the formal treaty of June, because not only was the text of the latter as yet unknown, but the State Department was still maintaining its silence concerning it. Of these resolutions, the two most important were those of Senator Arthur Capper, of Kansas, a member of the Committee on Foreign Relations, and Senator William E. Borah, Chairman of the Committee on Foreign Relations. There was also a resolution introduced by Congressman Burton which, while not directly connected with the Briand offer, had a definite bearing upon the subsequent discussion. These three resolutions received wide attention, not only in the press of the United States, but in Europe as well. This was as much due to their authorship as to their substance. There was nothing in the terms of any of them that had not been brought out in the private discussion of the preceding months, but the new fact was added that no longer was this discussion to be left in the hands of private individuals. The Government of the United States was now to be brought face to face with the question whether or not it was willing to give effect to the proposal of the Government of France.

The Resolution of Senator Capper was especially significant because, in the first place, it came from the Senator from Kansas. It was a unique incident in American history to have an authoritative exponent of the sentiment of the agricultural areas of the Middle West interpret, and as it proved ultimately, correctly interpret, the idealism of France. A member of the Republican Party and a consistent supporter of the Administration of President Coolidge, Senator Capper was not the kind of man to play politics by outbidding the Executive for popular approval. Nor was he the kind of man to be stampeded by popular movements into the support of measures which he did not himself study carefully and thoroughly; although a lifelong exponent of the farming interests, he had never been carried away by the extreme partisan views of radicalism, contenting himself with a program of forward-looking liberalism combined with a vigilant care for those practical measures by which democracy schools itself in statesmanship.

The text of Senator Capper's Resolution was given to the press on November 21, in the week preceding the opening of Congress and received wide publicity throughout the entire country.[1] The text of the Resolution runs as follows:

Whereas the Congress of the United States on August 29, 1916, solemnly declared it "to be the policy of the United States to adjust and settle its international disputes through mediation or arbitration, to the end that war may be honorably avoided"; and

Whereas Aristide Briand, Minister of Foreign Affairs of the French Republic, on April 6, 1927, publicly declared to the people of the United States that "France would be willing to subscribe publicly with the United States to any mutual engagement tending to outlaw war, to use an American expression, as between these two countries," and proposed that the two countries enter into an engagement providing for the "renunciation of war as an instrument of national policy"; and

Whereas there has been strong expression of opinion from the people and the press of the United States in favor of suitable action by our Government to give effect to the proposal of Monsieur Briand; and

[1] It was published by Senator Capper at Washington on November 21, 1927, and was introduced in the Senate on December 8.

Whereas the present arbitration treaty between the United States and France providing for the submission to arbitration of differences of a legal nature arising between them will terminate on February 27, 1928; and

Whereas the United States being desirous of securing peaceful settlement of international disputes and the general renunciation of war as an instrument of policy should not be under obligation to furnish protection for such of its nationals as aid or abet the breach of similar agreements between other nations: Now, therefore, be it

RESOLVED BY THE SENATE AND HOUSE OF REPRESENTATIVES OF THE UNITED STATES OF AMERICA IN CONGRESS ASSEMBLED, That it be declared to be the policy of the United States:

I. By treaty with France and other like-minded nations formally to renounce war as an instrument of public policy and to adjust and settle its international disputes by mediation, arbitration, and conciliation; and

II. By formal declaration to accept the definition of aggressor nation as one which, having agreed to submit international differences to conciliation, arbitration or judicial settlement, begins hostilities without having done so; and

III. By treaty with France and other like-minded nations to declare that the nationals of the contracting governments should not be protected by their governments in giving aid and comfort to an aggressor nation; and be it

RESOLVED FURTHER, That the President be requested to enter into negotiations with France and other like-minded nations for the purpose of concluding treaties with such nations, in furtherance of the declared policy of the United States.

Senator Capper's own comment on the Resolution was practically a part of the document, for in a few paragraphs he not only explained the meaning of the Resolution itself, but the attitude of those who like himself felt that the time had come now when the United States could not longer remain silent concerning the great issues of international war prevention. The comment follows:

I propose by this joint resolution to test the sincerity of our professions that America desires world peace. We have talked much about the desirability of peace, but have done little to advance the cause which the people have so much at heart. Nothing further is to be gained by repeating pious platitudes, by uttering high-sounding moral generalities or by professing to be devoted to international peace and opposed to war. More than ten years after the United States was dragged by circumstances into the most dreadful conflict in human history, half the world is still suffering acutely from the effects of that futile struggle of armed forces. It left bankrupt every European nation that took part in it. It cost nearly ten million young lives. Is it not time that the United States as the world's most powerful, secure and pacific nation should follow words with acts?

The resolution I shall present is not a radical or extreme statement of American policy. It has the merit of putting into plain and explicit terms the desire of the American people to advance the cause of peace. It omits meaningless moral generalities concerning the part this nation shall play in the world-effort to bring about an era of international understanding and, therefore, peace.

Our whole history and our best traditions summon us to participate in this effort—to lead it. Geographically the United States in its early history was almost isolated from the world. This isolation has ended. Now we are knit politically and economically by the closest ties with the world. The tremendous progress of science and invention has virtually abolished our geographical isolation. For generations we were the principal debtor nation. Now we have become the principal creditor nation. But whether debtor or creditor, we are a part of the world's political and economic organization and we cannot for a single day escape the responsibilities, obligations and dangers this relationship confers. The duty that rests upon us is to make the fullest use of our great power in the family of nations to promote understanding and peace. No one can make a friend of a neighbor, or reason with him, by arousing his combativeness. It was that spirit which led Europe, where much rivalry exists, into the greatest war of all time.

What is proposed by the resolution, are treaties with any like-minded nations to forego and renounce resort to war in difficulties arising in the relations of the contracting parties; to submit issues to arbitration or to judicial decision that cannot be settled by negotiation. Such a treaty was offered to the United States on the tenth anniversary of our entrance into the World War, April 6 last, by the Foreign Minister of France, M. Briand. "France would be willing," were M. Briand's words, "to subscribe publicly with the United States to any mutual engagement tending to outlaw war, to use an American expression, as between these two countries." In recognition of this specific offer my resolution specifies the willingness of the United States to enter into such a treaty "with France or any like-minded nation." Other nations will be found ready to follow that example, I believe.

As a member of the Foreign Relations Committee, I have followed with interest Lord Cecil's speaking tour in England for peace and reduction of armaments and noted the demand of the powerful British Labor Party for the conclusion of a treaty outlawing war between the two English-speaking peoples, and that party's demand for a drastic reduction of naval armaments.

In these times of peace, the navies of France, Great Britain and the United States cost their tax-payers not less than one billion dollars a year, a tremendous waste of human energy, and that is only part of it.

There is every reason to consider this proposal for civilized nations to renounce war as an instrument of public policy, a logical and necessary step toward peace. It goes farther, it seems to me, than merely declaring war criminal.

The resolution further proposes that governments engaging in such a treaty will not support their own nationals in giving aid to aggressor nations in war. And to give meaning to this provision the resolution defines an aggressor as any nation that, having agreed to submit issues to arbitration, plunges into war without making such an appeal. This part of the resolution does not prohibit nationals of the treaty nations from supplying aid to aggressors in war, but deprives them of national backing if they do. They must take their own chances in the game of destruction and ruin.

If M. Briand's proposal be accepted as between the United States and France and offers are made to extend it at once to Great Britain, to Germany, to Japan and to Italy, the chance of future wars would be reduced to a minimum so long as the other contracting nations keep the faith. As it is obvious that they themselves would not go to war with each other and by refusing jointly and severally to aid an aggressor nation, they would thereby make any war between two lesser nations virtually a local affair.

Finally there is the desirability and importance of having the United States resume the position of emphatic leadership in all that promotes international peace and understanding, a leadership it took and held under McKinley and Hay, Roosevelt and Root, and Taft and Knox. The adoption of this resolution would place our own government in the position of offering a practicable plan to any other nation of the same mind to put war outside the pale as between itself and the United States.

Within the next year, in February, June and August, the treaties of arbitration with France, Great Britain and Japan expire by their own terms. The adoption of this resolution opens the way for treaties in their place renouncing war between these important nations. Here is a vital matter. We have here a great opportunity to live up to our highest American traditions in this resolution to renounce war. We should make the most of it.

The text of Senator Capper's Resolution deserves careful study, more careful perhaps than it received at the time of publication, although it met with a cordial reception upon the part of most of the press of the country.

Most readers must have been surprised to read in the opening sentence that the Congress of the United States had already in August, 1916, declared that it was the policy of the United States "to adjust and settle its international disputes through mediation or arbitration, to the end that war may be honorably avoided." Nevertheless, this is part of the text of an act of Congress. It occurs in the preamble of the vote which authorized the creation of the new American navy, provision for the building of which was made in the heart of the World War and before the participation of the United States in it. The contrast between the high pacific ideals of the preamble and the rather ominous purpose of the act itself may account for the fact that every one had forgotten that Congress had once declared itself in favor of a policy nearly identical with that proposed by M. Briand. True, it did not go so far in the way of renouncing war as M. Briand, but it had more detail on the practical measures for avoiding war. Even although the cynic may have felt that this preamble was only a verbal concession to the pacifists, a precedent had been established of some value of which it was well to be reminded now.

The three articles of the Resolution itself will be seen to run closely parallel with those of Dr. Butler's proposal in Paris, a proposal which he had repeated in America upon his return in September. The first of the three sections of the Resolution was simply a combination of the Briand offer to renounce war, with the 1916 Resolution of the United States Congress quoted in the preamble. The heart of the proposal was that the United States declare in a treaty with France and other like-minded nations that its policy henceforth would be to renounce war as its instrument of policy and that it would employ as an alternative for war mediation, arbitration and conciliation. This part of the Capper Resolution has been substantially met by the Kellogg negotiations, but that instrument does not cover the second and third articles of the Resolution. In view of the fact, however, that they deal with a vital part of the problem of world pacification, it is not likely that the silence of the present treaty will be final in this regard.

The second clause supplies the definition of an aggressor nation, applying in broad terms the suggestion which was first advanced by the American unofficial committee of 1924 and incorporated first in the Protocol of Geneva and then in somewhat confused but still definite terms in the Treaty of Locarno. An aggressor nation is one which goes to war in violation of its given word to submit its international differences to conciliation, arbitration or judicial settlement. This definition is strictly limited and not capable of application outside of the treaties in which it is formally accepted, but a nation which definitely accepts the obligation to settle its differences by some form of peaceful agreement and then breaks this treaty by beginning hostilities without accepting the peace alternative, is to be regarded as guilty of that kind of willful violation of law as well as of honor which should be branded as illegitimate, and the war in which it engages becomes an act of anarchy. We shall discuss this definition at a later stage, but it must be admitted that the form in which Senator Capper's Resolution advanced the definition, calling for a formal declaration to accept a definition, is not easy to carry through in practical politics. There are few legislative bodies in the world which would be prepared to accept off-hand the statement of new principles even if they described agreed policies. The framing of a definition opens the door to infinite debate, and every legislator likes to make perfection still more perfect by changing the formula to one of his own authorship.

Having defined the aggressor nation in the second paragraph of his Resolution, Senator Capper goes on in the third paragraph to declare that no government which has joined in a treaty of this kind should connive at the aggression by protecting those of its citizens who are giving "aid and comfort" to the law-breaker. It is clear that some such proposal as this is necessary if the renunciation of war is to be made a reality, for if nations which violate the pact are to be accorded the same privileges of commercial or financial support as the victim of their onslaught, the only guarantee for peace will be in the increased armaments of nations faced with the continuing anarchy of the past. International peace is not a reality without some kind of international community, and there can be no community unless the governments of civilized states take some kind of stand against the nation which proceeds to disturb the whole structure of peaceful international dealing to which it has become a party.

The whole Capper Resolution might perhaps be boiled down to this,—the twofold obligation: in the first place, to use pacific means of settlement instead of war in case of international disputes, and, in the second place, not to help any nation which having taken the first of these pledges openly violates it. The

Pact of Paris contains the first of these two obligations in its text and the second in the preamble. But it has not faced the central question to which the second clause of the Capper Resolution is addressed.[1]

It is in connection with this phase of the Capper Resolution that mention should be made of the proposal of Congressman Burton which, although not called out by the Briand proposal, dealt with the question of the shipment of arms in terms which developed in some detail the Capper proposal not to assist an aggressor nation. There was one technical difference between the proposal of Congressman Burton and Senator Capper, for Congressman Burton did not suggest a treaty; instead of that, there was to be only the unilateral proposal of the United States itself. Behind this text there was also a precedent, for it was modeled verbally upon the joint resolution of Congress which had previously declared it to be the policy of the United States to prohibit the export of arms to Mexico when it was in a state of anarchy and, subsequently, under a revised formula, to China. The Resolution followed the wording of the previous one, merely making it applicable to an aggressor state instead of one in anarchy. The Burton Resolution passed the Committee on Foreign Affairs and was apparently making good headway when overtaken and overshadowed by the subsequent Briand negotiations. It has, however, not been withdrawn, and in view of the fact that discussion of the Capper Resolution will probably bring up the question of the possible alternative form of action proposed in the Burton plan—by statute instead of treaty—it may be well to have the text of the latter before us for reference. It reads as follows:

RESOLVED BY THE SENATE AND HOUSE OF REPRESENTATIVES OF THE UNITED STATES OF AMERICA IN CONGRESS ASSEMBLED, That it is hereby declared to be the policy of the United States to prohibit

---

[1] The Capper Resolution was introduced in Congress but was not brought to a vote.

the exportation of arms, munitions or implements of war to any country which engages in aggressive warfare against any other country in violation of a treaty, convention, or other agreement to resort to arbitration or other peaceful means for the settlement of international controversies.

Sec. 2. Whenever the President determines that any country has violated any such treaty, convention, or agreement by engaging in aggressive warfare against any other country, and makes proclamation thereof, it shall be unlawful, until otherwise proclaimed by the President, or provided by act of Congress, to export any arms, munitions or implements of war from any place in the United States or any possession thereof to such country, or to any other country if the ultimate destination of such arms, munitions, or implements of war is the country so violating any such treaty, convention or agreement.

Sec. 3. Whoever exports any arms, munitions, or implements of war in violation of Section 2 of this Resolution, shall, upon conviction thereof, be punished by a fine not exceeding $10,000 or by imprisonment not exceeding two years, or both. It shall be the duty of the Secretary of the Treasury to report any violation of Section 2 of this Resolution to the United States District Attorney for the district wherein the violation is alleged to have been committed.

CHAPTER X

THE RESOLUTION OF SENATOR BORAH AND THE OUTLAWRY OF WAR

THERE was an American phrase in M. Briand's original proposal which since then, and mainly because of M. Briand's use of it, has made the circuit of the world. It was the phrase "to outlaw war." M. Briand quoted it as an American expression and then went on to explain what it meant to him; it was simply the renunciation of war as an instrument of national policy, such as the signatories of the Covenant and the Treaties of Locarno were already familiar with. The American expression, however, had been used in a different setting in its native country, a country which had had no part in either of these two treaties, and when the phrase came home with this foreign accent upon it, there was a chance of misunderstanding on both sides. The consequences of this misunderstanding might have been to accentuate still more the differences in point of view across the Atlantic so that M. Briand's effort to unite the peace forces of both countries might have resulted in weakening them instead. It would almost certainly have done so had the American leaders of the movement to outlaw war held rigidly to a doctrinaire point of view. Instead of that, they joined with the rest of the peace movement in America in interpreting the French use of their own phrase in liberal and practical terms, and thus made possible a joint movement of all the forces working for international peace in the United States; which was a new and unprecedented thing.

This division of the peace forces of the United States in the post-war years is a political fact of greater importance than has hitherto been recognized. The failure to accept the League

drove a wedge into liberal opinion and split the peace movement into small groups of bitter, partisan sectaries, too busily
engaged in warring among themselves to do anything effective
for peace itself. As always happens in such cases, the more
ineffective the movement became, the more extreme were the
remedies proposed for it. That under such discouraging circumstances it could still be an active and powerful force in the
country is a clear proof that this movement does not any longer
depend for its vitality upon either individual leadership or individual bodies of dogma. With a sense of frustration constantly before it, it nevertheless remained alive, to belie utterly
that cynical interpretation of American democracy which sees in
the history of the United States only materialistic aims, pursued
in the consciousness of power and disguised by careless philan-
thropy. It was for no such purposes as these that the United
States had entered the World War. Because President Wilson
discerned the other and deeper interest of the country in the
establishment of decency and justice, the country rallied
to the call for war with such astonishing unanimity and readiness for sacrifice. Any other interpretation of the motives of the
United States in 1917 is false to history; and any interpretation
of its post-war actions which denies the continued existence of
these moral forces in American thought is an equally false
interpretation of American policies. Given the chance, there
could be no doubt that the great adventure of international
peace would be pursued with no less national enthusiasm and
strength by the United States than the adventure of war.

With such motive forces at its command, there was no reason
that the Ship of State should drift like a derelict across the
path of others seeking the same port,[1] if only a common chart
could be furnished for them all. But the possession of a common chart did not necessarily mean steering exactly the same

---

[1] The phrase is from a brilliant speech of Dr. Butler at the annual meeting
of the League of Nations Non-Partisan Association, January, 1927.

course and certainly did not involve accepting a common command. Where the dangers were as thick as in Europe, the convoy system might furnish the only safety in time of crisis, as it had both literally and figuratively in the heart of the World War; but at the calm distance from which America viewed the scene, this coöperation in defense seemed rather an involvement in danger. It was now seen, however, that though mapping our own course with the full freedom of unquestioned sovereignty, we might at least reassure those bent upon a similar peaceful journey that not only have we no black flag in our locker, but, on the contrary, if piracy should intervene, threatening to destroy that freight which held the hopes and aspirations of mankind, they would find us within hail.

The Briand use of the American phrase was a reminder of the fact that proposals for international peace are international proposals, and that the perfecting of plans suitable to one nation only, if that were possible, would not solve the problem. The preoccupation of Europe was, above all, to preserve and strengthen the League of Nations, a preoccupation which had become an anxiety upon the part of Continental statesmen. Indeed, everywhere except in the United States and Soviet Russia, the League was recognized as the heart and center of the organization of international peace, and in the subsequent discussion we shall find this view shared equally in the British Dominions and in Japan. There would be no surer way to wreck the proposal to outlaw war than to make it the expression of an American movement intent upon substituting for the existing world organization another and untried experiment. In the pages which follow, we shall see time and again how this concern for the welfare of the League on the part of the non-American countries brought a tone of hesitation into the negotiations.

The former opposition to the League upon the part of the American group supporting the program of outlawry was sufficiently clear. The fear was expressed that M. Briand had fallen into a trap which would make him, who had been the foremost champion and exponent of peace in Europe, the unconscious but responsible agent of an anti-League movement. In the absence of further official explanations from M. Briand as to what he had meant by the phrase which he had accepted from the United States, the European liberal press had given his project the doubtful assistance of an emphasis upon reservations which would prevent its use in any League-wrecking enterprise. Unless this doubt were cleared away by an interpretation of the movement for outlawing war which could make it the possible ally of the League, even although it offered only external support, there could be no hope of its success. The only way to do this was for the leaders of the outlawry movement in the United States to make clear both here and in Europe that if the League would accept the major premises which underlie the outlawry movement and distinctly disavow war as the instrument of national policy, that is the institution of war itself, then their chief objection to the League would be overcome and, while retaining full liberty of action for the United States, policies of peace and institutions for embodying them could be worked out in terms satisfactory both to the League and to countries outside of it.

It was the leadership of Senator Borah which made possible this double achievement. The American movement for the outlawry of war subordinated to its major purpose, which was to get rid of war, the further details of a program which at one time had been frankly advanced as an alternative to the structure of the League, or at least so thorough-going an amendment to it as to call for its reconstruction. The legalistic framework of a whole series of propositions for safeguarding peace by institutions yet to be created—which was in the American program—was seen to be entirely secondary to the immediate duty of joining with the rest of the world in a straightforward renunciation of war itself. It is not only the British who can subordinate theories of politics to practical fulfillment. With a ready and generous sense of the importance of M. Briand's use of their own phrase, the leaders of the outlawry of war movement in the United States engaged in no doctrinaire debate with him as to the other implication which that phrase had held for them in the past; and if the Briand proposal ultimately is written into the international law of the civilized world, a great part of the credit for that achievement is due to Senator Borah's leadership in this regard.

The originator of the American movement to outlaw war and the author of the phrase itself is a Chicago lawyer, Mr. S. O. Levinson, although his associate and friend, Dr. Charles Clayton Morrison, editor of the *Christian Century*, has perhaps done almost as much as Mr. Levinson to expound the latter's original proposal.[1] In fact, the one fully developed treatment of the proposal is that in Dr. Morrison's recent volume, *The Outlawry of War*, which is recognized as an authoritative presentment of the whole scheme. Its most important champion, however, has been Senator Borah, who has made it the basis of proposals in Congress and, while distinctly more cautious than Dr. Morrison in his application of its tenets, has lent the weight of his responsible position to furthering its claims. Equally weighty has been the support of Professor John Dewey, as conspicuous a figure in philosophy as Senator Borah in politics.

The statement of the original plan had been set forth by Mr. Levinson in a pamphlet which Senator Borah had printed as a Senate document on January 19, 1922, and which he then made the basis of a Senate resolution. That resolution was now revived and with only a few verbal changes was reintroduced in Congress on December 12, 1927. Its reintroduction at this juncture was stated by some of the outlawry group less cautious

[1] Cf. above, p. 47.

than Senator Borah, to be the interpretation in terms of American policy of M. Briand's offer, to which it must naturally be made to fit. The fact that the resolution came from the chairman of the Committee on Foreign Relations of the United States Senate gave it in any case a very real importance demanding careful scrutiny. The text of this Resolution reads as follows:

Whereas war is the greatest existing menace to society and has become so expensive and destructive that it not only causes the stupendous burdens of taxation now afflicting our people but threatens to engulf and destroy civilization; and

Whereas civilization has been marked in its upward trend out of barbarism into its present condition by the development of law and courts to supplant methods of violence and force; and

Whereas the genius of civilization has discovered but two methods of compelling the settlement of human disputes, namely, law and war, and, therefore, in any plan for the compulsory settlement of international controversies we must choose between war on the one hand and the process of law on the other; and

Whereas war between nations has always been and still is a lawful institution, so that any nation may, with or without cause, declare war against any other nation and be strictly within its legal rights; and

Whereas revolutionary war or wars of liberation are illegal and criminal, to wit, high treason, whereas under existing international law wars between nations to settle disputes are perfectly lawful; and

Whereas the overwhelming moral sentiment of civilized people everywhere is against the cruel and destructive institution of war; and

Whereas all alliances, leagues, or plans which rely upon war as the ultimate power for the enforcement of peace carry the seeds either of their own destruction or of military dominancy, to the utter subversion of liberty and justice; and

Whereas we must recognize the fact that resolutions or treaties outlawing certain methods of killing will not be effective so long as war itself remains lawful; and that in international relations we must have, not rules and regulations of war, but organic laws against war; and

Whereas in our Constitutional Convention of 1787 it was successfully contended by Madison, Hamilton and Ellsworth that the use of force when applied to people collectively, that is, to states or nations, was unsound in principle and would be tantamount to a declaration of war; and

Whereas we have in our Federal Supreme Court a practical and effective model for a real international court, as it has specific jurisdiction to hear and decide controversies between our sovereign States; and

Whereas our Supreme Court has exercised this jurisdiction without resort to force for one hundred and thirty-seven years, during which time scores of controversies have been judicially and peaceably settled that might otherwise have led to war between the States, and thus furnishes a practical exemplar for the compulsory and pacific settlement of international controversies; and

Whereas an international agreement of such judicial character would not shackle the independence or impair the sovereignty of any nation: Now, therefore, be it

RESOLVED, That it is the view of the Senate of the United States that war between nations should be outlawed as an institution or means for the settlement of international controversies by making it a public crime under the law of nations and that every nation should be encouraged by solemn agreement or treaty to bind itself to indict and punish its own international war breeders or instigators and war profiteers under powers similar to those conferred upon our Congress under Article I, section 8, of our Federal Constitution which clothes the Congress with the power "to define and punish offenses against the law of nations"; and be it

RESOLVED FURTHER, That a code of international law of peace based upon the outlawing of war and on the principle of equality and justice between all nations, amplified and expanded and adapted and brought down to date should be created and adopted.

Second, That, with war outlawed, a judicial substitute for war should be created (or, if existing in part, adapted and adjusted) in the form or nature of an international court, modeled on our Federal Supreme Court in its jurisdiction over controversies between our sovereign States; such court shall possess affirmative jurisdiction to hear and decide all purely international controversies, as defined by the code or arising under treaties, and its judgments shall not be enforced by war under any name or in any form whatever, but shall have the same power for their enforcement as our Federal Supreme Court, namely, the respect of all enlightened nations for judgments resting upon open and fair investigations and impartial decisions, the agreement of the nations to abide and be bound by such judgments, and the compelling power of enlightened public opinion.

One does not need to read beyond the opening paragraphs of the preamble of this resolution to see that M. Briand's conception of outlawry was quite different from this far-reaching plan of world organization. M. Briand had meant simply what he said: outlawry of war was the renunciation of war as an instrument of national policy in the way in which Europe had already renounced it under the Covenant and in the Treaty of Locarno. This meant a distinct recognition of the principle of enforcement or guarantee of peace by coöperative, international action. It would have been impossible for M. Briand to have accepted the assertion that "all alliances, leagues or plans which rely upon war as the ultimate power for the enforcement of peace carry the seeds either of their own destruction or of military dominancy, to the utter subversion of liberty and justice." The French point of view has always been the opposite to this, that plans for peace which make no provision for enforcement are much more likely to be subversive of liberty and justice because they leave the nation accepting them a helpless victim of anarchy or violence. But this French insistence upon adequate police had been the very basis of the most vigorous attacks upon the League by the proponents of the American plan for the outlawry of war. It goes without saying that European statesmen would find the American outlawry program, if stated in this form, exceedingly difficult to understand and still more difficult to accept.

Moreover, the experience of European history would refute two other propositions equally important in the American plan. The first is that the only antithesis of war is law; and the second is that a supreme court modeled on the basis of the United States Supreme Court would sufficiently safeguard a world organization and prove effective as the alternative for war. The emphasis upon law in international dealings which these propositions contain would seem to Continental readers to leave out of account almost the whole history of diplomacy, the greater part of the business of foreign offices, of departments of commerce, and many of the current international contacts of governments. It could hardly be widely known abroad that even before the debates over the Briand proposal, the proponents of the American plan for the outlawry of war had begun to escape from the legalism of the original program and were broadening the alternatives to war so as to include not only law but every other kind of pacific settlement or international dealing which definitely eliminates force and violence. But the documentary program stated in the Resolution showed no trace of this revisionist tendency; and in order to understand the subsequent debate as well as to appreciate the extent of the later adjustment which brought agreement, it is necessary to discuss the document rather than the historical evolution of the "outlawry" movement itself.

Fortunately that development makes it unnecessary in this historical survey to analyze in detail the argument presented by the plan for a world court of the kind envisaged here. Without entering into the question of the relation of the States of the Union to the Supreme Court, the outside world does not regard internal history of the United States as offering a fair analogy with the proper sphere of an international court. The contesting nations could place no such authority behind the decisions of an international body as resides in the Government of the United States, and indeed no stronger opponents of the super-state idea are to be found than in the American "outlawry" group. The Levinson plan seeks to avoid this by denying the use of force in giving effect to the decisions of the international court, falling back upon "the compelling power of enlightened public opinion" and the honor of the nations which would go to court instead of to war. There are, undoubtedly, two opinions concerning the sanctions of the League of Nations, opinions which have been forcefully expressed in the Assembly at Geneva, but the argument against sanctions based upon an analogy with the Constitution of the United States is another matter.

Moreover, the refusal to enforce the law because enforcement resembles war, seems to the European jurist to leave the "outlawry" plan in the paradoxical condition of not outlawing anything. "Outlawry" in the history of law has always meant an act of force and not merely an expression of opinion. The claim that the real outlawry of dueling, which had been cited as a parallel by the outlawry advocates, lay rather in the pressure of public opinion than in the enactments against dueling, is an open historical question; but even if it were true, it would mean nothing more than that the outlawry which had been asserted by the government had been ineffective, as all laws are which run counter to public opinion. The mere giving up of an ancient custom is not outlawry unless there is attached some formal enactment giving legal force to that fact. On the other hand, who, for example, would say that the Prohibition Amendment of the United States was not a formal outlawry of the saloon and the liquor trade, although it has not wholly prevented the use of intoxicants? The law proclaims principles and establishes the penalties for their violation, and outlawry is a part of this legal process, not a register of social pressures or moral attitudes. That is not to say that the moral forces may not sometimes have a validity stronger than the law. But we are trying merely to clarify terms which have led to a somewhat unprofitable debate across international frontiers and not to weigh the relative importance of public opinion and enforcible decrees. As a matter of fact, sometimes the one, sometimes the other, has seemed the more effective. It is possible to argue that the peace movement would be better off without an insistence upon enforcement. But "outlawry" in the strict sense of the term does not mean this. It is much more applicable to the European insistence upon enforcement and the implements of international police; and that is why the European observers were doubly puzzled over the American use of the term.

It was obvious that if this resolution had been left as the final authoritative reply to M. Briand, the path of negotiations would, to say the least, have been extremely difficult. But fortunately Senator Borah himself undertook to free the whole discussion from the doctrinaire element which had become embodied in the outlawry program and which had so long been a real obstacle to the unity of the peace movement in the United States. Senator Borah's chief preoccupation was not the splitting of juristic arguments but the earnest furtherance of international peace itself; and from first to last he sought to find the way to harmonize his plans with those acceptable to other governments so long as the negotiations kept in mind the honest fulfillment of a single underlying purpose. His policy henceforth was as practical as it was sincere, and once the Administration showed its willingness to take up the Briand treaty of the previous June, nothing further was heard during the course of the negotiations of the Senate Resolution to outlaw war. Those negotiations owe much to Senator Borah; just how much the contemporary historian can hardly say. But when all was over and M. Claudel was about to leave for Europe, he singled out Senator Borah as the one who had done most, not only to originate the plan, but to further the negotiations, and sent to him his formal thanks as representative of the Government of France.

It is striking to note that the term "outlawry" does not occur in any of the official commitments in the replies of governments. In its place stands an expression which is the real object of negotiation, the "renunciation of war as an instrument of national policy." It is not likely, however, that the term out-lawry will give way, in popular usage, to the phrase "renuncia-tion of war." For it carries with it just that sense of positive action which is needed as a slogan in the peace movement. Renunciation is suggestive of the pacifist ideal, it savors of self-abnegation; outlawry brings to the mind an act of force without being too precise as to how it might be used—hardly more than a vague threat of consequences. We are making others keep the peace, even if we must do so at the same time. There is a hint of that red-blooded benevolence, the kind of idealism that prefers to march to its goal of international peace singing a militant hymn, rather than to risk the mental struggle which confronts it in an analysis of its premises. The oriflamme of outlawry will probably be borne in front, no matter what follows after.

This is, after all, an important gain. The "peace movement" has found a slogan, a crusading call that can inspire to action, a shibboleth of victory. It has long been felt that the lack of any appealing symbol of this kind was one of the chief reasons for the failure of the movement to enlist any but that small fraction in any nation which lives for and in ideals. To the mass of humanity there is something weak and colorless in the word "peace." It has no suggestion of pageantry, no splendor of parade. Compared with the great adventure of war, it has seemed to most men the mere dull and commonplace routine, so lacking in vitality as to yield in crises to the sterner forces of events. So much has this been the case that the phrase "inter-national peace" has only in our own day begun to overcome a certain suggestion of cant and hypocrisy or at least of futile idealism. It is the strangest paradox in the civilization which calls itself Christian, that there should have been reproach at-tached to the word "pacifist." But the blame for this lay largely within the peace movement itself, for its pacifism had been both futile and extreme. It had never adjusted itself to the practical politics of a developing world, but, on the contrary, tended to erect for itself, like St. Augustine of old, a City of God on earth where perfect harmony should reign instead of the discordant and incomplete but vaster symphony of the historic civilization of today. Nowhere else had this extremist tendency of idealism shown itself so unpractical as in the United States, where the peace movement spent most of its energy in mutual antagonisms,—like the theologians of old,— instead of concentrating upon the common purpose of war elimination. Now at last the peace movement in America was united.

CHAPTER XI

THE ARBITRATION TREATY

EIGHT months had now elapsed since M. Briand had first launched his proposal, and six months since he had submitted a formal draft to the Government at Washington, but still the Administration withheld its reply. As time went on, criticism of this inaction had grown more and more outspoken,[1] and this, combined with the nation-wide attention given to the Capper Resolution, seemed to indicate that the initiative in the matter might pass from the executive to the legislative branch of the Government. The very people who had been most critical in the past of the Foreign Relations Committee of the Senate for its obstructive tactics, now began to turn to it instead of to the State Department.

As an excuse for the hesitancy of the State Department, the argument had been advanced in Washington and widely asserted in the press of the United States that M. Briand's proposal was in effect a bid for a disguised alliance of the United States with France, the very kind of entanglement which it would be the first business of any American Administration to avoid. This argument subsequently gained credence from its constant iteration and ultimately became an accepted part of what may be called the mythical history of the Briand peace proposal. We have already pointed out, in connection with the unofficial Draft Treaty of the preceding May, that had the French intended any such designs as those attributed to them,

---

[1] The most powerful exponent of this criticism continued to be Dr. Nicholas Murray Butler, who addressed important meetings in various parts of the country, especially in Indianapolis and Denver, in support of the Capper Resolution.

they could have been met by the simplest of devices, even while both Governments went on to bind themselves to policies of peace. All that was necessary was to insert in the treaty of peace a reservation that either signatory could recover liberty of action in case the other went to war with a third Power. This simplest of all provisions was finally incorporated in the multilateral treaty, at least according to the State Department's interpretation of that treaty. The argument that the Government at Washington was in danger of becoming involved in French politics because M. Briand's proposal did not extend to other countries would seem to be too apparent a fallacy to require argument, but, nevertheless, the authority of Washington secured nation-wide acceptance for this very point of view; and the Government of France apparently was unaware of the damage caused by leaving this impression uncorrected, and permitted the somewhat invidious interpretation of M. Briand's idealistic act to remain unexplained, at least officially. The intermittent but serious illness of M. Briand was perhaps partly responsible for this.

It was, of course, true that M. Briand had proposed nothing more than a Franco-American treaty, but there was no need for France to extend the proposal to its neighbors in Western Europe or to the world generally because it had already done this very thing and in stronger language and in more binding terms than were suggested for the United States. The Treaty of Locarno is much more of a renunciation of war than the Franco-American proposal; for it not only provides for all the renunciation covered by the Briand-Kellogg text, but both by the precision of its terms and the penalties which it provides for its own violation, it enacts the outlawry of war in the real sense of the word with reference to European Powers. The Covenant of the League carried this same principle of war renunciation, in less iron-clad terms, it is true, throughout the rest of the world. The United States was not within this circle of existing war renunciation treaties, and from the French point of view the engagement which M. Briand proposed was bringing the United States not merely into a new expression of friendly relations with France, but into harmony with the new world organization which France was exerting every effort to strengthen and develop. This world organization meant, in the eyes of the Government of France, but one thing, peace with security. The treaty with Washington would be a stepping-stone to further advances in which the rest of the world could participate, following the example set by these two democracies.

There was in the attitude of France, in its desire to lead the way and not be submerged in a cloud of other witnesses, something of the old-time feeling for national prestige which, while perhaps quite natural, is after all an element of weakness in diplomacy. It tends to cause the government to lose sight of the question at issue in order to uphold its own country's honor and dignity. The sensitiveness of France in this regard has been one of the chief weaknesses in its post-war diplomacy: a good example of this was its insistence during the Washington Disarmament Conference upon the theoretical right to possess more naval armament than it ever intended to build. The emphasis of Oriental nations upon what they term "face" is not limited to the Orient. In this case it found expression in the reactionary press in France, which the American reactionary press immediately copied, and the subsequent misunderstandings took on a color of recrimination; so that as far as the American public was concerned, it was faced with a situation that was growing more and more confused.

The historian has to deny the claim that the Administration at Washington first saved the country from the overreaching designs of clever European statesmen, and then turned the tables on Europe with a genuine proposal to renounce war. The proposal finally adopted was the original one of M. Briand; the intervening negotiations but served to go back to the starting point. Nevertheless, the United States did make a different use of this proposal from that which had been intended at the start, and any one familiar with even the rudiments of American history or American feeling must know that the American extension of the proposal was as inevitable as the French limitation of it was natural.

But while the historian will deny the partisan claim that Washington and not France was the real author of the peace treaty,—a claim which Mr. Kellogg himself was outspoken in repudiating,—nevertheless it would be equally wrong for him to ignore the difficult situation in which the State Department found itself. The Administration which had rejected the League of Nations and had failed to effect our entry into the World Court had recently been confronted with a multiplicity of plans for securing international peace, most of which would apparently involve casting aside the moorings at which the Ship of State had swung for nearly eight years upon the listless tide of inaction. True, there had been a Washington Conference, but it had worked within closely defined limits and had confined itself to an immediate reform which could be stated in terms of arithmetic. The summer months at Geneva had begun to show even in this field, apparently so highly technical, that the real heart of the problem escaped any such mathematical limitation, and that the very effort to avoid the larger view of the question prevented our seeing it correctly either in terms of science or of politics; for rivalry in armaments is, in the last resort, a competition in the field of science and of the resources placed at its disposal, neither of which has any known mathematical limit. Only the creative imagination can envisage the problems which are presented by the effort to rid the world of war or of its instruments, and the technician must yield to the statesman if they are ever to be solved. Washington had been reminded of this fact by the recent failure of the Geneva Conference, and, learning little by its disappointment, was preparing for greater failures in the future by a still greater surrender to the technician in the demand for the strongest navy the world had ever seen.

The Briand proposal lay at the other pole from this disarmament policy. Striking as it did at war itself instead of at the implements of war, it left all arithmetic behind. The Ship of State would be turned upon a course as yet untraveled by it; no wonder a nation's helmsman might refuse to listen to the insistent advice of passengers, who were not responsible for the safety of the vessel, to seek some way of satisfying their demand for adventure while yet holding to a formulated course. Fortunately, just such a chart lay at hand in the existing treaties with France, the Root Treaty of Arbitration and the Bryan Treaty of Conciliation. These, therefore, became the basis of the State Department's first counter-proposal which it sent back to France in the closing days of the year.

Then followed a confused chapter of diplomatic exchanges and public discussion. The two proposals, the Briand proposal for the renunciation of war and the revision of the Arbitration Treaty, were confused in the popular mind, and the press dispatches from Washington and Paris offered no light as to whether Washington was embodying the two proposals in a single treaty or whether it was keeping them separate. As the text was ultimately to show, this confusion passed somewhat into the negotiations themselves, for the revised Arbitration Treaty was recast so as to seem much more than an all-inclusive alternative for war, with provisions for conciliation alongside of those of arbitration so as to cover every possible item of dispute. The high claims set forth in the Preamble gave the Treaty still more the color of an American Locarno by the protestation that the signatories were actuated by a desire to demonstrate before the world "their condemnation of war as an instrument of national policy in their mutual relations."

For those who could take it as such, this formal tribute in the Preamble was supposed to make the Arbitration Treaty an answer to the Briand proposal. Happily, the Washington Administration was not the dupe of words in this regard, and was all the time going ahead with another treaty which should embody in its text the ideal which was here set forth in the Preamble.

The mistaken impression that the Arbitration Treaty was the American answer to the Briand proposal was strengthened by the speeches made upon the occasion of its formal signature. The negotiations had proceeded happily throughout the month of January and were successfully concluded in time for signing the Treaty on February 6, which was the one hundred and fiftieth anniversary of the signing of the Treaty of Alliance between France and the United States, so fateful in the struggle for American independence. Both in Washington at the time of affixing his signature, and the same evening in New York at a great Franco-American celebration, M. Claudel, the French Ambassador, made reference to the Treaty as though it really embodied the "outlawry of war," and chose the occasion to pay a public tribute to Senator Borah. But Senator Borah himself was under no such misapprehensions, as will be clear from the following chapter. Not only the outlawry of war but the renunciation of it was still to be dealt with in an entirely different treaty.

Nevertheless, this Arbitration Treaty lies directly along the path of the history of war renunciation. There are two parts to the proposal for renouncing war, the renunciation itself and the agreement to settle disputes by peaceful means. One cannot simply give up war without preparing an alternative for it; and the Arbitration Treaty dealt with the alternative. Examination of the text, however, showed that it had been badly drafted and was by no means the step forward which had been claimed for it, and that instead of strengthening the alternatives to war, it had weakened those already in existence. The existing Arbitration Treaty was repeated in Articles 2 and 3, and taking this section of the Treaty just by itself, there was a real advance upon the previous text because it no longer made formal exception of questions of national honor and vital interest. It was time that this phrase should disappear from the arbitration treaties of the United States, for the European nations had already discarded it, realizing how it could be used to frustrate every honest purpose of the treaty itself. All that a nation needed to do to escape living up to the terms of the treaty was to insist that the dispute in question was one involving its vital interest or its honor, and there was no one but itself to judge whether this was the case or not. The phrase had been doubly reactionary in the case of the United States, because in its arbitration treaties the Senate had reserved the right to investigate in every case whether or not the issue was one that might be arbitrated. This reservation of the Senate's power was still left in the French Treaty.

It was clearly the intention of the Administration to make the Treaty still more forward-looking by combining with the Arbitration Treaty the commitment of the existing Bryan Treaty so as to bring within one text the provisions for settling not only legal questions in an arbitration tribunal, but also the non-legal questions which were provided for in the Bryan Treaties of Conciliation. This linking of arbitration with conciliation in a single treaty was something that had not been done by the United States as yet. The Bryan Treaties had never been combined before with the Arbitration Treaties of Mr. Root. Yet this is just what had been taking place in a whole network of European post-war treaties for the settlement of international disputes, which held within their comprehensive scope a real and effective alternative for war. But in order to do this, there could be no emasculating and far-reaching reservations, excluding whole categories of serious problems from the scope of the treaties. Unfortunately, however, this is just what happened in the drafting of the American Treaty. The reservations concerning arbitration were not so extensive in scope, it is true, as they had been in the past, but still they excluded questions of domestic jurisdiction, or those which involve the interest of other nations, or those which affect either the Monroe Doctrine, or the obligations under the Covenant of the League of Nations. Now the Bryan Treaties had not contained any reference to these matters, but had applied to any and every kind of dispute. In the new treaty, by what seems to have been an oversight, the reservations concerning arbitration were apparently also applied to the Conciliation Commissions, thus lessening the scope of the Bryan Treaty and almost denaturing it. It was necessary, therefore, for the signatory governments to add to the text of the Treaty an exchange of letters stating that the original Bryan Treaty still held in its comprehensive original form. The Treaty, therefore, with this letter attached to it, finally drew into a single document the two outstanding alternatives for war to be used by the United States and France in the settlement of any possible dispute: arbitration for legal matters and those suitable for arbitral procedure, and conciliation for the more delicate or less definite questions which lay within or on the border line of politics.

We cannot leave this phase of the subject without recalling the fact that during the post-war years the United States had failed lamentably to keep abreast of the progress of the rest of the world in international arbitration. Although American initiative was so largely responsible for the early formulation and the extension of arbitration procedure, the United States had always set definite limits to its use. The movement for compulsory arbitration has made no progress in recent years in what may be called the Anglo-Saxon countries. It would be hard to secure for this proposal in 1928 any greater support than it received more than forty years ago when, in 1887, three hundred and thirty-two members of the British House of Commons memorialized the President of the United States in favor of an Anglo-American arbitration treaty, and nearly a million and a half signatures were secured for petitions in support of this movement. Public opinion then was stirring to such an extent that the Senate Committee on Foreign Relations unanimously passed a Resolution in 1888, calling for the universal and unrestricted employment of arbitration in the settlement of American disputes with all other countries. After two years' delay, this Resolution was agreed to by the Senate on February 14, 1890, and by the House of Representatives on April 3, 1890. In the form in which it finally passed it read as follows: [1]

RESOLVED BY THE SENATE (THE HOUSE OF REPRESENTATIVES CONCURRING), That the President be, and is hereby, requested to invite, from time to time as fit occasions may arise, negotiations with any Government with which the United States has or may have diplomatic relations, to the end that any differences or disputes arising between the two Governments which can not be adjusted by diplomatic agency may be referred to arbitration, and be peaceably adjusted by such means.

It would be carrying optimism to an unreal extreme to expect the present Congress of the United States to adopt so sweeping a resolution in favor of universal arbitration as that of 1890. For a purely American constitutional question was destined to interpose an almost insuperable obstacle in the path of international arbitration. The Senate, jealous for its right to advise the Executive in the making of treaties, refused to allow the process of international settlement to slip out of its hands through the wide extension of arbitration. It provided, therefore, that every proposal for arbitration should be made the subject of a special agreement calling for the Senate's approval. The issue came to a head under Republican administrations.

[1] Misc. Doc. No. 113, 51st Cong., 1st sess.; Cong. Docs., Vol. 2768. (Cf. World Peace Foundation Pamphlet, Vol. IX, Nos. 6-7, 1926, page 499.)

But from the opening of McKinley's first administration down to the close of President Taft's, neither the efforts of Presidents nor the skill and statesmanship of great Secretaries of State were able to make headway against the opposition in the Senate to the negotiation of general treaties of arbitration. All that was achieved was embodied in the series of treaties of 1908 and 1909 which bear the name of Secretary Root, treaties pledging the Executive "to make special agreements calling for Senatorial approval on the occasion of every proposed negotiation." [1]

In this connection it is interesting to note that Mr. Kellogg, prior to the submission of the Arbitration Treaty to France, consulted with the Senate Foreign Relations Committee and secured, in informal discussion, the presumption of its approval. This act of courtesy on the part of the Secretary of State was much appreciated by the Committee at the time. There is no good reason why it should not become an established procedure, for the Secretary does not yield his prerogatives in consultation of this kind, but merely assures himself of the attitude of the Senate, negotiating, as it were, with it just as he would with the representatives of the foreign Power in order to ascertain what projects are capable of fulfillment It may be argued theoretically that this is a step toward Cabinet responsibility to Congress, but it seems to be the only sensible way to prevent the foreign affairs of the United States from falling into utter anarchy, or at least the only way by which to assure giving effect to the policies of the Adminstration. It would not be beyond the realm of possibility that this method of consultation between the Executive and the Senate, which has ample precedent to support it, might help solve our greatest difficulty in treaty negotiation, permitting the Senate Committee on Foreign Affairs to give its advice to the Execu-

[1] The text of the Root Treaty of February 10, 1908, with France is given in the Appendix for purposes of ready comparison with the revised text of 1928.

tive—on the broad lines of policy at least—before, instead of after, the rest of the world has been involved in the consequences of an American Government proposal.[1]

Forty years of relative futility mark the path of the movement for universal compulsory international arbitration in the United States. It is because of this fact that the Bryan Treaties of Conciliation are so important. The United States has established a precedent here of an entirely different kind. It has agreed, or has been willing to agree, with some twenty other nations, to permit an international investigation into issues of disputes concerning which no Senate action is necessary, and no matter whether they affect questions of vital interest and national honor. Conciliation, rather than arbitration, is apparently the American procedure for settling those very disputes which are most likely to give rise to war. It is because of this fact that the friends of peace in the United States were most concerned to find in the first draft of the Arbitration Treaty a reference to the procedure of conciliation which seemed to apply to it some of the limitations which have been so serious a hindrance to the field of arbitration.

In spite of all these impediments, down to 1914 the United States joined with Great Britain in leading the world in the practice of international arbitration. In the post-war years, however, the Continental Powers of Europe have turned the tables on British and American history, and a vast network of arbitration treaties now draws together practically all nations in continental Europe. Both France and Germany, for instance, have declared their willingness to accept arbitration of every issue suitable for adjudication. The phrases "national honor" and "vital interest" no longer appear in the ordinary arbitration treaties of Europe. But more than this, they inter-

[1] Although Mr. Kellogg's act has precedent behind it, such formal consultations are still regarded as exceptional.

pose no Senatorial censorship or interference and, in form at least, realize the ideals set forth in the Hague Conferences, which seemed then almost an unreal dream and which the cynics ridiculed in the dark days of the World War. Running parallel with arbitration are the provisions for conciliation tribunals to cover matters not suitable for submission to a court. It is in this regard especially that the Franco-American Treaty was an approximation to European usage, although in tying up arbitration with conciliation it involved a step forward on the part of the United States.

This development of arbitration in European international relations is not well known in the United States. Therefore not many American readers will discover the unconscious irony in the statement in the Preamble of the Franco-American Treaty that it is to furnish an example to the rest of the world. For most of the Continental Powers of Europe, it would be an example rather to be avoided, for they already have gone beyond it. This can easily be seen by any one who takes the trouble to look through that vast collection of post-war treaties of arbitration which has been published by the League of Nations.[1] Already in 1923 the League had registered eighty-four treaties of arbitration and conciliation, most of them going much farther than the American model. It is not only the small Powers that have contributed to this great network of the machinery for pacific settlement but the great Powers as well. Great Britain and France have each made such agreements with over twenty other nations, and Germany with more than a dozen. The plain fact is that the United States, once the leader in the movement for international arbitration, has fallen behind the rest of the world.

[1] *Arbitration and Security*, League of Nations, Geneva, 1927.

CHAPTER XII

THE FRANCO-AMERICAN NEGOTIATIONS

THE Arbitration Treaty was not an answer to M. Briand's proposal for the renunciation of war, although in the confused newspaper comment it was at times so referred to on both sides of the Atlantic. The confusion was perhaps natural because the new Arbitration Treaty contained in its preamble an obvious reference to M. Briand's proposal. But the State Department kept the two projects separate. On the very same day on which he proposed the revision of the Arbitration Treaty, December 28, 1927, Mr. Kellogg sent a separate note to the French Government in which at last he dealt with M. Briand's proposal of the preceding June. This letter and not the Arbitration Treaty was the real beginning of the official negotiations by the United States for a treaty to renounce war.

The chapter of diplomatic history which followed is one so full of human interest that even in retrospect one is tempted to delay too long over it. In its sudden turns and dramatic surprises, it recalled the play and counterplay of old-time diplomacy; and yet the interchange of notes was given to the world at the time and challenged a nation-wide discussion. While it dealt with the most serious question within the scope of politics and invited the expression of the most lofty sentiments, at the same time it showed how childish and petty great nations can be and how it is possible for statesmen to misunderstand even their own projects when presented to them at the hands of others. It was public diplomacy in a full-dress debate with all the world watching and a goodly portion of it joining in. At intervals for the next two months and more, the two governments wrote each other notes of explanation which were in turn explained in contradictory ways by the press of each country. On each side there were nationalist and reactionary editorials which took it for granted that the whole negotiation was insincere and that each government was simply playing for political advantage at home by attempting to outbid the other in an unreal proposition which both of them were supposed to be at heart attempting to sabotage, or else that the government in question had been the blind dupe of a clever opponent. One would think to read some of this comment that France and the United States were enemies instead of friends, and that the diplomatic exchange was more or less of a war in itself. The liberal press did not quite succeed in correcting this impression, and the extreme Left wing helped it along by joining with the nationalists to give vent to their suspicion and the continuing prejudices of both wartime and post-war hostility to Franco-American friendship. In France, there was the widespread antipathy to things American which had grown out of the unsympathetic attitude of the United States to French post-war policies, and this found ready expression. In addition, as the French press is traditionally more in touch with official opinion than the press of the United States, the cool reception to the American proposals was taken to indicate that the whole negotiation was headed for failure.

But public diplomacy, like most other things that democracy tries, may be clumsy and confused and slow-moving, but it has behind it whatever reality there is in national purpose and ideal; and in the long run its achievements mark steps of permanent advance. The actual negotiations moved tortuously within a very narrow circle of ideas, but, ultimately, the circle was rounded and the proposal came back to the exact terms in which it had been first given to the world, and in those very terms was accepted at last with practically unanimous acclaim, not only in the two countries which originated it, but throughout the whole civilized world. It is not too much to say that this ultimate success was due to the very fact of public participation in the long debate which seemed at first to be an obstacle to ready agreement. It is not the first time in the history of democracy that an obstacle has become a stepping-stone.

It is unnecessary now to follow this debate backward and forward through the winter months of 1928. We confine ourselves to the actual dispatches.

Mr. Kellogg's first letter of December 28, 1927, proposed that "the two Governments, instead of contenting themselves with a bilateral declaration of the nature suggested by M. Briand, might make a more signal contribution to world peace by joining in an effort to obtain the adherence of all of the principal powers of the world to a declaration renouncing war as an instrument of national policy." In fulfillment of this suggestion he stated that the United States should prepare to "concert with the Government of France with a view to the conclusion of a treaty among the principal Powers of the world, open to signature by all nations, condemning war and renouncing it as an instrument of national policy in favor of the pacific settlement of international disputes."

The answer of M. Briand to this first note of Mr. Kellogg was immediate and direct. It was delivered in Washington on January 5, 1928. France readily agreed to the enlargement of the proposal and accepted the invitation to join with the United States in presenting a draft treaty embodying the suggestions of M. Briand to the other nations of the world. But before asking the other nations, "it would be advantageous immediately to sanction the general character of this procedure by affixing the signatures of France and the United States." In other words, the bilateral treaty of M. Briand's first offer could be retained in the making of a multilateral treaty, as a model to be followed and a guarantee of the sincerity of the two governments which were taking the initiative. Thus by a simple device in procedure the American proposal might still preserve the original one.

So far the path of agreement was easy, and the Government of France went on to state its definite acceptance of its own proposal which came back to it in such enlarged form. But in this restatement, it substituted for the original formula, "the renunciation of war as an instrument of national policy," another phrase which called for the renunciation of "all war of aggression." This was the only attempt to introduce a variant formula, and the sequel showed how valuable, and indeed necessary, had been the original term "war as an instrument of national policy."[1]

It was at this point that the popular debate broke loose emphasizing the differences in the formula, almost forgetting that the governments were clearly not at variance as to the underlying principle of the proposal, and were merely seeking to find a way to give it expression that would not be misunderstood, and forgetting as well that both Foreign Ministers frankly declared that the draft of the treaty was still at the initial stage. It may have been partly due to the long public discussion of unofficial proposals that popular comment treated the first beginnings of the official negotiations as though they were in the final stages and seemed to take it for granted that any divergence of statement at the start could not subsequently be overcome. So far as the procedure went there was no real difficulty in harmonizing the American proposal with the turn given it in the French reply. All that was needed was a diplomatic recognition of the special claim of France as the initia-

---

[1] There is more than incidental significance in the fact that this expression of Clausewitz, the theorist of war, was now taken over from strategy to politics. The statement in the Paris press that the phrase was advanced by jurists of the Quai d'Orsay to give meaning to "the American expression 'outlawry of war' " would be interesting if true; but that element of interest is lacking.

tor of a proposal, with the United States in the rôle of friend and supporter. We shall see that this problem was by no means serious and was soon got rid of.

But there was a real question as to the change of formula. What are wars of aggression? The view was widely held in England and the United States that there was no possible way of defining a war of aggression so as to distinguish it from any other kind of war. We shall refer to this point later on. But the press comment in Paris made it equally clear that there were those in France to whom the phrase "war as an instrument of national policy" was less definite and clear than the term "war of aggression." It turned out in the long run that both phrases meant substantially the same thing, but this was not the view of most American commentators. M. Briand's note was interpreted as a step backwards, and those who had been hostile to France throughout were not slow to claim that the insincerity of the French proposal had been shown up by Mr. Kellogg in this first exchange of letters.

No one who knows the history of post-war Europe and of the place in it occupied by M. Briand as the outstanding exponent of international peace can accept this interpretation of the French reply. Nevertheless, from this time on, the initiative in the negotiations passed from Paris to Washington and the world came to regard the proposal as an outstandingly and definitely American project. It was not referred to henceforth as "M. Briand's plan" but as "the Kellogg proposal."

The opening of this new phase was Mr. Kellogg's note of January 11. It dealt with the new procedure and content in straightforward fashion. The procedure would be simple, for France should join with the United States in communicating to the British, German and Italian Governments the text of M. Briand's original proposal and the copies of the subsequent correspondence between the United States and France, on the understanding that this preliminary discussion in no way committed any of the participating governments, pending the conclusion of a definitive treaty. The French suggestion that all governments should be invited to a ready-made treaty was open to the objection that some Powers might delay or refuse acceptance, and so the treaty would not come into force at all and "the present efforts of France and the United States would be rendered abortive." A practical solution would be to begin negotiations for the multilateral treaty by submitting M. Briand's short text of June 20 as a basis for discussion or agreement. This method of procedure turned out to be the one which was ultimately followed, although with slight variation. As a historical document, however, the note of January 11 is more important for the fact that it now published for the first time the text of the original proposal of M. Briand of June 20, 1927. This text was also ultimately to be made the text of the final treaty with only a few verbal changes so that Mr. Kellogg's note of January 11 is a historical forecast of the whole subsequent achievement.

The purpose of Mr. Kellogg in quoting the draft treaty proposal of M. Briand was to point out that it contained no mention of the word "aggression." "On the contrary, it provided unequivocally for the renunciation by the high contracting parties of all war as an instrument of national policy." The question was directly put to the Government of France why it had changed the formula and whether or not this revision implied a change of purpose.

The answer of the French Government was contained in its note of January 21, which will always present a difficult problem to the historian, for the most cordial friend of France can hardly fail to interpret it as anything else than an effort to withdraw from the whole negotiation. There was even a tone of irritation in the text itself and a suggestion that the United States had been maneuvering the Government of France into a false position. The argument was as weak as the implication was misleading. But as events turned out it helped along the negotiations toward final success perhaps more than any other single document; for it led to the forward-looking incident of the United States Government interpreting the obligations of European treaties and especially of the Covenant of the League in a way which made American coöperation possible in ways which had hitherto been commonly denied.

The French letter gave color to the American suspicion that the original proposal had been an effort to involve the United States in the policies of France, by repeating that all that France had intended was to give expression to the historical relations between the two republics. This limited declaration had been denatured by the American proposal to bring in other Powers, and once it had become so general as this, France was indifferent as to whether the instrument should be first signed by the United States and France. But if these other Powers were to be invited to sign, then the treaty must harmonize with their existing obligations under the existing treaties for the maintenance of peace; the Covenant of the League, the Treaties of Locarno, and those which guarantee neutrality. While the United States was a stranger to these obligations, all other nations must bear them in mind, and they could not make treaties with the United States without taking into consideration their obligation to help maintain those treaties. In the Treaty of Locarno, for example, Britain and Italy undertook to go to the help of France in case it were attacked by Germany, or to the aid of Germany if it were attacked by France. If the Kellogg proposal to renounce war went so far as to conflict with this police engagement, France could not accept it. France was ready to "join in any declaration tending to denounce war as a crime and to set up international sanctions susceptible of preventing or repressing it. There has been no change in its sentiments in that respect: its position remains the same." This linking of the denunciation of war and the police action to prevent it was, to say the least, not helpful to the American Administration, for the American refusal to accept the obligations of an international police had been the one chief obstacle to the acceptance of the League of Nations. It almost looked as though the French Government were taking the occasion to accentuate the fact that the United States was moving in an orbit of its own while all the rest of the world was bound together in the system of the League, and that, therefore, the best that could be done was to accept some such declaration as that which Poland had proposed in Geneva at the last Assembly, denouncing aggressive war as an international crime. The French note was the real test of public opinion in the United States, for it played directly into the hands of the opposition to the Kellogg proposal. But the current of public opinion was working strongly at the time and, by a strange but happy coincidence, was expressing itself as it had seldom done in the memory of the present generation in overwhelming popular protests against the big navy program which had been sponsored by the Administration.

The failure of the Geneva Conference for the Reduction of Armaments had won over the Administration to the plans of the Navy Department which called for the building of the greatest navy the world had ever seen and an expenditure of money extending into the billions. It was expected that this grandiose scheme of imperial splendor, making visible the symbol of world power, would appeal to popular American sentiment. On the contrary, no other act of any Administration in recent times had proved so overwhelmingly unpopular. There was, of course, the organized opposition of the peace forces of the country, but it was not this which carried the day against the navy plans. It was the unorganized but indignant protest of thousands of individuals who took the trouble to write personal letters to their representatives in Congress protesting both against the wild extravagance of this unprecedented expenditure and the implication that it carried with it. The shock which Congress received from this deluge of protests on the desks of Congressmen and Senators can be partly measured by the fact that, instead of billions, nothing whatever was finally voted throughout the entire session of Congress. It is probable that much of this protest was in no way connected with pacifism, even in its mildest forms. It was more likely a common-sense protest against needless waste, for few of those who vote the money for a navy stop to think much about its actual use in war. At most, it is for them an instrument of threat and menace rather than of warfare itself. But Congress took the other meaning out of the protest and there was jarred into its consciousness a belief that the country had been gained heart and soul by the ideals of international peace. It is, of course, impossible to say how far this popular clamor against naval armaments affected the negotiations of the Kellogg proposal, but that it strengthened the hand of the Administration at a time when it most needed encouragement is a fact beyond argument.

The first answer of Washington to the Briand note did not come from the Secretary of State but from the Chairman of the Foreign Relations Committee of the Senate, Senator Borah. In a notable article in the New York *Times* on Sunday, February 5, he answered point by point the note of the French Government, and clearly showed that a treaty to renounce war as an instrument of policy would be simply strengthening both the Covenant of the League and the Treaties of Locarno, and presumably any legitimate treaty of neutrality. If France could sign a treaty with the United States to that effect, without violating the Covenant of the League, then any other member of the League could do the same, for the French renunciation would be the same as any other renunciation. If all the members of the League renounced war it would be a reinsurance of the Covenant, a reinsurance which would at the very least mobilize the moral forces of the world against the institution of war, and one to which the United States would, for the first time, be a party.

Senator Borah's argument was irrefutable; he went behind the façade of the structure of the League of Nations to emphasize its purpose and its fundamental principle, which is the maintenance of peace. But his statement did not stop with this assertion of a common purpose. While he repeated his belief that the United States would never join the League as it stands today, because it "will never become identified or coöperate with a system for peace based upon 'pledges to wage war,'" nevertheless it can coöperate with the League from the opposite angle. "At the present time," said Mr. Borah, "we have a network of treaties and understandings relative to peace—arbitration treaties, conciliation treaties, the Hague Tribunal, World Court, peace machinery of the League and the machinery of Locarno. The effect of the Kellogg proposal is a solemn pledge to let that peace machinery work. It is a solemn pledge to rely upon the peace machinery of the peace plans and not upon the war machinery. It is a solemn pledge among the leading nations that they will not resort to war, that they are forever pledged to the employment of peaceful methods for the adjustment of their controversies. This gives us international laws based upon peace and not upon war. This pledge strengthens every piece of peace machinery in existence."

Without pausing to analyze Senator Borah's conception of the peace machinery of Europe, the significant fact was that the weight of his influence was definitely thrown in favor of continuing the negotiations with France and working out a formula which would harmonize the two points of view. The hesitancy of France found now no answering hesitancy at Washington. And the next letter of Secretary Kellogg, that of February 27, not only repeated the argument of Senator Borah but also stated that, if France could sign a bilateral treaty renouncing war as an instrument of national policy it could just as well become a party to the multilateral treaty, for the difference between the two was one of degree and not of substance. "If, however, members of the League of Nations cannot, without violating the terms of the Covenant of the League, agree among themselves and with the Government of the United States to renounce war as an instrument of their national policy, it seems idle to discuss either bilateral or multilateral treaties." To clinch this argument, Secretary Kellogg recalled a resolution of the recent Havana Conference of the American Republics condemning war as an instrument of national policy, adding that seventeen of the twenty-one states accepting this resolution were members of the League of Nations. The proposed treaty, therefore, instead of running counter to any obligations of the League, might be regarded as "a most effective instrument for promoting the great ideal of peace which the League has so closely at heart."

So far, the Secretary was undoubtedly on solid ground. But the agreement with Senator Borah extended to something more than the method of negotiation. There was an unqualified acceptance of Senator Borah's opposition to any attempt to distinguish by definition between aggressive and defensive war. The renunciation must not have any exceptions and qualifications which would destroy its value "as a guaranty of peace." [1] "The ideal which inspires the effort so sincerely and so hopefully put forward by your Government and mine is arresting and appealing just because of its purity and simplicity; and I cannot avoid the feeling that if governments should publicly acknowledge that they can only deal with this ideal in a technical spirit and must insist upon the adoption of reservations impairing, if not utterly destroying the true significance of

[1] The word "guaranty" is distinctly open to criticism in this connection, for the whole insistence of the United States was upon avoiding responsibilities for peace enforcement.

their common endeavors, they would be in effect only recording their impotence, to the keen disappointment of mankind
in general."

Unfortunately, a complex problem cannot be made simple
by ignoring its complexities, and the effort of the United States
to avoid discussion on this point, of clarification and definition,
merely led to continuing debate in which each nation stated its
point of view, the United States along with the rest. There is
no final way of settling this question of peace and war which
does not involve the definition of aggression and defense, for
the one is prohibited and the other is retained, and we must
know which is which. This is exactly what Mr. Kellogg refused
to do.

If the French notes of January were somewhat less than
encouraging, the next one, that of March 30, was still further
removed from the spirit of the original proposal. At least, so
it seemed at first reading, and so it will always seem to those
who read such documents but once. One was almost tempted
to suppose that the phrases of M. Briand had been retouched
by one who had never learned to yield the logic of an argument. A legalistic tone pervades the note and legalism is negative when its caution intervenes to place limits upon those sentiments and ideals which call humanity to new adventures. In
any case, the reply which now came from the Government of
M. Poincaré was interpreted widely in the United States as a
convincing argument that the Government of France had never
seriously intended its original offer. Instead of attempting to
surmount the qualifications and exceptions which it had previously noted, France proceeds to state them in greater detail
than before, and in language which implies a rising doubt as
to the trend of the new treaty. The reservation that the signatories are to recover full liberty of action against any state
which violates the treaty is necessary "in order not to turn an
instrument of progress and peace into a means of oppression."

There is a clear implication in this turn of the phrase that unless the treaty is properly framed, it may prove a menace instead of a blessing; the French Government prefers to take no chances. Not only is the right of legitimate defense definitely asserted, but as well as that, the new treaty must not run counter to any existing treaty obligations, not only those of the Covenant and of the Locarno agreements, but also treaties guaranteeing neutrality; and, finally, the multilateral treaty must be made worldwide and not go into effect until all nations will have signed and ratified it. As for defining an aggressor, the French reply avoids that point, but defines "war as an instrument of national policy" as being that kind of war which nations use "as a means of carrying out their own spontaneous independent policy." It is the renunciation of attack or invasion, or the use of force to settle international differences. If aggression is not to be defined, as Mr. Kellogg insists, well and good; but the phrase "war as an instrument of national policy" can at least be elaborated.

It is only fair to the French Government, however, to remind ourselves that there was reason for its caution. It would have had a short memory, indeed, if it did not recall at this juncture the persistent and trenchant criticism of Senator Borah directed against the post-war policies of France and more especially those of M. Poincaré. The tone of the French note may, therefore, be partially explained as a warning against any attempt to turn the anti-war treaty into an instrument for the undoing of the European state system based upon the Treaty of Versailles. The sensitiveness of France upon this point seems to have been chiefly responsible for the fact that from now on it resigned the leadership in the negotiations to the United States; and yet Ambassador Claudel himself was later to be chief witness for Mr. Borah's singleness of purpose throughout the negotiations. At no time did Mr. Borah permit the major issue of a worldwide reform to be lost sight of in the issues of current politics. Had this fact been better appreciated in Paris, the French text might, perhaps, have had less reference to the sanctity of existing treaty obligations. However much Senator Borah might dislike the Treaty of Versailles, he was not dealing with that subject here.

The French note marks, in a way, the closing of the first phase of the negotiations. There were many, indeed, who thought at the time that it was the end not only of the first phase, but of the proposal itself. Liberals, not only in America but in other countries as well, registered their strong protest against the negative tone of the French reply and its discouraging outlook. The reactionary press in Paris claimed that those who concocted this document were hoping that they had seen the last of the Kellogg plan. But they had failed to see what the Government at Washington fortunately detected, that beneath the surface of this somewhat rugged text there lay, after all, the fundamental basis of a possible agreement. M. Briand had stated once more in clear and unequivocal terms that France would join with the United States in the effort to eliminate war as an instrument of national policy, and the reservations with which the note dealt were only those which were rooted in the necessity for preserving the defense of France itself and the coöperative defense of the world's peace against a violator of the treaty pledge.

The French Government declared that it was ready to join with the United States in submitting to the Governments of Germany, Great Britain, Italy, and Japan, the correspondence between France and the United States from the first treaty proposal of M. Briand in the preceding June, and at the same time to propose for the assent of these four governments a draft agreement in almost the identical language of the general proposal.

Owing to the way in which it is printed in the collected texts, the reader may easily overlook the fact that this apparently negative document of the French Government really contained once more the actual outline of the treaty. This outline, in which the original suggestion is kept alive by the French Government, occurs in the closing phrase of the fourth last paragraph and the opening sentence of the paragraph following, as will be seen clearly if the text of these two sentences is disengaged from their context. The proposal is that M. Briand's original plan be reworded in multipartite form by the United States with only verbal changes.

The signatory powers of such an instrument, while not prejudicing their rights of legitimate defense within the framework of existing treaties, should make a solemn declaration condemning recourse to war as an instrument of national policy, or in other words, as a means of carrying out their own spontaneous, independent policy.

They would specifically undertake, among themselves, to refrain from any attack or invasion, and never to seek the settlement of any difference or conflict of whatsoever nature or origin which might arise between them save by pacific means.

This letter was to mark the end of the distinctly Franco-American negotiations. In the month following, both countries turned from this mutual exchange of letters to the framing of treaty texts and their submission to the other Great Powers for comment or approval. Since, however, the French draft was destined soon to be eliminated from the discussion, we may, perhaps, turn to it at this point and then dismiss it from the story. There is an additional reason for this, in that its text simply and frankly does not convey the impression of an attempt to reach agreement with the American proposal, but rather an effort to subordinate it to the exigencies of practical politics. The French Draft Treaty was submitted to the governments of the Great Powers on April 20.[1] It still repeated in the heart of the text the principles of the Briand offer, but it so circumscribed them by recalling and emphasizing existing

[1] Cf. Appendix IV.

treaty obligations, as to make them seem mere vague generalities which would melt away at the touch of the hard facts of a world in which war is still used, if not as an instrument of a nation's policy, nevertheless for the maintenance of all those conditions which determine policy. The right of legitimate self-defense is reserved "within the framework of existing treaties"; and it was expressly stated that the provisions of this treaty should "in no wise affect the rights and obligations of the contracting parties resulting from prior international agreements to which they are parties." It is not too much to say that this provision, set forth in Article IV of the French draft, shocked and alienated liberal thinkers in all countries; for it seemed as though the French Government was insisting in these terms on the sanctity of the *status quo* to an extent that really denatured the American proposal and threatened "to turn an instrument of progress and peace into a means of oppression," to repeat the very words of the last French note to the United States. It is quite possible that the Government of M. Poincaré had no idea that it was leaving the new proposal so far behind in its insistence upon the fact that nations must honor their given word. It is undoubtedly true that a fundamental condition of enduring peace is the sanctity of treaties; and this must have been the interpretation which Sir Austen Chamberlain put upon the French text when he declared in his reply to the United States that the British Government also would prefer to have some such provision as Article IV of the French draft in the final treaty. Nevertheless, public opinion, as contrasted with official opinion, reacted strongly against this emphasis upon the *status quo*; and in England even more strongly than in the United States, the critics of France, and there were many, used the French Draft Treaty to confirm them in the opinion that the Government of M. Poincaré was not in full sympathy with the high ideals of M. Briand. So strongly did this current run, that the French draft received no public adherence from any other government. Instead, the French Government, itself, was to witness in the following months the worldwide acceptance of its own original draft treaty of the previous June, but under the title of the Kellogg, rather than the Briand, proposal.

CHAPTER XIII

THE KELLOGG PROPOSAL

THROUGHOUT the winter months it was evident that the Governments of the United States and France were moving steadily farther and farther apart instead of towards agreement, both as to content and procedure. For a time the misunderstandings seemed not only to threaten the failure of the whole negotiation but to accentuate the none too cordial attitude of a number of the French newspapers which seemed to reflect an opinion in governmental circles. If the issue had not been so serious a one, there was something almost humorous in the charge that Mr. Kellogg had taken an unfair advantage of M. Briand by treating his first sketch or outline of the points of a treaty as though it were the finished and final form of the treaty itself. Diplomacy does not move this way. Treaties are contracts; they are legal documents, and unless carefully drafted are likely to create misunderstandings and disputes between nations instead of settling the questions at issue. When Lord Salisbury, as Foreign Minister, drafted his projects of British policy, he did so in broad and untechnical terms like those which M. Briand used. Then he would call in experts on his Foreign Office staff and tell them to restate that "in diplomatic jargon." In the opinion of the diplomatic world, Mr. Kellogg was mistaking the draft of an idea for the legal terms of a treaty. The French wanted the job done with all the careful detail called for by the importance of the commitment. This further drafting would not in their eyes falsify the original proposal, but it would state the terms under which it was being worked out. But in the eyes of the American Government the statement of the conditions was regarded as a statement of limitations, and the more the French developed their reserves, the more the American insisted upon the generalities.

The divergence in procedure naturally grew with the divergence in contents. In all of the American notes of December, January and February, Mr. Kellogg had proposed the joint action of France and the United States. They were to sign together the note which would transmit the proposition to the other Powers. The French avoided a reply until, in their concluding note of March 30, they had fully stated the reservations and conditions to be embodied in the text. Then, instead of meeting the American suggestion directly, the French Government stated that it was willing to join with the United States to ask the other governments to study the situation so as to see how they could reconcile their previous obligations with the terms of the contemplated new treaty. This was not going very far with the United States, but the French caution added a still further condition stating that the plan as now conceived originated with the American Government and that it was to take the responsibility for success or failure. Evidently, at the time, failure was expected by the goverment that penned this note.

From now on the project had definitely become an American one, and the American Government made it its own in the fullest sense of the word.

In identic notes sent to the Governments of Great Britain, Germany, Italy, and Japan, on April 13, the history of the French negotiations were summarized in a few words with sympathetic reference to the ideals and purposes of France, but with a frank appeal to the other Governments to take up the question henceforth directly with the United States. The other members of the League were appealed to, to support the opinion of the American Government that membership in the

League of Nations did not conflict with the broad proposal to renounce war as an instrument of national policy and that therefore the restrictions and reservations which France was now insisting upon were not really necessary, so far, at least, as the League and the Treaties of Locarno were concerned. American diplomacy was directed, in the first place, towards having the Great Powers state whether or not they were free to sign a new treaty, and only after that, whether or not they were willing to do so. Perhaps not the least benefit arising from the whole negotiation may turn out to be this clarification of the meaning of the Covenant and of the Treaty of Locarno, showing that these instruments of peace instead of conflicting with the general renunciation of war as an instrument of policy, are strictly in harmony with it. The American Administration, which had rejected the Covenant, was now in the strange position of insisting to League members that the obligations of the Covenant were solely those of the maintenance of peace. If nothing else were to come of the Kellogg proposal, it was well worth while for the service it rendered in this regard. A new emphasis was given to the central purpose of the existing framework of peace quite apart from the multilateral treaty.

But this was not all that the Kellogg note contained. It actually submitted a preliminary draft of a definite text. It is true that this was offered only as "a preliminary draft . . . representing in a general way the form of treaty" which might be adopted, but the text of the note of April 13 is the final text of the multilateral treaty, with the exception of a few slight changes in the preamble.

The reception given this letter was something more than a complete justification of the persistence of the American Government; it was even a justification of public diplomacy. The outburst of popular approval which it called forth throughout the whole world showed that the public opinion of democracies is in advance of the cautious policy of their governments. However diplomacy might regard it, however difficult it might be for international law to interpret it, there was in what Mr. Kellogg called "the purity and simplicity" of his proposal to renounce war an appeal to the common conscience of the civilized world which found expression in a new and most effective way.

Once more we find exemplified the truth of what Ambassador Houghton had so eloquently depicted in his address at Harvard University in the preceding June, that the governments even in democratic countries are poor vehicles for the expression of the moral purposes of nations when dealing with each other. Embodying as they do traditions and precedents, and feeling strongly the responsibility for the maintenance of existing rights, they tend to emphasize the difficulties and the obstacles in the path of reform or even of fair accommodation.[1] They do not readily yield to the demands of those mere common-sense ways of doing things which rub off the trappings from the world of business. The point raised by Ambassador

[1] This address was printed privately and, except in Germany, never received the attention it deserved. We can quote here only a single paragraph of the concluding argument: "It would seem that the time is at hand when a new experiment in democratic control must be made, and those peoples who have demonstrated their competence to govern themselves within their own national frontiers must assume direct responsibility for their relations with each other. Our governments have shown themselves unable to protect us against war. They continue to act along well-defined grooves and in accordance with the dictates of a political theory which exalts nationalism and relies frankly upon the use of force, when necessary, to attain these ends. We have no apparent reason to hope for any change in their methods and in their aims. The future, if they control it, seems likely to be merely an intensified repetition of the past. Personally I believe we cannot safely continue to be democratic within our national frontiers and autocratic in our relations with the other self-governing peoples. A durable peace cannot be based upon force. It must, if it exists at all, be based upon goodwill. And I believe profoundly that that practical goodwill exists, that the great self-governing peoples may safely trust one another, and that only a method of dealing between them, inherited from an outgrown system of autocratic government prevents our recognition of that great beneficent fact. We are caught in a process of our own making. And we must unmake it."

Houghton is a fundamental one, to which both governments and peoples will come back in years to come, long after the Pact of Paris is a page of history. For it is not only in matters of peace and war, but in all other vital concerns of nations, that the way must be found for making governments more and more responsive to the will of the people. On the other hand, responsiveness to the popular will is not any more important than consistency in policy and a regard for existing obligations. There would be no progress but only disorder in the state if the government surrendered all directives in times of crises. That is just when nations feel the need of government most, and when they are least likely to divest themselves of its protecting care. Plebiscites alone will not suffice; there must first of all be popular instruction in the alternatives to war, so that when disputes arise the people may know what chance there is of avoiding war while maintaining a just cause. Without the instruments of international dealing there can be no effective appeal to the popular opposition to war itself. For, unless the nation is in possession of appropriate means of pacific settlement, popular feeling will insist upon recourse to war. However, this discussion is carrying us too far afield; the Houghton suggestion was no part of the Kellogg proposal.

It had been American public opinion which had kept alive the initial proposal of France throughout the summer and autumn of 1927. It was now to be principally British public opinion which was to galvanize the American proposal into something which its own Conservative Government was obliged to accept. Pacific Germany spoke out, also, with practically unanimous demand for German adhesion, and the prompt action of the German Government in sending a complete acceptance of the American scheme stimulated even those whom it annoyed. In a few days' time, the American proposal had become one of the definite facts in the world's history.

The chief interest for the time being shifts to the British

Empire. It is not too much to say that there had been little interest in Great Britain in the Franco-American negotiations during the preceding months. The newspapers had paid slight attention either to the Briand proposal or to the American notes; and such comment as there had been during the winter was of that restrained politeness which is so often the British way of registering disapproval. With a strange lack of foresight the British had apparently never expected that the proposal would come around to them. Now suddenly it was a British problem and, although the Government delayed before replying, the British public began its answer immediately and in no uncertain terms. What is more, it responded with an enthusiasm and unanimity that was something new in recent British politics. With the exception of one or two extreme conservative and reactionary newspapers, like the *Morning Post,* there was a nation-wide demand upon the Government to accept the proposal and join with the United States in furthering its acceptance throughout the world. The London *Times* was almost as outspoken in its favor as the Labor and the Liberal press, although reminding its readers of the seriousness of the step proposed and the problems which it left unsolved. Meetings were held all over the country and resolutions passed in favor of the Kellogg proposal; and the delay of the Government in replying to the United States increased rather than lessened the momentum of public opinion.

Although British public opinion was practically of one mind, the Government held back the answer to Mr. Kellogg for over a month. There were reasons for this delay, as we shall presently see, but the result was that it was not Britain but Germany which sent the first affirmative reply to the United States. No other Great Power in the world today has made such a radical change in its attitude towards peace and war as Germany. The new German Republic is an unprecedented experiment in the politics of peace. Shorn of armaments by the Treaty

of Versailles and deprived for the time being of the reassertion of its military and naval power, it has been forced from
the very exigencies of its post-war situation to find and apply
the practical equivalents in terms of peace for the arbitrament
of the sword. It has concentrated upon this task both theoretically and practically, and the new German Republic is a laboratory for the study of pacific international affairs, such as the
modern world presents nowhere else. The popular reception in
Germany of the American proposal was therefore overwhelmingly favorable.

But there were practical reasons as well, which no person
could ignore, why the German Government should adhere to
a proposal of this sort from the United States and so phrase its
acceptance as to indicate identical purpose and outlook with that
of America. This the German note succeeded fully in accom-
plishing; it was one of the most successful documents in this
whole chapter of diplomatic history, for it gave the impression
of a complete and unreserved acceptance of the American note,
and yet managed to repeat the major reservations which France
had insisted upon. It stated that "respect for the obligations
arising from the Covenant of the League of Nations and the
Rhine pact (Locarno) must in the opinion of the German Government remain inviolate." But immediately one had to agree
with the United States that its proposals could "only serve to
strengthen the fundamental idea of the Covenant of the
League of Nations and of the Rhine pact." There was a plain
implication, therefore, that if France found any difficulty in
adjusting its previous commitments to the Kellogg proposal, it
must be on account of its other treaties "guaranteeing neutrality" to which Germany, for a very good reason, was not a
partner. But this was too good a point to be left for mere implications; Germany crossed the "t's" and dotted the "i's." It
remarked that so far as it was concerned it had signed no other
treaties than the Covenant or Locarno "which might affect the

substance of the new pact." Other international obligations of this kind had not been entered into by Germany. It did not need much foresight to see that in this deft reminder Germany was preparing the way either to ascertain the real bearing of the French alliances or to lessen any menace to itself which they had been thought to contain.

The position of the British Government was now becoming an uneasy one. It had before it not only the American proposal, which was so strongly backed by public opinion, but it had as well to consider the abortive French counter-proposal of April 20, to which passing reference has been made. Although this counter-proposal does not come fully into this story because it was so soon discarded by its authors, still, for the time being, it had a claim upon the attention of the British Government equal to that of the Washington proposal. Moreover, from the standpoint of professional diplomacy and the traditions of the Foreign Office, the French draft was preferable to that of Washington, and in some form or other the British reply would have to say about the same things which were incorporated in the French text. Then, while the public grew more impatient, the technical situation grew more confused. Under such circumstances, past experience showed only one method of solution, and that was by calling together a conference of experts of the different governments charged with the task of securing a text to embody the principles already agreed upon. A suggestion of this kind was therefore thrown out by the British Government in the course of a debate in Parliament.

Although this suggestion was not in the form of a communication to the American Government, the State Department lost no time in stating its emphatic disapproval of any such course. It issued a statement, or rather allowed a statement to be issued, that it was absolutely opposed to any such reference of the drafting of the treaty to a committee of experts. This killed the suggestion so far as the British negotiations with America were concerned, but it did not end the matter for the European Powers. The answer which the Government of Italy sent to Washington on May 4 stated quite plainly that plans were under consideration in Europe for a preliminary meeting of the legal experts of the Powers directly interested in the proposed treaty, and that it had adhered to this procedure but was of the opinion that nothing would come of such a meeting unless the United States participated. Signor Mussolini did not commit himself with reference to the treaty itself, but confined his reply to this question of procedure.

As a matter of fact, the suggestion of a meeting of experts was a sound one. Public diplomacy calls for something more than an exchange of notes through the public press or the public discussion of policies in international conference. Agreement between nations as to fundamental principles is not enough; treaties must embody these principles in the frail vehicle of words, and the experience of history has shown only too often how difficult it is to phrase a commitment in language which docs not lead to ultimate misunderstanding. Impatience with the mistakes of the old diplomacy should not lead to the thoughtless conclusion that the casual methods of an open forum should be substituted for the proper work of tried and responsible specialists in international affairs. We must still use the official channels of intercourse for the business of governments and leave in their hands the technical framing of proposals when it is clear that the nations themselves have reached an essential agreement on the large questions of policy. Then the problem shifts from the issue itself to the statement of it in terms which will be understood by and meet the needs of each of the negotiating parties. This second phase of negotiations, which is the proper business of State Departments and Foreign Offices, even under the régime of public diplomacy, will continue to play its legitimate part, although perhaps even in the casting of a phrase, these agents of the governments will be more keenly aware of their responsibility because the whole world will pass judgment on the text which they produce.

Public interest may become impeding interference if it prevents the formulation by technical experts of an essentially technical statement. Only those who have a sufficient knowledge of the details can put those details into language, and the framing of a contract is essentially a matter of detail. Good intentions will never be a substitute for clarity of expression in an international treaty. There comes a point where public diplomacy must use the machinery of those schooled in the language and trained in the history of international relations.

This does not mean that public diplomacy is valid only in the discovery of problems and not in their solution. It must keep alert in criticism and judgment and in the stimulation of expressed purpose, to the very end of the proceeding; but there is danger that there may be no achievement at all unless the matter is turned over at the proper stage to those who can frame specific texts which take into account the intricacies of existing relationships and the definite setting and results of the proposed change.

Now, this cannot be done without an international consultation of the specialists of the different Foreign Offices.

It is not enough for each Foreign Office to prepare its own case with care and precision, and then send its plenipotentiaries to international conference. Every time that this has been done with reference to the larger problems of world politics it has resulted in failure. The failure of the Naval Disarmament Conference, as well as the success of the negotiations at Locarno, have both been attributed by the most competent judges to the technical preparation of the preliminaries to the negotiations themselves. There was undoubtedly much preparation for the Disarmament Conference, but it was not shaped up for agreement through previous exchanges on technical problems;

on the other hand, this was exactly what was done prior to
Locarno. The world has given the credit of Locarno to the
three outstanding statesmen who presided over the Foreign Offices of Britain, France and Germany, and imagines that the
work was done in conferences like that of the dramatic boat-
ride on the lake when M. Briand persuaded Herr Stresemann
to accept the terms of a difficult compromise. But there would
probably have been no boat-ride at Locarno, and certainly no
treaty of the complicated and surprising contents of the document there agreed to, had it not been for the previous meeting
of the experts of these Foreign Offices, Dr. Gaus, M. Fromageot and Sir Cecil Hurst in London preceding the Locarno
meeting, and more especially if the German Foreign Office had
not, even before that, studied the strategy of peace in terms of
a European problem. Something like two years elapsed between
the first Cuno offer of Germany and Herr Stresemann's dis-
patch in the Cologne *Gazette* in March, 1925, which led to the
final negotiations at Locarno.

In the conversations with France, the United States had now
about reached the point where France and England stood six
months or more before the conference at Locarno. The great
project of a world-Locarno presented more difficulties for the
technician to solve than those which lay between the first German suggestion and the final signature of the European agreement. Any short cut through it was likely to result in misunderstandings either before or after the signature. This is a
lesson forced home by almost every experience of recent years.
Mr. Lloyd George is still suffering from his failure at the
Genoa Conference of 1922 at which M. Briand joined him in
the effort to extemporize a European settlement. Even these
two past masters in politics found themselves faced with failure from inadequate preparation. On the other hand, it is a
well-known fact, universally admitted, that the successes which
have attended so many of the efforts of the League of Nations

have been due to the scientific preparation of the problems themselves by the highly qualified Secretariat, which shapes up its projects solely with reference to the points at issue and not for the sake of furthering any one nation's case.

The suggestion of the British Government to have a conference of experts was a sound one in itself; but such a conference must deal only with the details of statement and not with policies. That is for governments to determine and the experts must be the agents of their will. The recent Conference on Disarmament in Geneva had shown conclusively the mistake of permitting experts to determine general principles. The United States had apparently learned its lesson in this regard so thoroughly that the European suggestion found practically no support across the Atlantic. The case might have been different had the European governments first stated their full agreement with the Kellogg proposal and made it clear that the expert advice was to be limited solely to the embodiment of the proposal in a working document. But the last note of the French Government and the continued silence of the British Foreign Office left a certain doubt as to whether, after all, there was agreement on the fundamental principle. Under these conditions, if Mr. Kellogg was to ensure the success of his proposal, there was much to be said for his refusal to have anything to do with an international conference of technical experts.

The result was that the European experts did meet, but only in the closest of official secrecy. As a matter of fact, the English, French, and German experts who met to discuss the treaty were the very same men who had worked together on the preliminaries of Locarno, M. Fromageot of the French Foreign Office, Dr. Gaus, representing Germany, and Sir Cecil Hurst.

While these deliberations were going on, the State Department, although not a party to them, was itself busy with the study of the practical bearings of the proposed treaty upon

American policy. The result was embodied in two formal statements by Mr. Kellogg: one before the Council on Foreign Relations in New York on March 15; the other, which largely repeated and elaborated the first statement, was in the form of an address delivered on April 28 before the American Society of International Law. This latter address so fully covered the ground in debate and so clearly laid down the practical application of the proposed treaty that it was ultimately made a part of the official record and will stand alongside the treaty itself as an authoritative commentary. Indeed, it is even something more than this, for the explanations which Mr. Kellogg made on that occasion were not so much textual comments as a statement of the way in which the American Government might expect the existing obligations to be interpreted and the new proposal to be fitted in with them. It contained nothing new or startling, for practically all that was said by the American Secretary of State had been previously stated by Senator Borah and had become a commonplace of the discussion. The significance of the address was rather in the fact that this interpretation was taken over officially by the American Administration. (1) Self-defense was to be taken for granted and there was no need to define it, but each state should decide for itself what was aggression and what was defense. (2) The League Covenant "imposed no affirmative primary obligation to go to war." It might authorize a war but each member would decide for itself whether the authorization was legitimate and necessary. (3) Similarly, the Treaties of Locarno might call for police action, but only against a nation which had "resorted to war in violation of its solemn pledge thereunder." (4) Treaties of neutrality, which France had referred to, were presumably of the same defensive nature and if all the signatories were equally to join this anti-war treaty, it would simply add to the guarantee of peace. (5) This strengthening of the existing guarantees of peace was inherent in the multilateral treaty because it would go without saying that any violation of it would "automatically release the other parties from their obligations to the treaty-breaking state."

This last statement is the all-important item in Mr. Kellogg's explanation. It was already foreshadowed in Mr. Borah's first public explanation of February 5, but from now on, this point as to the application of the treaty was destined to receive fully as much attention as the text of the treaty itself. If the signatories were released from the obligation to remain at peace when the Peace Treaty was violated, there was something more than real renunciation of war in the multilateral treaty; there was a hint, and rather a stern one, of the solidarity of peaceful nations, which is an idea to build upon and one not less important for the maintenance of enduring peace than the formal renunciation of war. It involved, however, a wholly different set of questions, which the United States has so far absolutely refused to consider. International peace does not rest upon the mere negative renunciation upon the part of sovereign Powers. It must be the natural expression of a community of interests if not a community of nations. Europe was to emphasize this positive conception of peace in the negotiations which followed. The United States continued to think in terms of the negative act of renunciation. This was to furnish the germs of a subsequent misunderstanding, but the full implications were not evident at the time.

CHAPTER XIV

THE BRITISH REPLY

THE old adage that the British have built their empire in successive fits of absent-mindedness is generally interpreted as being highly complimentary to their political capacity. Where other nations plan and theorize, the British are supposed to come at once to conclusions with reality. The critical historian can hardly share to the full this estimate of British capacity. He will have in mind too many major blunders in the long process of British imperial development. But he will at least have to agree that general theories in the field of politics do not reach within the consciousness of British statesmanship until those theories involve in some definite way the real interests of the British nation. No other nation, not even Germany under Bismarck or France under Poincaré, has ever so consistently directed its affairs according to the dictates of *Realpolitik.*

Fortunately for Britain and for the world at large, enlightened British opinion has discovered that the interests of the empire are those of prosperity and settled government the whole world over. It was the earliest of the great nations to discover what all the rest are slowly learning now—that none of them can be wholly self-contained, either in peace or in war, under the conditions of modern life. A generation before the League of Nations was dreamed of it had begun the creation of its own league of nations, held together across the Seven Seas by less formal constitutional devices than the Covenant of the League itself. If it has developed a sensitiveness to realities in international affairs which surpasses that of any other state at the present time, this is not due to any Anglo-Saxon superiority in race or natural aptitude. The British Foreign Office stands out in international policy as the Bank of England has stood out in the world of international finance, because of the schooling of necessity. When a nation develops beyond its natural means of supply, it becomes dependent for its very existence upon the healthful functioning of the worldwide organization of trade and credit in the economic sphere, and of confidence and integrity in political relations.

The reaction, therefore, of British public opinion to the Briand-Kellogg proposal of a treaty to renounce war as an instrument of national policy was something more than a purely nationalist reaction. It was an index of the reality of the proposal itself in terms of international policy. It was something even more than this. For British policy has not only to keep in mind the two great formal leagues of nations in which it is involved, that of the British commonwealth of nations on the one hand, and of the Geneva organization on the other; it is also a member of a third covenant, an unwritten one, but, if anything, more vital than the Covenant of the League, namely, an understanding that there shall never be war between the British Empire and the United States. This third element in British foreign policy is the nearest approach to a general guiding principle in all its international dealings. Next to the sentiment of loyalty within the empire itself, it is the strongest single motive in British external policy—so strong as to become the touchstone for the realities of its dealings with other nations through the League at Geneva. The Kellogg proposal had to be judged by Downing Street in the light of this treble orientation.

And then, over and above them all, the Imperial Government must not forget the empire that is not wholly a commonwealth, the far-flung colonies and dependencies, and the lines of trade and of protection which constitute the most intricate design in all the complicated pattern of political institutions in the history of civilization. The commerce of China is much more an element of empire than the possession of Hongkong; the garrison of Suez is infinitely more important than the entire military establishment of Canada. The problems of peace and war on such a background reveal something of their true significance.

In the light of these facts there is much to be gained by a close scrutiny of the reception given in Britain to the Kellogg proposal. In general it may be said that this was a composite of three different attitudes: a strong desire to accept it, both because of its substance and also of its origin; a puzzled doubt as to how much the United States was really behind it, and a further doubt as to what it actually meant. Of these three attitudes, the first was by all means the dominant one, and was voiced in the Conservative press as strongly as in the Liberal or Labor organs. British public opinion was strongly behind that very kind of proposition which British statesmanship instinctively avoids, a proposition cast in the broadest terms of unrestricted generalities.

But when one turned from the reception in the press to the formal action of the British Government, one found that this cordial approval of the main idea in the Kellogg proposal was hedged about with doubts and reservations as to its practical application. Indeed, at first it seemed as though Sir Austen Chamberlain were leaning more to the French draft than to the American. In a speech in Birmingham before the Anglo-French Society in the latter part of April, he referred to the "unwisdom of sacrificing old friends to gain new ones," a phrase which aroused impatient protest and a certain uneasiness even in the editorial columns of the London *Times*, which definitely aligned itself with the American draft and against that of France. "The attitude of the last French note," said the *Times*, "was specifically and narrowly French. It did not represent the British view, nor could there have been a question of this country ranging itself on the French side as opposed to the American side of the discussion. . . . It is impossible that the British Government should not explore to the full and in a cheerful spirit the possibilities of this American initiative."

The protest of the *Times* was echoed in Parliament. In the House of Commons, Mr. Ramsay MacDonald's whole-souled endorsement of the American proposal and the prodding of Mr. Lloyd George brought from Sir Austen Chamberlain the definite statement that the British Government looked for a successful conclusion of the negotiations with America, and that its delay was due only to two causes, the need of careful technical study of the text itself and the consent of the governments of the Dominions to participate in the signature. It was while he was on the defensive in this debate that Sir Austen made the statement which was so quickly challenged by the Labor leaders of the House, that Great Britain "has never treated war as an instrument of national policy." It was an incautious statement, for when his opponents reminded him of the South African War, Sir Austen Chamberlain insisted that he would not "go back to ancient history and the Crusaders." So swift is the movement of events these modern days that it apparently seemed to the son of Joseph Chamberlain that centuries had intervened since the day of Britain's last great imperial adventure,—when war had been used as an instrument of policy,—and yet hardly a generation had intervened.

The debate in the Commons was not a criticism of the caution of the Government but of its not having made clear to the United States that its efforts were being directed toward making a success of the negotiations. There must be no appearance of lukewarmness in the coöperating with the United States to pursue a common aim. Sir Austen's reserve might be mistaken in the United States for a disguised negative. It would be all very well for the Government to act this way if it were speaking for Britain to Britons; but as it was speaking to the United States, the attitude should be very careful and the acceptance positive. America should know that the British Empire was whole-heartedly with it in the effort to rid the world of war.

The debate in the House of Lords throws a flood of light upon the double preoccupation of British opinion, to leave no doubt about the acceptance of the new proposals and yet to make sure that they did not place the empire in an impossible position. The record is that the Peers unanimously passed a resolution endorsing the Kellogg plan. Headlines in the papers very properly called attention to this vote, and editorials pointed out how remarkable it was that this last citadel of conservatism in the British constitution should have come out for so revolutionary a doctrine as that of the renunciation of war as an instrument of national—i.e., British—policy. The House of Lords is not given to accepting general doctrines of any kind, and its action in this regard was all the more noteworthy. But when one studies the debate a little more closely, one finds a good deal more in it than the headlines indicate.

The resolution was introduced by the Marquis of Reading, Ambassador at Washington in 1918, later Viceroy of India. It called upon the Lords to express a cordial welcome to the American proposal "whilst recognizing the desire of His Majesty's Government to coöperate in securing the peace of the world." No one could question the good will behind this plea for coöperation with America, and Lord Reading's speech in support of the resolution was cordial to a still greater degree. Yet, there was at least as much statesmanship as sentiment in the terms of the resolution, for the words had been carefully chosen to recall those other obligations of the British Government embodied in the Covenant of the League. It was not the Kellogg proposal which called upon His Majesty's Government "to coöperate in *securing* the peace of the world."

This phrase carries us at once over into the question of sanctions and the enforcement of peace, and is completely out of the atmosphere of the Kellogg proposal. These few words are a reservation in themselves; it was not for nothing that the proponent of this resolution had been Lord Chief Justice of England. The careful reader will discover in it simply an endorsement of the caution of Sir Austen Chamberlain's reply. But there are so few careful readers! It is not likely that there were many even in England who went behind Lord Reading's applauded statement, that the American proposal was "the most momentous that the House had had before it for years," to examine the exact text of his resolution. The listening Peers, however, had less reason to be confused; for in the midst of the debate Lord Reading frankly admitted that he was with Sir Austen Chamberlain to the full and agreed "with every word that has fallen from him on this subject."

But to stop at this point would be to misinterpret the spirit of the Lords' debate. There is something in the tone as well as in the choice of words; and when it seemed as though Lord Cushendun, the very embodiment of Ulster and Conservative caution, had failed to grasp imaginatively the possibilities which the American proposal opened up, there was a high note of earnest protest from Lord Reading speaking for the Liberals, Lord Cecil for liberal conservatism, Lord Phillimore as the outstanding expert on international law, and the Archbishop of Canterbury, for whom the proposal was "one of the most remarkable in the history of civilization." Witnesses of the debate have spoken of the compelling effect of this combined plea for a clear acceptance of the opportunity to work together with America for the elimination of war.

The reply of the British Government to the Kellogg offer was delivered by Sir Austen Chamberlain to Ambassador Houghton on May 19. It was at once apparent from the text of this note why the British Government had taken over a month in its preparation and had deliberately delayed its sending in spite of a growing protest which almost reached the extent of a national demonstration. In its few paragraphs, for the note is not a long one, it not only sought to harmonize the persistently practical view of the Government of M. Poincaré with the ideals enunciated by Mr. Kellogg, but it covered as well another problem which British statesmen instinctively seek to avoid, namely, the tracing of the invisible frontiers of imperial policy throughout the world. There is a frontier to policy as well as to empire; there are obligations and duties which transcend the narrow limits of a country's territory; obligations and duties registered in treaties or acknowledged by established precedent. A world empire has to face the complications of time as well as of space, of history as well as of geography; and the network of these complications increases in geometric ratio with every new addition to the fabric. The British Empire has not only to adjust itself to the European continent, where, for the present, the writ of the Locarno peace may be said to run, but it rubs shoulders with danger from Cairo to the hinterland of China and is not free from problems of police throughout the whole continent of Africa. It is easy for the arm-chair idealist to make light of these responsibilities, but the progress of civilization, which is the real embodiment and only lasting hope of international peace, owes more to those who have assumed the white man's burden in the far corners of the world than to their facile critics who would reform the world by abstractions. There is a trace of all of these preoccupations in the British reply.

First of all, Sir Austen Chamberlain takes up the two draft treaties, the French and the American, and attempts to harmonize them by stressing their common purposes and pointing out that the French are merely trying to state more precisely the conditions under which the treaty would be applied. There is no concealing the preference of the British Foreign Office for a greater precision than is to be found in the American text, but it finds the way for harmonizing the two by putting Mr. Kellogg's explanation of the treaty "on record in some appropriate manner so that it may have equal value with the terms of the treaty itself." Thus the American text, broad and general in terms, may remain unchanged, but the conditions under which it is applied will be stated by each country for itself.

The textual problem which this situation presented is one of great interest to the student of diplomatic history, however trying it may be to the general reader. How could the British Government at one and the same time secure precision in its commitments and yet preserve the text of the treaty which deliberately avoided this precision? The traditional device of diplomacy might in part be used, to insert the explanatory phrases in a preamble; and this was ultimately done. The other device most commonly used would be the addition of qualifying terms in a protocol attached to the treaty and recognized by all the signatories as equally binding with it, although its terms might vary in their application. But any such formal addition to a worldwide treaty would tend to envelop the original document in such a flood of protocols as to leave the whole treaty a mass of confusion and a ready source of future misunderstanding. There remained, however, a third device in the technique of diplomacy and one which had been used effectively in the negotiations at Locarno, namely, the exchange of letters paralleling the treaty and interpreted as substantially an agreement concerning their operation.[1] The British note suggested this way out of the difficulty, but, out of deference to the

---

[1] At Locarno, the German inquiry as to how the League might apply the sanctions provided for under Locarno as well as under the Covenant was met by a joint letter from the other Powers, interpreting Article XVI of the League Covenant.

American point of view, did not insist upon having the notes redrafted and placed alongside the treaty itself as part of the formal treaty document. It merely stated that "means no doubt can be found without difficulty" for giving Mr. Kellogg's explanation of the treaty equal validity with the terms of the treaty itself. Neither the British nor the French Government went on to elaborate this point. No further letters were exchanged embodying reservations, and the treaty text finally signed made no reference to either the exchange of letters or, with one exception, the reservations mentioned in them. The result is that this British note of May 19 remains simply a statement for and by Britain. It has never been formally agreed to by the United States or any other signatory any more than the reservations of France have been agreed to. Whether a unilateral reservation of this kind binds other signatories or not will be discussed in detail below.[1]

The detailed points made in the British note are so clearly stated in the text itself that it is almost unnecessary to summarize them here. They might, however, be listed as follows:

1. The right of self-defense is taken for granted and need not be referred to in the text.

2. The provision "that violation of the treaty by one of the parties should release the remainder from their obligations under the treaty toward that party," which the French note insisted upon, need not be incorporated in the treaty if Mr. Kellogg's speech accepting this interpretation be put "on record in some appropriate manner so that it may have equal value with the treaty itself."

3. The obligations of the Covenant of the League and of Locarno are not endangered by the proposed pact because "the new engagement will cease to operate in respect of a party which breaks its pledge and adopts hostile measures against one of its co-contractants." The position of the British Government

[1] Chapter XVII.

is identical with that of the German Government toward the Covenant and Locarno; no new treaty should be accepted which would weaken or undermine these engagements "upon which the peace of Europe rests. Indeed, public interest in this country in the scrupulous fulfillment of these engagements is so great that His Majesty's Government would for their part prefer to see some such provision as Article 4 of the French draft embodied in the text of the treaty." To this procedure the British Government understood that there would be no objection, since Mr. Kellogg had made it clear in his speech that he had no intention of interfering with the obligations of the Covenant or the Treaty of Locarno. But although Mr. Kellogg was quite explicit on this point in his public utterances, nothing came of the British Government's endorsement of the French proposal. There were two good reasons for this. In the first place, Article IV of the French draft was far too sweeping, for it safeguarded not only peace treaties like Locarno and the Covenant of the League, but all prior international agreements; a provision which might easily nullify the whole of the renunciation treaty. In the second place, the Government to which Mr. Kellogg belonged would not find it easy to become the sponsor for the League of Nations through any such treaty commitment. This suggestion for a change in text was ignored by the United States in its subsequent reply, and nothing further was heard about it.

4. So far, the discussion was on familiar ground; the British Government was merely restating the points that had been raised in the discussion with France. But in the tenth paragraph, the British note turned from European to imperial problems and stated a purely British reservation. The defense of the Empire is not merely protection of its frontiers; "there are certain regions of the world the welfare and integrity of which constitute a special and vital interest for our peace and safety. . . . It must be clearly understood that His Majesty's Govern-

ment in Great Britain accept the new treaty upon the distinct understanding that it does not prejudice their freedom of action" in preventing "interference with these regions." Since the United States, under the Monroe Doctrine, has similar interests "any disregard of which by a foreign Power they have declared that they would regard as an unfriendly act," the British Government believes that the position of the two countries is substantially alike and that Great Britain is as free to accept the principle of renunciation of war as the United States itself, thus implying that neither the Monroe Doctrine nor the new Chamberlain pronouncement is fundamentally anything more than an application of the principle of self-defense.

The British Monroe Doctrine, as it was immediately termed in the press commentaries throughout the world, received no comment from the American Government, but the British Government, in signing the treaty, repeated this reservation once more in emphatic terms. It is discussed in a separate chapter below.[1]

The remaining points in the British note were of less importance. The French proposal that the treaty should not go into force until all the nations of the world had signed it was rejected for the more practical American plan of immediate signature by a limited number of nations and subsequent adherence by the rest; and finally we have an indication of the complexities of the Empire in the statement of the British Foreign Minister that the Governments of the Dominions would be glad to have separate invitations to participate in the conclusion of the treaty and so become independent signatories of the commitment to renounce war as an instrument of their national policy.

The American Government lost no time in taking up this last suggestion of the British Government. On May 22, only four days after Sir Austen Chamberlain's note, the invitation was

[1] Chapter XVIII.

extended to all the Dominions and to India to join in the multilateral treaty. Nor did the Dominions lose any time in replying.
Inside a week, on May 30, New Zealand, the Irish Free State,
and Canada had answered, and a few days later came the replies of Australia, India, and South Africa. All of the replies
were in the affirmative and only two of them, Canada and
South Africa, took pains to recapitulate the conditions of their
acceptance and their interpretation of the text.

The answer of Canada is especially important, one of the
most important documents, indeed, in the whole collection, for
it discusses its obligations under the League of Nations in terms
which have a direct bearing upon the American policy with
reference to the League. As a neighbor of the United States,
but also a member of the League of Nations, Canada has consistently maintained at Geneva a policy very similar to what the
United States might have adopted had it accepted the Covenant. While retaining an absolute loyalty to the spirit and
purposes of the Covenant, it has always claimed that it was
for each sovereign state to say when and how it would join in
the police action of the League against a recalcitrant member.
It would stand to reason, therefore, that members of the
League were just as free as any other Powers to make a treaty
of the kind proposed, and the fact of their previous covenant
of peace would only strengthen the presupposition that this
treaty, as well as the previous one, would be honored and
kept.

There is little more to add in this chapter of British diplomatic history. After Mr. Kellogg's final note of June 23, which
is discussed below, Sir Austen Chamberlain desisted from the
attempt to modify the American text beyond the slight change
in the preamble which had been introduced, and confined himself to a short but emphatic repetition of the claim that signature of this new treaty did not in any way affect the freedom

of action of the British Government in those unnamed regions of the world whose "welfare and integrity constitute a special and vital interest" for the peace and safety of the Empire.

Once more, the Dominions joined in with a chorus of approval, and the British Commonwealth of Nations declared itself ready to sign away the right to use war as an instrument of its national policy.

CHAPTER XV

MR. KELLOGG'S LAST NOTE

On June 23, 1928, almost exactly one year after M. Briand had submitted his draft of a treaty to the United States, that original draft was re-submitted by the Government of the United States to the governments of fourteen countries. This practically brought the end of the story, so far as the formal negotiations were concerned; for although the State Department, in this document, still presented the treaty text in tentative form and expressly stated that it was not insisting upon the exact wording of the draft but would be open to suggestions for any improvement in that regard, none of the governments addressed took advantage of this invitation, and the treaty as finally signed was simply the unchanged text of the note of June 23. This alone would make Mr. Kellogg's note the most important communication in the whole collection, more important to the historian than even the historic parchment signed and sealed in Paris on August 27 following. But an added importance is given to it by the fact that acceptance of the treaty by the other signatories was in most instances accompanied by either direct or implied reference to this letter, containing as it did, not only the text of the proposed treaty but the interpretation of it by the American Government. Whether the note thus acquired equal validity with the treaty, as some commentators have stated, is another question, the discussion of which we may leave for a later chapter. All that need be said here is that Mr. Kellogg's interpretation of his text removed difficulties and doubts, sufficiently at least to secure its acceptance by all of the governments to whom the note was addressed. Ample assurance was given that the treaty in no way infringed upon the "inalienable right of national defense" or measures of coöperative defense under the Covenant of the League or treaties like those of Locarno. The French Government saw its reference to treaties of neutrality interpreted to cover its defensive alliances and not merely its formal guarantee of the neutrality of Switzerland, as some legalists thought might be the case. It became clear that the purpose of the proposed reform, the "renunciation of war as an instrument of national policy," was a fair summary of the condition of legitimate international dealings; and, once the American Government had shown that this was the meaning of its whole proposal, there was immediate readiness to accept it on all sides.

There was only one government which continued to feel that perhaps not all difficulties had been cleared away by Mr. Kellogg's frank explanation, and that was the government whose foreign relations were more complicated than any other because they reached throughout the whole world and brought responsibilities not always easy to state in universal formulae. The British Government, as we have seen above, reminded the United States once more that under the caption of legitimate defense must be reserved the right to prevent disturbances to peace in parts of the world not within the frontiers of the Empire itself. Neither in this note nor at any other time did the United States make any reference to the statement of what was popularly but misleadingly termed "The British Monroe Doctrine." All other doubts and problems were apparently met by Mr. Kellogg's note,—at least so the other governments were convinced. No suggestions were made for revising the actual text of the treaty, and with the universal consent thus received, there was nothing left for the American Government to do but to proceed with the actual arrangements for its signing.

By a happy inspiration the State Department, rejecting the

suggestion that its own treaty be signed at Washington, proposed signature at Paris; and, to mark his sense of its importance, Mr. Kellogg prepared to break precedent and attend the ceremony himself. This was interpreted outside the United States as a generous and tactful suggestion, but it would seem to have been due not to any diplomatic calculations upon gaining French public opinion but rather to a very sincere appreciation of M. Briand's part in initiating the whole matter, for which this signal act of recognition was due to him and to the Government of France. This last incident in the story of these negotiations is an important part of them; for the history of diplomacy is not merely a history of ideas. It deals, or should deal, almost as much with the form and manner of action as with the content of international dealing. Manner in diplomacy is almost as important as strategy in war; a lesson which the Old World had applied long ago but which it hardly thought America had learned. Tact demands imagination, and imagination in political affairs is grotesque unless it is based upon a knowledge of the world. Our diplomacy had suffered at times in the past from an absence of these qualities.

Whatever opinions one may hold about the substance of the Kellogg proposal, there can be but one opinion as to the diplomatic success of its handling. It was not only in this last phase of the negotiations that the State Department deserves credit for successful diplomacy. From the time that it became convinced of the validity, as well as the importance of M. Briand's proposal, it maintained a policy of persistent optimism which argued not only seriousness of purpose but a confidence in the equal good will of other governments which steadily overcame hostility, both silent and expressed, and forced all but the most pronounced of cynics to silence or at least partial agreement. This was not an easy task. Public opinion in other countries, even among our friends, was dubious as to the sincerity of our provisions for international peace, in view of what we had actually done or failed to do in the past. Some of the bitterness of post-war psychology had been turned against us on account of the American policy with reference to the war debts, added to our complications in Nicaragua and elsewhere. Then had come the plans for a huge American navy, on the heels of a disarmament failure at Geneva. This was not a promising background for negotiation by the American Government of a treaty of universal and enduring peace. But Mr. Kellogg paid no attention to these hindrances. He took for granted the good will which his own offer was destined chiefly to create, and the result was a triumph for American diplomacy which is all the more remarkable in view of the fact that every government which gave its signature at Paris did so with the full knowledge that Mr. Kellogg represented only a part, and not the whole, of the treaty-making power of the United States. In this regard, the diplomatic success of Mr. Kellogg will measure fully as high with or without the ratification of the Senate.

But with all credit to the persistence and tact of the State Department, the reason that this negotiation is something more than an episode in diplomacy is not because of Mr. Kellogg's direction of it, nor the care which he took not to go too far in his commitment; it was because the negotiation gave expression to a public opinion which had become ready for the proposal before he made it. From the standpoint of the stability of the act itself, it is well now to recall how slowly the State Department moved at first rather than how definitely and strongly it persisted at the last. There is, after all, something to be said in justification of this initial delay in taking up the French proposal. When a matter of international policy depends, as this does, upon public opinion and national attitudes for its reality, the Foreign Office of a government should make sure before accepting it that the nation is really ready for it. It was only when Congress met in December that the state of public opinion here with reference to M. Briand's proposal became defined. There is a world of difference between the adherence of either academic or idealistic groups as expressed in irresponsible debate and the action of the governments themselves. Mr. Kellogg waited his time with conservative caution. He then tried out the possibilities of the treaty to renounce war in the incomplete treaty of arbitration, and it could hardly have escaped him that the only criticism of that document was that in its drafting it had not embodied enough of the instruments of peace as between the United States and France. The tremendous outburst of protest against the navy-building program was, as has been said above, an added element of popular endorsement. It became quite clear that for the first time in American history, at least the first time since the World War, the peace movement in the United States was united on a single objective. The strength which the movement thus attained is surely a true index of what the nation really stands for; and it is because there is no doubt upon this point that this chapter of the history of American foreign policy is to be appraised not in terms of diplomacy but of statesmanship.

CHAPTER XVI

THE SIGNING OF THE TREATY

AROUND the corner from the tomb of Napoleon and adjoining the buildings of the Chamber of Deputies, stands the Foreign Office of France. It is called the Quai d'Orsay, partly because it fronts the Seine, and partly no one but the student of history knows why, for the name has that flavor of half-forgotten memories which live on in Europe even when they have ceased to have a meaning. It looks across the river to the Place de la Concorde and the gardens of the Tuileries, but from its back windows one sees, spreading out, behind mimic defenses of low wall and filled-in moat, the gabled roofs of the Invalides, built by Louis XIV as a hospital for old soldiers, but now become as well a museum of war. Nowhere else in the modern world, not even in the Military Museum of Berlin, is war more glorified than here. It is the historic center of military France. Hung high along the chapel walls, long rows of battle flags attest her victories on a hundred battlefields, and her great soldiers rest below. In the dome by the altar, the sunlight, falling through light draperies, spreads day by day a pall of imperial purple on Napoleon's tomb. Compared with this reminder of power and national glory, the drab courtyards and unpretentious halls of the legislative building to the east have little for the eye. The politics of peace have no such pageantry as that of war.

This has been a fitting setting for the home of French diplomacy, halfway between the businesslike parliament, at work on the problems of the present, and the monument of a military past. For the Foreign Office partakes of both the routine and the display. It is the one civilian department of government which still perpetuates in a democratic age something of that splendor which once surrounded and disguised the business of the sovereign. Most of the other ministries are almost indistinguishable from the offices of any great private concern. Etiquette no longer stands in the way when there is serious work to do. But, although this is growingly the case in the handling of home affairs, a trace of the old-time manners and display is still to be found in diplomacy, because in it the nation meets the outside world; and nations, like private individuals, do not like to receive their guests without formality, in everyday dress. On great occasions, when ambassadors or foreign statesmen assemble in conference, diplomacy may even rival or outshine the glitter of military parade. The Quai d'Orsay has been no exception in this regard, for although republican France shares with the United States, and with the new spirit of democratic Germany, the cult of simplicity in the ordinary dealings of its government, it can when representing the majesty of the state assume the trappings of power with something of the old-time grace. It is doubtful, for instance, if Versailles ever witnessed greater military pomp—even when Louis XIV received the great Condé returning from his victories—than when the Treaty of Versailles was signed at the close of the World War. Through miles of ranks of cuirassiers with pennants flying from lances at rest and regimental colors gleaming in the sun, the diplomatic cortège passed into the great courtyards of the old château; and when the German delegate laid down the pen that had acknowledged a world defeat, reverberating cannon sounded the salute to peace from the southern hillsides of Saint Cyr, the school of war for France.

The relation of diplomacy to war was expressed by the scene at Versailles; its relation to peace was witnessed at another scene two months earlier, at the Quai d'Orsay, itself. There was no evidence of pomp and very little ceremony when, in the great hall of the Foreign Office, the representatives of the Allied Powers accepted the obligations of a covenant creating a society of nations. And yet this event and not the signature of the Treaty of Versailles was the epoch-making moment of the Peace Conference. It marked the dawn of a new diplomacy, a diplomacy more befitting the new business affairs of nations; and though the shadows of the older day were still to cling across the western horizon, Europe from that time on found its state system steadily changing to the other mold.

Years intervened, years of controversy and of much international misunderstanding. But in spite of the heritage of hatred which war always leaves, and the unparalleled problems of reconstruction and reparation and the blindness of partisan policies, the technique of the new diplomacy which brings nations together instead of holding them apart, as in the formal methods of the old régime, radiated from Geneva back into the Foreign Offices with ever-growing strength. Diplomacy was steadily shifting its interests from war to economics. The business of the world had created a community of nations; it sought now to carry on the business of that community in businesslike ways. It is not too much to say that if there had been no League of Nations, there would have been no Briand proposal, no Kellogg plan, no Pact of Paris. There was no place for them in the diplomacy that registered the weight of armaments. But while the Covenant had been framed to safeguard international peace, it did not go the whole length of calling upon the members of the League to renounce war as the instrument of their national policy. Indeed, it had distinctly left open the possibility of war where no other means could be found for the redress of grievances; in the last resort the sovereign state could assert the prerogative of sovereignty. This was as far as the world was prepared to go in 1919. Now the same room of the Quai d'Orsay which had witnessed the acceptance of the

Covenant was to be the scene of the signature of a treaty which proposed to complete the diplomatic revolution by severing the historical dependence of diplomacy on war.

Paris was gay for the signing of the Pact that was to bear its name. There were flags of all countries down its long avenue, and on its government buildings the German flag was flown beside those of England and America. Even the red insignia of Soviet Russia with its sickle and hammer floated beside the stars and stripes in sign of the ultimate adhesion of that revolutionary power. Within the Quai d'Orsay itself there was a touch of ceremony lacking when the delegates of the Peace Conference crowded to their places at the reading of the Covenant. This time the plenipotentiaries were guided to their places at the great horseshoe table by ushers clad in blue and gold, with red velvet breeches and white silk stockings and a "superbly uniformed Swiss Guard with a halberd, an inheritance of the court procedure of centuries ago, led the solemn procession of statesmen from the reception room to the clock room, where the signing took place." The correspondent of the Associated Press in noting these details commented upon the contrast of this ancient ritual with the simplicity of the scene which followed. For it was a civilian gathering with no military trappings and differed in no other way from any ordinary business meeting. Yet the scene was not lacking in solemnity; for the successor of Bismarck, who was also the initiator of Locarno, by his presence alone, evoked the twofold memories to which M. Briand gave expression in the only public address of the occasion.

The central figure was, of course, M. Briand himself. No one else there had known, as he had known, the responsibilities of wartime government. He had been Prime Minister of France through the heart of the World War and during the long agony of the battle of Verdun. It was this experience, as he has stated many times, that made him devote his energies in the post-war years to the furtherance of the peace movement in Europe. And so for those whose imagination could reach outside the setting of that passing moment, there was in this renunciation of war as an instrument of national policy a symbol of consecration. After all, perhaps that crusading call which rallied the forces of America, that this was to be "a war to end war," was not a phrase to be left for the cynic and the disillusioned. For in so far as the Pact of Paris was to be a reality, it gave in turn a meaning to the World War,—the only meaning it could have in which the whole world could possibly agree. Nowhere else had modern war been judged so correctly as by those who saw most of it, the private soldiers in the trenches; and their sense of its crushing futility was known and remembered—with poignant memories—at almost every fireside of Europe. It was this fact, even more than the agreement of governments, that gave to the scene in the Salle de l'Horloge, in spite of all its simplicity, a grandeur and an elevation of spirit which, far more than the pageant of an hour, will remain in history to embody the hopes and aspirations of a world at last becoming civilized.

Fortunately, there is no further need to comment or describe, for the text of M. Briand's speech on this occasion so fully conveys the sense of this high reality that it may stand as a final summary of the history and meaning of the Pact of Paris.

M. BRIAND'S ADDRESS

Gentlemen, I am fully conscious that an occasion so solemn most truly calls for silence. And it would be my own wish simply to have each of you rise in turn and, in the name of his country, affix his signature to the greatest collective act and document that has been born of peace. But I would fail in my duty to my own country if I did not tell you how deep an honor France feels it to be to welcome the first signatories of this general agreement for the renunciation of war.

If this honor has been left to France as an acknowledgment of the moral standing she enjoys, thanks to her constant efforts in the cause of peace, I gladly accept such a tribute on behalf of the Government of the French Republic, and I express the gratification of her whole people, happy that the inmost recesses of their national psychology should at last be understood by the world.

While extending to you, gentlemen, this welcome, I rejoice to see gathered here all (save those kept from coming by duty or ill health) who as statesmen and Ministers of Foreign Affairs have had a personal share in the conception, the drafting, and the working out of this Pact. Special thanks are due to those who have undergone the fatigue of long journeys in order to be present at this manifestation.

I have no doubt that you are all at one with me in the same feeling of gratefulness to one of our colleagues who has unhesitatingly brought us, with all the moral authority of his own name and that of the great nation he represents, the seal of his faith in the scope of the agreement that we are about to sign. Today, sitting with us in that same hall where his illustrious predecessor, President Wilson, brought to the works of peace so high a consciousness of the mission of his country, the honorable Mr. Kellogg can now, with a rightful pride, see how far we have gone, and how quickly, since together we first weighed the possibilities of bringing to completion so vast a labor of diplomacy. In the negotiations which today have reached this happy ending, no one was so well qualified to take that great rôle that fell to him, and that will forever do him honor in the memories of men. His optimism and his tenacity have got the better of the skeptics. His entire fairness and good faith, and the readiness with which he has satisfied legitimate questionings by clear and definite explanations have given him the confidence of all his collaborators. And, lastly, his clear vision has taught him what we can hope from governments that are inspired by the deep yearnings of their peoples.

What more exalted lesson can be offered to the civilized world than an assembly in which, for the signing of a compact against war, Germany of her own free will and on an even footing takes her place among the other signatories, her former enemies? The example is still more striking when, for the first time in more than half a century, it is given to a representative of France to receive a German Foreign Minister on French soil and accord him the same welcome as that given to all his foreign colleagues. I would add, gentlemen, that when this representative of Germany bears the name Stresemann, you can believe me particularly happy as I render homage to the loftiness of spirit and to the courage of this eminent statesman who for more than three years has been willing to assume full responsibility in the work of European coöperation for the maintenance of peace.

Since I have gone so far in mentioning names, you will not take it amiss, and certainly Lord Cushendun will give his approval, if with thoughts as of a brother, I evoke the name of Sir Austen Chamberlain; and to him we send all our hopes and wishes for a full and speedy return to health. When I think of the unwearying devotion that the cause of peace has always aroused in his noble soul, I can envision the joy that would have been given to so determined an enemy of war by the sight of a meeting such as this. We, at any rate, know that whether visible or invisible, he is at this hour, and in every true sense, still with us.

It will, I hope, be no exaggeration to say that today's event marks a new date in the history of mankind.

For the first time, and on a general plan that is open to all the nations of the world, a congress of peace has done something more than make a political settlement of the immediate conditions brought about by some particular peace imposed as the results of war. For the first time, on a scale as absolute as it is vast, a treaty has been truly devoted to the very establishment of peace, and has laid down laws that are new and free from all political considerations. Such a treaty means a beginning and not an end. We have not met to liquidate a war. The Pact of Paris, born of peace and breathing freedom and law, is of its nature a true treaty of concord. That, no doubt, is why Mr. Kellogg, when he insisted on leaving to the French Government the privilege of receiving you in Paris, told the French Ambassador that it seemed to him very fitting that the neighborhood of the Place de la Concorde should witness the signing of the Pact.

The Treaties of Locarno, after the Dawes Plan, first bore witness to that new spirit which has now found full expression. All the signatories of the Locarno Treaties were entirely familiar with the concept of the renunciation of war as an instrument of national policy. I had occasion to point that out in the message to the American people which I sent on April 6, 1927. But those particular treaties, designed to give political guarantees of peace to one definite part of Europe, could not, of their very nature, take on that universal character from which a general pact against war must derive its whole value.

The League of Nations, deeply imbued with the same spirit, likewise issued a declaration designed to secure the same result as this present Pact. But, apart from the fact that the United States had no share in it, the formula and the methods of the League could not be equivalent to those to which it has been possible for us to have recourse for such a general agreement as the Pact provides. The League of Nations, a vast political undertaking for insurance against war, and a powerful institution of organized peace in which there is room to welcome all new contributions to the common task, cannot but rejoice at the signing of an international contract by which it must benefit; for, far from being inconsistent with any of its obligations, on the contrary this new agreement offers the League a kind of general re-insurance. Thus, those members of the League who will soon be in a position to ask it to register the agreement of today may justly feel that they are bringing to the League a precious token of their attachment and loyalty.

The essential feature of the Pact is that for the first time, in the face of the whole world, and through a solemn covenant involving the honor of great nations who all alike have behind them a sad record of political conflicts, war in its most specific and dreaded form—selfish and willful war which has been regarded from of old as springing from divine right, and has remained in international ethics as an attribute of sovereignty—has been at last deprived by law of what constituted its most serious danger, its legitimacy. For the future, branded with illegality, it is by mutual accord truly and regularly outlawed so that a culprit must incur the unconditional condemnation and probably the hostility of all his co-signatories. It is a direct blow at the institution of war, a blow against its very life.

It is no longer a question of a defensive organization against this scourge, but of attacking the evil at its very root. War as a means of arbitrary and selfish action, is no longer to be deemed lawful. No longer will its threat hang over the economic, political and social life of peoples. Henceforth the smaller nations will enjoy true independence in international discussions. Freed from their old bondage, the nations that have signed the new contract will gradually abandon the habit of associating conceptions of national prestige and national interest with the idea of force; and this single psychological fact will not be the least important element in the evolution there is needed for the final stabilization of peace.

But, you say, there is no true realism in this Pact. And where are its sanctions? Well, is that realism which excludes from the realm of facts all moral forces, among them that of public opinion? Indeed, any state which would so act as to incur the reprobation of all its co-signatories would run the positive risk of seeing them gradually and freely unite against it, with results which very soon it would have reason to fear. And where is the country, a signatory to this Pact, whose leaders would on their own responsibility expose it to such danger? The modern law of the interdependence of nations makes it incumbent upon all statesmen to lay to their hearts those memorable words of President Coolidge: "An act of war in any part of the world is an act that injures the interests of my country." [1]

We can realize how important it is to extend the scope and range of an international solidarity which tends, as an ideal, to encompass the entire world.

When on June 20, 1927, I had the honor of proposing to the Honorable Mr. Kellogg the formula which he decided to accept and embody in the draft of a multilateral pact, I never contemplated for one moment that the suggested engagement should exist only between France and the United States. Indeed I have always thought that in one way or another through multiplication or extension, the proposed covenant would in itself possess an expanding force strong enough to reach rapidly all nations whose moral adhesion was indispensable.

It was, therefore, a source of gratification to me to see Mr. Kellogg, from the beginning of the active negotiations that he was to lead with such a clearsighted and persevering mind, advocate extension of the Pact and assign to it that universal character that fully answered the wishes of the French Government.

It may be said that this element of the universal that was always in the Pact has already found its application in actual practice, for the intentions expressed by many governments enable us even now to consider the spiritual community of the nations that are morally represented at this first signature as being a much greater one than may appear. All those peoples whose delegates have not been in a position to sit among us today must realize in this hour of complete union our

[1] From President Coolidge's Memorial Day speech at Gettysburg, May 30, 1928. President Coolidge's exact words were: "Whether so intended or not, any nations engaging in war would necessarily be engaged in a course prejudicial to us."

unanimous regret that for purely technical reasons it was found imperative to adopt a procedure best calculated to ensure and expedite, for the benefit of all, the success of this great undertaking.

But the mind's eye broadens this solemn assembly of first signatories to a general pact for the renunciation of war, and extends it beyond the walls of this room, and even over all frontiers whether of land or sea. Surrounded by the whole great community of mankind we well may believe that there are more than fourteen of us about this table. Indeed, you may have seen for yourselves that the Government of the Republic has purposely ordered that the flags of all nations should be raised over the edifice that shelters us today.

Gentlemen, in a few moments the cables will be telling the entire world of the awakening of a great hope; and from now on it must be our sacred duty to do all that can be done so to bring it that that hope may not be disappointed. Peace has been proclaimed, and that is well. That is much. But peace has yet to be organized. For settlements by force we must substitute settlements by law. That must be the work of tomorrow.

At this unforgettable hour the conscience of peoples, freed from all national egotism, is making the truest of efforts to reach those high regions where human brotherhood can be felt in the beatings of one and the same heart. Let us seek a common ideal within which we can all merge our fervent hopes and put away all selfishness. There is no country represented here that has not poured out the blood of its children on the battlefields of the last war. I ask you to dedicate to your dead, to all those who died in that great war this solemn agreement which we are now about to consecrate with our signatures.

PART THREE

THE MEANING OF THE PACT

CHAPTER XVII

EXPLANATIONS AND A RESERVATION

THE negotiations were over and the Pact was signed. But what, after all, did it mean? The text itself was one of the shortest and simplest of all treaties; two short paragraphs, hardly more than two sentences, stated the obligations assumed. Seldom had so important an event so little text behind it or so direct and simple a history. It might have been expected, therefore, that there would be universal agreement as to what had actually been accomplished, especially since the governments themselves professed to have reached perfect accord. But in spite of these facts, there still remained questions in many minds, doubts which found expression on the part of both friends and opponents of the treaty. Was it, after all, only an act of faith, a moral gesture; or did it really mark the actual relinquishment of war as an instrument of policy; if so, how would it be applied and worked out in actual practice, and, above all, what obligations were assumed by the United States of America in virtue of it? There was as well another series of questions still more insistently asked and not fully answered at the time; what was the effect upon the treaty of "reservations" by the separate signatories? Had they robbed it of its real purpose, or merely stated the conditions under which, in any case, it would have to be worked out? These are questions which must now be faced.

If the treaty raised questions in the minds of American observers, this was still more the case in Europe. Not all the doubts expressed in the course of the negotiation were ended by the signing of the treaty, although a study of the published comments shows a growing appreciation of its value, and a reluctance to give expression to anything which might hinder its ratification. The comment in the British press was especially instructive. It will be recalled that so long as the negotiation lay between France and the United States, almost no notice was taken of it in Great Britain. This was not because of a lack of interest in the subject itself, but because the method pursued was not the British way of doing things. British policy prides itself on keeping away from general abstractions, and here was the widest kind of generality with nothing of that practical approach, an obligation without any stated limits either in time or space. No wonder that the most experienced observers of international affairs were apparently the most puzzled; for instance, the Manchester *Guardian*, the enlightened exponent of British liberal policies, had contradictory editorials on succeeding days. The *Times* was more consistent, but its editorials seemed to lack conviction as to the fundamental value of the proposal itself. But the chief preoccupation of the British press was to meet the American proposal in a way which would encourage rather than discourage the movement for international peace in the United States. It did not pretend to understand all the idiosyncrasies of that movement but wished to make clear that by and large Great Britain was fully as deeply concerned in the maintenance of peace as the United States. The French press as usual followed the government lead; but the echo of its former skepticism was not entirely silenced. Opinion in Germany was somewhat more optimistic than that in England but differed little in substance. There was only one point upon which there seemed to be unanimous agreement and that did not deal with the treaty itself. On all sides there was a hope that the initiative of the United States marked the definite end of a period of aloofness from general international affairs. This interpretation was bluntly stated by the nationalist press.

If things were to go on this way, it was not a happy augury

for the future history of the treaty. The nationalist press in the United States was quick to point out the nature of so much of the European comment. There was at once an emphatic reply in kind to their confreres in Europe, denying that the United States would ever permit this or any other treaty to involve it further in foreign complications. Thus, the treaty renouncing war furnished the nationalists on both sides of the Atlantic with another opportunity to repeat the time-honored warning that policies of peace are synonymous with national betrayal! Fortunately, nine years of controversy and of education had steadily lessened the influence of American jingoism; but it also sobered liberal opinion and made it more practical. Common sense demanded that instead of running away from a treaty of this kind, which had received the endorsement of so many governments and the leading statesmen of the world, the text should be studied for what was in it and not as represented by those opposing it or failing to understand it in other countries. The direction of future American policy is a question in itself and will be dependent upon many questions which lie entirely outside the scope of this or any other treaty.

The apparent divergence between European and American interpretations was, after all, not so serious as opponents of the treaty seemed to think. It was chiefly due to the fact that the Pact of Paris had been vague upon the point which Europe emphasized and definite where Europe had been vague. There are two things in the suppression of war, the suppression itself and the substitution of something else for it. Europe had been developing the substitution; America insisted upon the renunciation. This was the basis of the whole misunderstanding; and once we narrow the issue down to it, we find that there is no real reason for misunderstanding at all. As both Senator Borah and Mr. Kellogg have pointed out, the treaty renouncing war as an instrument of national policy is in harmony with the fundamental principles of the Covenant of the

League; but it does not entail acceptance of that obligation of the League which America has refused to assume: the enforcement of peace against a recalcitrant state.

An entirely different problem was added by the so-called reservations in the acceptances of the other signatories. In his note of February 27, Mr. Kellogg had expressly asked that there should be no qualifications or limitations which would weaken or destroy the treaty "as a guaranty of peace." "The ideal which inspires the effort so sincerely and so hopefully put forward by your Government and mine is arresting and appealing just because of its purity and simplicity; and I cannot avoid the feeling that if governments should publicly acknowledge that they can only deal with this ideal in a technical spirit and must insist upon the adoption of reservations impairing, if not utterly destroying, the true significance of their common endeavors, they would be in effect only recording their impotence, to the keen disappointment of mankind in general." This paragraph is now recalled by those who claim that the "purity and simplicity" of the original plan have been completely obscured by the insistence upon reservations. This, for instance, was the point of view set forth at the Williamstown Institute of Politics by a professor of international law, who, with shrewd strategy, chose this method of indirect attack upon the treaty itself. His listeners were warned above all that in accepting the signature of Britain under the conditions it laid down, the United States would be endorsing all of these British conditions, and there was one of them which might carry us over into a tacit approval of British imperialist policies. Enlarging upon this theme, it was stated that, treaty and reservations taken together, the proposal to renounce war was turning out to be the most dangerous endorsement of war that the world had ever seen. This amazing statement was based upon the theory that the treaty, itself, was so vague as to contain no practical commitment, while the reservations, on the other hand, were so definite that they held the only real commitments there were. Follow this line of reasoning one step further and the legal argument is complete; the conclusion reached is that the only thing the treaty really does is to secure an agreement justifying defense—in its two forms of national defense and coöperative defense under the Covenant or treaties like those of Locarno. Thus, said the jurist in question, the Pact of Paris, instead of getting rid of war, fastens it upon the world, if only by enlarging the conception of defense. So deftly was this argument advanced and so logical did it seem that it received wide attention throughout the country and won adherence from some of those who had hitherto supported the treaty. This is not the first time, especially in recent American history, that legalism in the guise of caution has linked itself to policies of reaction or that public opinion has mistaken special pleading for an impartial judgment.

It is, of course, utterly false to state that the treaty is denatured by the acceptance of Mr. Kellogg's own explanation of it. This covers all the "reservations" with the exception of the "British Monroe Doctrine," discussed below. They are not reservations at all but merely explanations. Reservations in the proper sense of that term cut in upon the original proposition or run counter to it. The reservations attached by the United States Senate to acceptance of the World Court protocol were regarded by the other nations as being of this negative nature and that is why they have not been adopted. Similarly, the reservations to acceptance of the Covenant, although not passed, were regarded as lessening the full scope of its provisions. Mr. Kellogg's plea in his note of February 27, quoted above, had reference to what seemed to him to be a reservation of this kind, the French proposal to deal only with "aggressive war." Because of Mr. Kellogg's feeling that this did constitute a reservation in the real sense of the word, the French Government immediately gave it up and nothing further was heard of it.

To define the scope of a reform in the terms of its application is, after all, but an essential part of its statement, and no such definition can be made without excluding from it not only those things which are contrary to it but also those things which run parallel with it but which are already in existence. For instance, to show how the renunciation treaty fitted in with the Covenant of the League was merely a further description of the renunciation treaty. All that the European Powers had done in this regard was to accept the statement of Mr. Kellogg. It is not likely that Senator Borah, whose convincing argument that Treaty or Covenant could operate side by side, independent in setting as in action but mutually helpful, was engaged in denaturing the treaty any more than he was trying to distort the Covenant. He was simply explaining the real purpose of both. Similarly, Mr. Kellogg was engaged in showing how the treaty would work by describing its scope. This is a commonplace in any act of governments, like a debate in Congress on the proposal for a law,—it must be set into an existing political framework, and the proponent of the law should show how this can be done. It may happen, and often does, that in such cases the cautious or conservative legislator has to be reassured that the proposal is neither too much nor too little and that it leaves intact things it never was intended to touch. That is not denaturing the proposal unless the explanations run counter to the real intent. Mr. Kellogg explained the working of an unfamiliar formula, the renunciation of war as an instrument of national policy. Because there was no precedent to explain it, the explanation had to be given then and there, and when the other Powers in their replies explicitly noted the interpretation, it merely added a further guarantee of the validity of their signature. Otherwise, they might later have advanced a whole series of contradictory explanations of what they thought they had done. Viewed from this angle, it cannot be said that there was any conditional signature whatever—with a possible exception of one British proviso—which was not in Mr. Kellogg's list of explanations. With that possible exception, the treaty was accepted and signed on the terms set down by the American Government and expressly embodies its understanding of its own proposal.

But for the sake of argument, let us treat all the qualifications noted in the correspondence as though they were reservations in the strict sense of the word, making the most of the objections that have been raised against them; they merely mark the limits of the proposed reform by preserving the existing state of affairs in the field covered by them. To denounce them is therefore to denounce the existing state of things; which, as every one knows, is not what the international lawyer intends to do. If it be objected that the United States had not hitherto noted the existence of the international commitments between other states arising from the Covenant and that the so-called reservations in mentioning them introduced something novel to the American Government, the answer is that this conception of the conduct of American foreign affairs, which does not admit the validity of treaty obligations in full force between other nations with which we are dealing, is a doctrine of anarchy instead of law. The co-signatories to the Pact of Paris had every right on their side in making clear that their existing obligations which were not covered by the scope of the proposed treaty should remain as they were; and the United States did not become a party to these previous treaties when it replied with the assurance that the new engagement dealt with something else. It is true that this implied that the previous treaties did not conflict with the present one, but the argument that the State Department in eliciting from other countries a statement to this effect had underwritten their engagements, when it expressly stated that they lay outside the scope of its proposal, was the kind of argument to which the lawyer would be the first to object.

Some of the points of this discussion have been covered in the course of the narrative; others will be dealt with in the pages which follow. But in dealing with these details, we must not permit ourselves to lose sight of the character of the Treaty as a whole. While there is much to be said for the argument that it would have been a better treaty had it included in the text some of the description given in the notes, it has at least avoided the danger of being lost in that form of legalism which emasculates the purpose of a great reform by an impossible effort to list all the conditions under which it would operate. That this is a real danger in international affairs has been shown by the discussions over the League of Nations and the World Court. The tendency of the lawyer to attempt to foresee and to meet every conceivable circumstance of the future would reduce statesmanship to impotence in dealing with most of the major problems of an age like this. It is far more important to know whether or not the Kellogg treaty gives expression to the real needs and aspirations of the nations signing it than whether its terms embody the proposals in final form satisfactory to the legalist. The school of experience is not closed by the acceptance of any one document. On the contrary, the chance is offered for improvement and amendment, for clarification and definition. The only really vital point which the lawyer should raise in a matter which has secured in principle the assent of the civilized nations is whether or not the form of the proposal is such as to mislead or betray the hopes built upon it.

This means in plain English that the proposal to renounce war as an instrument of national policy must be so stated as not to lessen the safeguards of liberty at home and peace abroad by a failure to reckon with those forces which might conceivably falsify the proposal itself. In the case of the United States, this narrows down to two definite questions. Does the Pact of Paris involve the United States in the wars of other countries from which it would otherwise be free; and have we given guarantees to the policies of other nations which either tend in this direction or may be contrary to either our own vital interest or the furtherance of international justice?

These are the political questions which the treaty raises and, like all political questions, they look to the future. But there remains a historical and to some extent a sentimental problem which must be answered even if upon examination it hardly seems to be worth delaying over. Does the renunciation of war apply to the past? The answer is an emphatic "no." The proposal before us has no relation whatever to the wars which have been fought in the past. It does not call for an examination of the rights and wrongs which war may have caused or rectified in the days when it has been the recognized instrument of policy upon the part of every nation. The proposal before us is not for an *ex post facto* treaty denying the facts of history according to new principles of international dealing never before employed. The question becomes absurd in itself when one begins to discuss it in these terms, and yet there is a lingering doubt in many minds as to whether by admitting the renunciation of war today we are not also condemning its past use.

The reason for this doubt lies in the way in which war has been attacked in the theories of pacifism. The moralist has been too often an absolutist, paying no attention to the local and temporal conditions under which people live, conditions which progressively change with advancing civilization. The historian, constantly mindful of these conditioning facts, judges human conduct differently; he sees the frontier line between right and wrong moving forward with the increase of knowledge and intelligence. The establishment of new criteria, which is the process of history itself, does not invalidate the old; but on the other hand the validity of each new step in advance must be determined on its own ground and not on the basis of outworn circumstance. For example, the validity of the Treaty of Locarno is not to be found in the denunciation of war as such, but in the denunciation of war as an instrument of the policies of the great European nations at a time when they had learned the futility of the instrument of war and the need for realizing their community of interests across war-worn frontiers. The major problem of statesmanship here, as elsewhere, is to determine the legitimacy of actions on the crude basis of present and future realities. The guide to these realities may lie in an appreciation of the past but the realization itself belongs to the future.

To take but one other example, it is, of course, impossible to imagine that the Foreign Minister of France should have proposed anything which in the slightest degree would deny the legitimacy of America's action in 1917. On the contrary, his proposal was set forth as a memorial of that act ten years later, and what memorial could be more in keeping with the purposes which animated the United States and to which President Wilson gave expression in terms at once universal and enduring? As a matter of fact, it was not as an instrument of policy that the United States used its armed force in 1917; it had no selfish purpose of national aggrandizement, and that would cover the whole case, even had the present treaty been in force. The renunciation of war as an instrument of policy would not apply to a nation which had set itself the task of making conditions safe for democracy throughout the world. It is historically unjustified to allow the disillusion of a later day to deny for us the moral aspect of the response of the United States to the call to arms in the World War. There were, of course, material interests at stake, and the United States was also defending its own right, but the real issue placed before the whole country and accepted by it was one whose appeal was not to selfish policy but to an ideal. All great movements of history have more than one cause and respond to more than one stimulus; but it was the higher motive which dominated in the opening months and weeks of our participation in the

World War. Subsequent years have obscured and blurred the memory of those days, but there was nothing in our action of 1917 that would have to be renounced in the light of the present proposal to deny ourselves the use of war as an instrument for the attainment of purely national interests.

One final caution, however, is due the reader at this point. We are not arguing here the question of the causes of the World War nor the responsibilities of the governments which were drawn into the conflict in 1914. It is possible to refer to America's participation without in any way becoming involved in that other controversy, because it was the existence of war itself which involved the United States and not the warlike trend of peace-time policies. The entry of the United States into the World War happily fits within the admitted categories of the Pact of Paris; but had the European nations prior to 1914 been brought face to face with the test now embodied in the Pact of Paris and accepted it as a principle of international European policy, not only would the present controversy as to who was the aggressor in those fateful days be quickly solved, but the war itself might perhaps have been avoided. This would almost certainly have been the case if to this treaty of war renunciation were added the implements of peaceful settlement provided by the League. Such at least is the judgment of the Foreign Ministers of France and Germany today.

CHAPTER XVIII

A BRITISH MONROE DOCTRINE?

IN the British reply to the Kellogg proposal to renounce war there was one reservation which may prove to be a doctrine in itself. The other reservations cover familiar ground: the right of self-defense and the obligations of mutual or coöperative defense under the League of Nations and the Treaty of Locarno. These Mr. Kellogg substantially agreed to in his note of June 23. But quite a new problem is thought to have arisen from the British claim to exclude from the operation of the proposed treaty such areas as are strategically necessary for imperial security, even if they are not parts of the Empire. To this part of the British reply, referred to frequently in the press as constituting a "British Monroe Doctrine," the American Government has never made any reply.

"There are certain regions of the world," said Sir Austen Chamberlain, "the welfare and integrity of which constitute a special and vital interest for our peace and safety. His Majesty's Government have been at pains to make it clear in the past that interference with these regions cannot be suffered. Their protection against attack is to the British Empire a measure of self-defense. It must be clearly understood that His Majesty's Government in Great Britain accepts the new treaty upon the distinct understanding that it does not prejudice their freedom of action in this respect." Sir Austen then went on to say that "the government of the United States has comparable interests, any disregard of which by a foreign Power they have declared that they would regard as an unfriendly act," and therefore the British Government believes that it is expressing the intention and meaning of the United States Government in presenting this reservation.

The parallel with the Monroe Doctrine which Chamberlain himself suggested at once led the press, especially on the Continent, to regard this statement as a new assertion of British imperialism, a Monroe Doctrine for the British Empire. It has been denounced as having in it something sinister, a buttress for reactionary and imperialist policy. The British Liberals were just a little troubled for fear this might be the case; for, no matter what may be the ultimate fate of the Kellogg proposal, the Chamberlain pronouncement, being a unilateral statement of British policy, will have taken its place as a formal notification of British policy in this regard. The Continental criticism has been more outspoken and, by one of those paradoxes so familiar in the world of international politics, it is chiefly the reactionary Continental press which is most disturbed at its discovery of this new expression of British imperialism.

It would, indeed, be a strange result of the negotiation for a treaty to renounce war if one of its major consequences were to be the formulation and the international acceptance of a policy of aggressive imperialist strategy. It is, therefore, important to see if this is really the case.

It is commonly taken for granted that what Sir Austen Chamberlain had in mind in stating this reservation was the situation in Egypt; but unfortunately for the popular understanding of it, he did not state this fact in so many words. When pressed in debate to explain what "regions of the world" he had in mind, the Foreign Office refused to be more specific, and the result was that both in Britain and outside of it the geographic vagueness was emphasized as though it might include the whole frontier line of British interests from Gibraltar to China, and even perhaps the concessions in China itself. A careful reading of Sir Austen's words brings us back to Egypt. His statement that "His Majesty's Government have been at

pains to make it clear in the past that interference in these regions cannot be suffered" can hardly have any other reference
than to the specific statement made with reference to Egypt,
for there is no parallel to this in British dealings with other
sovereign states. We may, therefore, dismiss the apprehen-
sions entertained as to a new worldwide British Monroe Doctrine, for it is explicitly stated that the doctrine is neither new
nor worldwide but only the statement of a local condition previously established by Great Britain. This means Egypt. It will
be necessary, therefore, to look closely into the Egyptian situation in order to see exactly what the British reservation involves. It happened that just when the Kellogg offer came to
the British Government the Egyptian problem had reached another crisis through the refusal of the Egyptian Government to
accept the treaty with Great Britain which it was hoped would
settle that long and bitter controversy. Fortunately, we can discuss the reservation which applies to Egypt without discussing
the Egyptian problem, for our sole interest is whether or not
that reservation tends to invalidate the proposal to renounce
war as an instrument of national policy. Limiting the question
thus, we come upon the fact that there is nothing new in the
reservation; that it is, indeed, but a reminder of previous declarations of British policies in this regard. Whatever else may be
obscure in British-Egyptian relations, there has been no ob-
scurity in the statement by Great Britain of its refusal to allow
any other state to interfere in Egypt.

The British Government had already declared to all the
world that it would "consider any aggression against the territory of Egypt as an act to be repelled with all the means at its
command." This declaration of British policy was set forth in
the most precise terms in a circular letter to all other governments on May 15, 1922, following upon the declaration which
established the new Kingdom of Egypt. The text of this statement, and not Mr. Chamberlain's backward reference to it in

his reply, is the fundamental document of this so-called British Monroe Doctrine. The final paragraph reads as follows:

The welfare and integrity of Egypt are necessary to the peace and safety of the British Empire, which will therefore always maintain as an essential British interest the special relations between itself and Egypt long recognized by other governments. These special relations are defined in the declaration recognizing Egypt as an independent sovereign state. His Majesty's Government have laid them down as matters in which the rights and interests of the British Empire are vitally involved, and will not admit them to be questioned or discussed by any other Power. In pursuance of this principle they will regard as an unfriendly act any attempt at interference in the affairs of Egypt by another Power, and they will consider any aggression against the territory of Egypt as an act to be repelled with all the means at their command.

A careful analysis of this statement will show that it is not a Monroe Doctrine any more than our policy with reference to the Panama Canal is a Monroe Doctrine. It is a part of the problem of the defense of the Empire, for the Suez Canal is a link in that Empire much more vital than Panama is for us. There is no parallel overland route. If we could imagine a California in India or Australia and no other way to reach it than by the sea routes and the canal we should have some apprehension of the problem of Egypt for the British Empire. It is an interest of which Britain has been fully aware for more than a century and which determined its Near Eastern policies long before there was any canal at Suez. The reference to this fact in the Chamberlain note is, therefore, simply a statement of long existing realities.

From the standpoint of Great Britain, recognition of this essential fact of British vital interests in Egypt is hardly open to debate. In any case, when Mr. Ramsay MacDonald was called upon to speak for Britain in this regard, in his dual capacity as Prime Minister and Foreign Secretary, he was every bit as emphatic in the assertion of British claims as Sir Austen Chamberlain has been. It was, therefore, not to be expected that the Kellogg proposal should have brought about any change in Britain's Egyptian policy. But it is another question whether the reassertion of that policy in the answer to Mr. Kellogg introduced a new element into the American proposition. Is it a fact that the assertion of a Monroe Doctrine, or a doctrine of protectorates and special interests in different parts of the world, is incompatible with the renunciation of war as an instrument of national policy? If this were so, the British reminder of the existence of our own Monroe Doctrine takes on a more subtle character than is evident at first reading. For we ourselves could hardly propose what we could not carry out. The supposition, therefore, is that the British see no contradiction between the essential principles of the renunciation of war and the maintaining of such doctrines as that of the Monroe Doctrine whether in Egypt or in the Western world. We, too, must, sooner or later, work out the setting of the renunciation of war in terms of our existing obligations to others and the maintenance of our own security. In facing this problem we may find that, as Sir Austen Chamberlain suggests, there is some light to be thrown upon our own obligations by a detailed study of those of Britain in its canal zone.

The Egyptian problem is complicated and far reaching and suggests parallels with practically everything in the entire range of our relations with other American nations. But those elements of the problems in this area, which are involved in the acceptance of a treaty for the renunciation of war as an instrument of national policy, fall into three familiar groups: the Monroe Doctrine, intervention, and the problems of the Canal Zone. Keeping these three points in mind, let us see what light may be thrown upon our own policy by a study of the parallels in Egypt.

Time and again, prior to the World War, the British had

declared that their occupation of Egypt was only a temporary
necessity. Finally, to make good the promise which had been
held out to Egyptian nationalism, they proclaimed a formal
recognition of the independence of Egypt under its own king.
This was in 1922, after Lord Milner's historic report advising
liberal measures. But Britain reserved to itself, until these matters should have been regulated by treaty agreement, (1) the
security of the communications of the British Empire in Egypt;
(2) the defense of Egypt against all foreign aggression or interference, direct or indirect; (3) the protection of foreign interests in Egypt and the protection of minorities; (4) the
Sudan. During the last six years negotiations concerning these
four points have dragged along with little promise of settlement until, in the course of this last winter, a draft treaty was
finally accepted by both the Prime Minister of Egypt and the
British Foreign Secretary. Unfortunately, upon his return to
Egypt, Sarwat Pasha was unable to secure the ratification of
the agreement and the negotiations are once more at a stand-
still. It is, therefore, rather difficult for the student of the Kellogg peace proposal to draw definite lessons from a situation
still more or less in political chaos.

Keeping, however, to our own problem of discovering in the
position of Britain in Egypt parallels to the position of the
United States in the American continents, we find the nearest
approach to the Monroe Doctrine in the insistence of Britain
that no other Power shall interfere in Egyptian affairs. This
claim runs through the draft of the British-Egyptian treaty,
as it has been in evidence in every dealing of Britain with
Egypt since the Egyptian occupation. It comes to light in the
second article of the British-Egyptian draft which binds Egypt
"not to conclude with a foreign Power any agreement which
might be prejudicial to British interests"; and especially in
the third article, which reads as follows:

If, by reason of any attack or act of aggression whatsoever, His Majesty the King of Egypt should be involved in war for the defense of his territory or for the protection of the interests of his country, His Britannic Majesty will, subject always to the provisions of the Covenant of the League of Nations, come immediately to his aid in the capacity of belligerent.

Now it is interesting to see that this claim of Britain to stand between Egypt and the outside world was not the part of the agreement which awakened the violent nationalist attack upon it. That was reserved for the other clauses dealing with Britain's claim in Egypt. It was intervention rather than a Monroe Doctrine which was most objected to—such provisions as those for the maintenance of British troops in Egypt and the limitations imposed upon native Egyptian armaments. These have to do primarily with the question of internal police, although indirectly they also bear upon the question of European foreign relations in the denying to Egypt the right to prepare adequate armaments for its own defense. The right of protection over the canal zone by Great Britain is taken for granted; although, as in Panama, a new problem arises in connection with the development of an air base which may yet become almost equally important with the canal as a link for the empire.

The Pact of Paris does not deal with peace-time arrangements of this sort, even if they have to do with armaments and military occupation. It is only the use of war as an instrument of national policy which is forbidden. Why, then, did the British Government raise any objections or reservations with reference to Egypt? There could be only two possible occasions for them: if Britain should become involved in war with a foreign Power over Egypt, or if it should become involved in war with Egypt itself. The parallel with the Monroe Doctrine, strictly speaking, applies only to the former case; interference in the internal affairs of Egypt falls under the category of intervention, which is a different matter.

Taking up first the relation of Egypt to other foreign Powers, we come to some interesting conclusions. Great Britain, according to the draft treaty, proposed to replace its protectorate over Egypt by an alliance between sovereign states, stating that in future it would act as one ally to another. But the terms of this alliance contain one condition which at once makes all further parallel with the Monroe Doctrine invalid. For Article 3, already quoted, states that the protection accorded Egypt by Britain shall be "subject always to the provisions of the Covenant of the League of Nations." This can only mean that Article 21 of the Covenant, which reserved the Monroe Doctrine from that document, is distinctly not invoked by Great Britain. The external relations of Egypt are to be safeguarded by the League, of which Egypt is to become a member (Article 10). There is no provision here for complete freedom of action in British protection of Egypt against external aggression, such as was implied in the British note to the Powers in 1922 to which Sir Austen now makes reference; and no such freedom of action as the United States might assert under the Monroe Doctrine.

When one turns to the problem of intervention, one comes at once upon the hot center of dispute. The Egyptians want the British to leave Egypt and the British are convinced that they cannot go without imperiling their "vital interests." For this the British-Egyptian draft treaty had no immediate remedy, but it provided means for future settlement. Again, the League may have a say in the matter. Article 7 provides with reference to the British garrison in Egypt that after ten years, in case of disagreement, "the question may be submitted to the Council of the League of Nations." It is only when one studies texts of this kind in the numerous post-war treaties that one realizes the extent to which the League of Nations is writing itself into the international law of the civilized world.

Had this treaty been ratified by Egypt, the British might

have regarded their case as largely covered by the one reservation as to the sanctions of the League. That one sweeping reservation, which all members of the League are equally insisting upon, would surely have met most, if not all, eventualities in the British defense of Egypt. It reserves the right to defend not only one's own territory but the territory of other states when the League of Nations declares that a case of aggression has arisen. The fact that Great Britain should insist that it is to be the original, and perhaps the sole, executor of the League's sanctions in this area is the only apparent difference between British claims in this regard with reference to Egypt and British obligations to execute the sanctions of the League in other parts of the world in case of flagrant violation of the Covenant. But in its reply to Mr. Kellogg, the British Foreign Office decided, instead of building upon the hopes and plans of 1928, to go back to the original situation set forth in the proclamation of 1922. It took the risk of criticism upon the part of liberal opinion rather than give promises which it might not be able to fulfill. It would be a most serious mistake upon the part of American opinion if it were to fail to realize the sincerity of such a line of action.

Both Britain and Egypt apparently place the ultimate solution of their problems in a reference to the League of Nations. The parallel with the situation of the United States under the Monroe Doctrine, therefore, does not hold; but an analysis of that doctrine would also show that it, too, is definitely directed toward the development of peaceful means of settlement of international disputes, although it may keep in reserve the right of a war of defense against the intrusion of aggressive forces in the Western world. In either case there are no fundamental difficulties of adjustment with the terms of the Pact of Paris.

CHAPTER XIX

DEFINING WAR WITHOUT A DEFINITION

IT WAS only once that the note of asperity crept into the negotiations and that was when M. Briand proposed that the renunciation in the multilateral treaty should apply only to aggressive war. To attempt to define aggression and defense, said Mr. Kellogg, would be to weaken and virtually destroy the positive value of the renunciation of war. This was also the opinion of Senator Borah and the proponents of the outlawry of war in the United States. On the other hand, Senator Capper's Resolution had definitely accepted a definition of an aggressor nation "as one which having agreed to submit international differences to conciliation, arbitration or judicial settlement, begins hostilities without having done so." Behind this definition there was also a chapter of history which we may leave aside for the moment. In fact, the whole matter might perhaps be left to history if it were not that, as we have just seen, the British reservation raises once more the question of what is legitimate defense. The definition of defense is merely the obverse of that of aggression, and if this definition holds or if any other can be found, it would solve the last remaining problem which the treaty raises.

It is not an academic question; it is a very real one. Most wars of modern times have been waged as wars of defense, and the absence of an agreed definition has been an incentive to diplomacy so to camouflage its aggressions that the nations waging war would in each case believe that they are fighting in defense of either their homes or the vital interests of their country. With the rise of democracy, or at least of responsible government, even the most realistic of statesmen have had to disguise their venturous enterprises as defensive measures, if not for their own people, at least to gain the support of the outside world. Thus Bismarck succeeded in putting France into the position where it would strike the blow he most desired in order to have with him what he called the "imponderable" element of public opinion.

Now if practically all modern war is either real or pretended defense, the treaty which renounces all war except defense should find some way for defining the exception. But the acceptance of any formal definition in matters of this kind is extremely difficult, quite apart from the substance of the definition itself. It would be almost impossible to secure agreement in Congress on a definition of Euclid, if that definition had become involved in the politics of the country. On the other hand, it may be possible to work out a distinction in practice between legitimate and illegitimate defense and then state that practice later in short and formal terms. It is this latter method which has been employed in the course of the present negotiation. In his statement of the conditions accompanying the renunciation of war, Mr. Borah first, and Mr. Kellogg after him, have practically defined aggression and defense without a definition. The test proposed is still somewhat incomplete, but it is along the right direction. In any case, it is in harmony with the recent developments in Europe which have embodied the progress made there in connection with the work of the League of Nations.

The statement in the preamble of the treaty that nations violating this pledge "should be denied the benefits of this treaty" furnishes the clew to the answer to our problem. This will become clear not by argument so much as by description of an incident when this test was actually applied.

In the autumn of 1925, almost at the very time the Great Powers were signing the Treaty of Locarno, a Greek army marched over the mountain frontiers of Bulgaria. In a border skirmish some Greek citizens had been attacked by the Bulgarians of Macedonia. In the name of defense, the defense of its citizens against Bulgarian outrages, a Greek army corps crossed the frontier, with all the accouterments of war. A second army corps was sent to its support and a third lay close at hand to follow. The refugees from sixty villages came fleeing into Bulgaria with tales of a Greek invasion and memories of the horrors of past Balkan wars with all their atrocities. Bulgaria, disarmed by the Treaty of Neuilly—its counterpart to the Treaty of Versailles—appealed for help to the League of Nations. The Council of the League was summoned by telegraph to meet immediately at Paris, the Foreign Minister of Sweden flying by airplane to reach the meeting-place in time. M. Briand presided. The representatives of Greece and Bulgaria in Paris were summoned to the Council table and the session began. First, the Bulgarian Minister was turned to, but as he began to speak of the justice of Bulgaria's case, M. Briand raised his hand and refused to listen. He stated that the Council was not there to judge the justice of the case but to arrange that subsequent justice should be done. There was therefore just one question to which the Bulgarian should reply and that was whether or not Bulgaria would withhold hostilities and accept the judgment of a commission appointed by the League of Nations to judge the facts in proper form. The Bulgarian Minister, mastering his disappointment, accepted the League proposal and stated that Bulgaria would not engage in hostilities either before or during the negotiations of the commission.

M. Briand then turned to the Greek Minister. But Greece was already involved, and its situation was more difficult. Instructions had to be received from Athens before the Greek assent could be given to the demands of the League. Next day, however, that assent was forthcoming and a Commission of Inquiry investigating the facts both on the scene of invasion and at the capitals of the two countries assessed the costs of the invasion upon Greece, which paid to Bulgaria some 30,000,000 levas ($210,000). The frontier posts were drawn back on each side of the hilltops which constituted the frontier, and a few Swedish gendarmes watched over peace in the Balkans.

This was not a mere incident in European history. Had the two nations actually gone on with the struggle, their neighbors would inevitably have been drawn in; the flames in southeastern Europe could hardly have been held behind the Danube. And if the Little Entente were engaged, the Great Powers could hardly have escaped as well. At least this much can be said, that the murder of Sarajevo seemingly held no greater potentiality of war in 1914 than the events which promised a general Balkan conflagration in 1925. Instead,—the League of Nations applied the definition of aggression.

This will become clear if we recall Senator Capper's definition of the aggressor nation as that one "which having agreed to submit international differences to conciliation, arbitration or judicial settlement, *begins hostilities without having done so.*" Both Bulgaria and Greece had agreed to submit their differences to "conciliation, arbitration or judicial settlement" in the Covenant of the League. If either one had gone on with hostilities when the Council of the League presented the alternative and forced the choice, then it would have been the aggressor. The violation of its own promise, in the Covenant, to accept pacific means of settlement instead of force is the simplest and clearest possible test of aggression. It is not the act of violence alone, but even more the violation of a previously given pledge. The pledge is the condition of the test. It is not too much to say that without it there cannot be any test at all. Violence by itself is not aggression. There is violence as well in defense and police action, neither of which can be called aggression. There must be some agreement as to the conditions under which force is permissible, and as it is impossible to formulate beforehand all the conditions and circumstances which may arise, the only solution is to provide the proper means for determining each issue as it arises, such as a court for cases arising under international law or other justifiable issues, arbitration, also a judicial procedure, or conciliation and conference. The refusal of these means of peaceful settlement by a nation which has formally accepted them and its employment of violence in their stead is an act of aggression concerning which there can be no two opinions. Without an agreement of this kind it will always be possible for the aggressor to think itself the aggrieved and seldom possible for both sides to agree as to where the aggression lies.

Perhaps the clearest way to state this point is that the definition of aggression,—that the aggressor is the Power which in going to war violates its already given pledge to settle its disputes peacefully instead,—erects a juristic frontier alongside the geographic one. The nation which attacks another not only crosses the natural boundaries of mountain or river but the boundaries of actions themselves set forth in agreements. And it is this juristic frontier which alone furnishes an adequate test of aggression and legitimate defense.

The mere crossing of a nation's geographic frontiers is no sure test of aggression. Nowhere has this been more frankly stated than in the British reply to Mr. Kellogg's note. The Suez Canal does not lie within the Empire, yet the maintenance of connections with India through that canal, as well as at the Straits of Gibraltar, is perhaps the most vital single link in imperial defense. The very existence of the British Empire depends upon maintaining its connections, and any attack upon them whether on foreign soil or on the high seas will be resisted by the British Empire as an act of self-evident defense. This is what the so-called Monroe Doctrine of Mr. Chamberlain's note amounts to; "there are certain regions of the world, the welfare and integrity of which constitute a special and vital interest for our peace and safety. . . . Their protection against attack is to the British Empire a measure of self-defense." This statement might well be made on any necessary occasion by an American Secretary of State with reference to the Panama Canal. Legitimate defense is not confined to repelling invasion within a country's frontiers. Yet this is all that Mr. Kellogg had in mind when he referred to the inalienable right of self-defense. "Every nation is free at all times and regardless of treaty provisions to defend its territory from attack or invasion." [1] The inadequacy of this conception is not only borne home by the British reply, which we have just been discussing, but is a commonplace of military and naval strategy. All soldiers are agreed—and they should be the judges in this matter—that the defense of a nation's territory against attack should not always be awaited within the territory itself. To take the simplest case, there seems to be no adequate defense against airplane attack once the squadrons are overhead. The only sure method of warding off this danger is to destroy the enemy bombers before they leave their hangars, just as wasps can only be destroyed within their nest. Moreover, frontiers have been drawn disadvantageously to certain states so as

[1] Note of June 23. This reference to defense regardless of treaty provisions has been objected to in certain liberal quarters as containing the doctrine of Bethmann Hollweg that necessity knows no law. But Mr. Kellogg is talking of something entirely different from the proposition of the German Chancellor. What he means to say is simply that when a nation's territory is invaded, the right of defense takes precedence over all other obligations, for they are conditioned upon it. Any other theory would lessen instead of increase the validity of treaties, for the state which admits an enemy on its soil is confessedly no longer sovereign. This is a very different thing from regarding treaties as scraps of paper when they stand in the way of national policies or of national action even in times of crises. Had Mr. Kellogg's critics been fair to him, they would not have separated this phrase "regardless of treaty provisions" from the very narrow setting of its use in the sentence here; it is only when the territory is actually invaded that Mr. Kellogg suggests that defense is legitimate, whatever the treaty obligations of a country. The proper answer, of course, is that no treaty obligations should be entered into which would be violated by the act of defense against an invader.

to deprive them of their natural defense, and if the attack is coming from that quarter where the frontiers have been purposely left open for easy invasion and conquest, the only hope of an otherwise defenseless nation may lie in reaching first the natural ramparts which lie outside their political frontiers. From the strategical standpoint there has been not a little criticism of the act of the French Government at the opening of the World War when it ordered its army to retreat within its own frontiers in order that the crossing of those frontiers by the enemy should be seen by all the world to be an act of aggression. Politically this gesture will not have the weight with historians proportionate to its good intentions. For there is no sure test of aggression in the act of crossing the frontier. Aggression is a political and not merely a military act, for the distinction lies in the political conditions which are violated and not in the violation of actual territory.

But there is another reason, hardly less important, for not regarding the defense of frontiers as a criterion of legitimate defense; if all the emphasis were put upon it, then whole nations would be more and more the victims of disorderly elements along the borders. Nearly every nation has its Macedonia, and it would be a sorry theory which would force governments to the lawless standards of these backward communities. If every time a border brawl occurred the two nations were obliged to take up the feud in the name of national honor, the inalienable right of self-defense would indeed become the outstanding obstacle to the progress of civilization. It was by suppressing the feud through the alternative settlement of courts of law that barbarism and anarchy were put down within the state itself, and the frontier feuds of nations must similarly yield to the greater interests of the common weal; yet the only way to suppress the feud is to supply the common weal with adequate instruments of justice and make recourse to them the test of honest citizenship. Similarly, in the community of nations, the test of aggression which is the crime against the common weal must be established at a juristic frontier which a nation crosses when it violates its previously given word to resort to pacific means of peaceful settlement instead of war.

Now let us go back to that scene in the Council of the League of Nations when M. Briand applied the definition of aggression. There was no mention of a definition, possibly no conscious thought of it. Nevertheless, the action of the Council was a perfect instance of its application. M. Briand was right in refusing to be led into any discussion of the causes of the Greek invasion or the assertion of Bulgarian innocence. Aggression in this technical sense of the word does not reach back into any question of grievances, but has only to do with the method in which those grievances are redressed. The only question was that which M. Briand asked: were the disputants ready to have the grievances redressed through peaceful means or did they intend to fight? This point should be self-evident, but there has been much misunderstanding about it. The definition of defense and of aggression is only a denial of improper means of redress; and no means are improper in the hands of a sovereign state unless it has previously renounced them by treaty with other nations. The definition of aggression does not apply except where nations have definitely given up the right of feud, which is the right to use war as an instrument of their national policy. Perhaps the shortest way to state the definition of aggression is that it is the legitimation of peaceful ways of settling international disputes. Therefore, without specifically saying so, this treaty, which renounces war as a national instrument and calls for the resort to peaceful means of settlement instead, constitutes in itself a universal test of aggression.

Thus far, the problem is really a simple one, so simple that there must be something more involved or Mr. Borah and Mr. Kellogg, as well as Sir Austen Chamberlain, would not be so emphatic in their refusal to accept the definition as adequate. The real difficulty lies in determining just what acts constitute a violation of the treaty. Who is to determine whether the frontier acts or other acts of hostility are really in violation of the pledge or any measures of defense against a violator? Mr. Kellogg has no doubt upon this point, for it is now necessary to quote the whole sentence of which we have only quoted part before. "Every nation is free at all times and regardless of treaty provision to defend its territory from attack or invasion, *and it alone is competent to decide whether circumstances require recourse to war in self-defense.*" The importance of this last clause in interpreting the Pact of Paris can hardly be overstated. Each nation is to remain the judge of its own actions. This is the real reservation to the Pact of Paris. Others which have been noted are of relatively slight importance compared with this assertion that each and every nation remains free to judge whether or not it or the other signatories have violated the terms of the treaty in case of war or are acting merely in their own defense. It is in this connection that one sees how much less of a guarantee of peace lies in the Pact of Paris than in the Covenant of the League, which provides a machinery of investigation for the hour of crisis, and by recalling the obligation to employ it instead of arms for the settlement of disputes forces an application of the test of aggression then and there. The choice under the League is definite and clear, a commission of investigation awaits each international disorder; the Pact of Paris merely states that pacific means—the vaguest of terms—should be employed instead of war. As a practical measure, therefore, the Pact is by no means so well implemented for effective action as the Covenant of the League.

Mr. Kellogg's statement that each nation must be the judge

of its own actions is merely an honest statement of the American point of view; it has been the British point of view as well, as British statesmen have repeatedly emphasized at Geneva. Both nations held back from anything resembling a super-state which could sit in judgment upon their actions in matters of war and peace. No one has been more emphatic in this regard than Mr. Borah; but, at the same time, Mr. Borah saw the way for preventing this reservation from emasculating the whole proposal by emphasizing the consequences of a violation of the treaty instead of keeping attention fastened upon the reservation itself. The world would have to leave the United States free to judge on its own account as to which nation, in case of war, had violated the juristic frontier of its given word. But at least this much would be accomplished, that any war in the future will be judged not so much with reference to the ends to be attained by it as with reference to the method used for attaining those ends. The legitimacy of war is denied by the Pact of Paris, and the use of the illegitimate method is henceforth aggression. It makes no difference what the policy of a nation may be, war is no longer to be its instrument.

The Pact of Paris defines aggression and defense without a definition. This is also true of the Treaty of Locarno. Indeed, the Treaty of Locarno could never have been signed had it not involved the same definition which we have been discussing here. The chief point of that great treaty is that Great Britain becomes the guarantor of peace between France and Germany by pledging its support to the victim of aggression on either side the Rhine. With the experience of the World War behind them, the British people are strongly opposed to anything resembling a one-sided alliance which might drag Britain into war for the maintenance of policies of other countries; the American hostility to involvement of this kind is just as strong as that of Britain. And yet Great Britain had a moral responsibility and a vital interest in maintaining peace upon the Continent. How could it avoid entanglement with Continental policies and still insist that those policies should be pacific? If a flagrant aggression should occur, there would be no difficulty in securing British action against it. Flagrant aggression meant crossing the geographic frontier and that was the first thing provided against. But Article 5 dealt with the crossing of the juristic frontier as well, and so made the Treaty of Locarno an all-inclusive guarantee of peace. Article 5 stated that the provisions of Article 3 of the Treaty—that the signatories would settle all disputes by peaceful means and in the manner laid down in the treaty itself—were placed under the guarantee of the High Contracting Parties; and that if one of them refused "to submit a dispute to peaceful settlement or to comply with an arbitral or judicial decision" and openly attacked another signatory, the other signatories (and by this was chiefly meant Great Britain) should join to maintain the treaty as against the aggressor. Article 5 of the Treaty of Locarno is the juristic heart of the most effective outlawry of war which has yet been enacted. War was not only renounced by each of the signatories for itself, but they were to suppress it on the part of others. This was really outlawry of war. M. Briand had this in mind in his initial offer to the United States when he used the phrase "outlawry of war" to describe what had been done at Locarno. Outlawry implies the action of police, the enforcement of peace against its violator, not merely the practice of pacific policies. Is there any such commitment of peace enforcement in the Pact of Paris? This question brings us back once more to a familiar controversy which it is impossible to avoid but which, happily, the formula of the Kellogg treaty and the accompanying explanations of Mr. Kellogg have largely solved.

CHAPTER XX

THE ENFORCEMENT OF PEACE AND THE LEAGUE OF NATIONS

How can the United States support the cause of peace throughout the world without giving some guarantee that it will help to suppress violations of peace when they occur? This, next to its renunciation of war as an instrument of policy, is the most important thing for the United States to consider in connection with the Pact of Paris. It may be stated at once, and with the utmost emphasis, that the United States has no intention of accepting the duty of policeman even in the way laid down for Britain by the Treaty of Locarno. The formal obligation to intervene in the interests of peace when other nations go to war is a complication which the United States is not prepared to accept. It has registered this decision in ways which no statesman at home can overlook and which no foreign statesman should ignore. It was chiefly because this was believed to be the fundamental characteristic of the League of Nations that the opponents of the Covenant were able to carry the day. The mere apprehension of any possibility of this kind has been the chief argument for America's withdrawal from the whole peace movement of post-war Europe; for there, especially on the Continent, the emphasis has been upon enforcement.

It has, to say the least, been an unfair picture of the League of Nations which presented it to the American public as though the suppression of violence on the part of the League was merely war under another name and that the League actually perpetuated war in the name of peace. But the fear that this was so became almost a national obsession. Its basis, however, lay not in the reluctance of the United States to perform its duty as a civilized Power, but simply an abhorrence of entanglement in that kind of politics which played with war as an instrument of policy and that brought in peace-loving peoples to redress the balance of justice. While fully admitting the moral slump which this country suffered in withdrawing from the great experiment which other nations were working out, the reason for remaining aloof must not be interpreted as showing any sympathy with any Power which might attempt to overthrow the League by force or trickery. It was only because American opinion feared the continuance of these elements in international affairs and their possible use by League Powers themselves. The misunderstanding was chiefly due to the fact that the World War had so largely destroyed good faith among nations, and that the League seemed to many Americans still to emphasize this absence of good faith by its insistence upon measures of police, that the United States withheld its assent. Now the chief merit of the Pact of Paris is that it is a supreme assertion of international good faith and under it the moral purposes which persist in the American outlook are finding a way of expressing themselves, clear of entanglement but in full harmony with the real purpose of the League.

There is no legal obligation in the Pact of Paris upon the United States or any other Power to join in police action against a state which runs amuck in the world, and no external body is called upon to point out the duty to the signatories in case violation occurs. The only reference to the problem is in that phrase added to the preamble in its final form which states that "any signatory Power which shall hereafter seek to promote its national interests by resort to war should be denied the benefits furnished by this treaty." The novelty in this method of approach is that instead of enumerating the duties of the law-abiding states it denies the aggressor the right to calculate upon the continuance of friendly relations. It does not say that those relations will be broken, but, in leaving the signatories free to take this step, points to it as a moral duty. No measures of coercion are provided beyond the fact that the aggressor states should receive no aid or comfort from the co-signatories. If the United States is unwilling to go to the extent of dissociating itself from a nation which goes to war in violation of its pledge of peace in a treaty to which the United States is a co-signatory, when that treaty leaves the United States its own judge as to whether the violation has actually occurred or not, then the United States has really put itself on the side of the aggressor. For to supply such a belligerent with the resources of war and to insist upon our right to do so would be making ourselves the accomplices in the aggression. The article in the preamble goes no farther than to warn a nation planning such aggression that it cannot calculate upon our joining it in this way. Our own good faith would count for little if we were to give it aid and comfort in such a violation of the peace. The treaty indicates that once convinced of the nature of its violation we could notify it that we recover full liberty of action with reference to it, and in view of the financial power and the control of resources at the command of the United States, a notification of this kind, that we regarded its act as canceling our obligation to remain at peace, would make any adventurous state pause on the threshold of its adventure. It is a way of using the influence of the United States for peace without assuming any obligations to join in positive measures of suppression.

It will be claimed by the legalist that this departs from the traditional policy of America in maintaining neutrality while other nations go to war. But the time has come to recognize that the concept of neutrality must now be changed to fit the conditions of modern warfare. When nations went to war dependent upon their own resources, and the conflict did not extend beyond the immediate scene of operations, neutrality was easy, for it meant simply remaining away from the actual fighting. Modern industrial warfare has changed this entirely, as the United States knows well. The arsenals of the European belligerents before we entered the war were to be found in Bridgeport, Pittsburgh and the Bethlehem Steel Works, as well as at Woolwich and Creusot. The existing international law permitted this because it had not been adjusted to the new era. We must recognize this fact if we are to deal honestly and squarely with the problem of war itself. If the nation whose forces are supplied with arms is in our opinion an aggressor nation, we become morally, if not legally, the accomplices in its aggression by the support rendered through finance and industry, upon which its chance of victory may depend. No one has seen this more clearly than Congressman Burton whose experience in the International Commission on the Export of Armament gives added authority to his proposal, which calls for a purely American pronouncement that it is an established policy of the United States not to supply with arms a nation which goes to war in violation of its specific pledges. Senator Burton's Resolution, however, is not up for discussion at this point other than to indicate what might be done by the United States to square itself with its moral duty in time of war. The Kellogg proposal does not go so far as this. But in releasing the signatories from the obligation to remain at peace with an aggressor, it procures that liberty of action which both saves us from involvement with the aggressor and enables us to perform the least of all moral duties, which is to refuse our aid in the perpetration of an international crime.

So far we have merely dealt with the negative consequences of the clause which reserves our liberty of action in case a nation goes to war in violation of the treaty, the point that we should not be helping the aggressor. But it is not likely that, in the case of a perfectly clear violation, the United States would stop short with this. Senator Borah, in an interview in the New York *Times*, March 25, 1928, expressed the opinion that the country would not rest content with a merely negative sanction.

Another important result of such a treaty would be to enlist the support of the United States in coöperative action against any nation which is guilty of a flagrant violation of this outlawry agreement. Of course, the Government of the United States must reserve the right to decide, in the first place, whether or not the treaty has been violated, and, second, what coercive measures it feels obliged to take. But it is quite inconceivable that this country would stand idly by in case of a grave breach of a multilateral treaty to which it is a party. . . . Of course, in such a crisis we would consult with the other signatories and take their judgment into account. But we should not bind ourselves in advance to accept their decision if it runs counter to our own conclusions.

Some sentences in later portions of the interview strengthen still further the statement, as, for instance, the following reply to the query as to what effect the Kellogg proposal would have upon the League of Nations:

At present we have a network of treaties and understandings relative to peace—arbitration treaties, conciliation treaties, the Hague Tribunal, World Court, peace machinery of the League and peace machinery of Locarno. The effect of the Kellogg proposal is a solemn pledge to let all this peace machinery work.

We reach the conclusion, therefore, that the warning in the preamble to the Pact of Paris that any nation using war as an instrument of its national policy cannot in future depend upon our indifference, is the missing formula which solves for the present at least our relations with the League of Nations as well as with the individual governments of the world. There is a moral obligation not to frustrate measures of peace or to become an accomplice in any effort at frustration; but there are no involvements in police measures, no formal obligations of enforcement. The problem of the "sanctions," which had seemed at times insoluble, is at last nearing solution. If this alone were to the credit of the Pact of Paris, it would make it an outstanding milestone on the pathway of international peace. It is hardly to be wondered at that European countries concentrate their attention so largely upon it. At the same time, in their anxiety to secure American coöperation, there is some tendency to overstate what has been done. It is as important to emphasize the freedom of action which is reserved as the moral duty which is admitted.

It is impossible to close this discussion without appending a historical note. The suggestion of a negative instead of a positive sanction was first set forth in the plan of the American Committee which, in 1924, furnished some suggestions—especially the definition of aggression—embodied in the Geneva Protocol. The Protocol itself, however, definitely and emphatically rejected this particular idea and put all emphasis upon the obligations of joint action against the aggressor. The originator of the suggestion in the plan of the American Committee was Mr. David Hunter Miller. It was rejected in Geneva because the continental states felt the need of a more definite obligation to maintain the peace, an obligation which Locarno has since provided for the Continental Powers. But the British Empire as a whole has not been a member of the Locarno pact, the Dominions holding back from participation in the policing of Europe, much like the United States itself. The formula of 1924 left the aggressor state uncertain what action would be taken against it and decreased by that much the risk of aggression. The same conception is once more before us in different working in the preamble of the Pact of Paris. The Continental Powers now recognize its validity in the support of the Covenant itself; thus it may serve to bridge the gulf not only between the League and the Powers outside it, but also that continuing difference of opinion within the League itself expressed by the reluctance of the British Empire to assume universal obligations of police on terms almost identical with the external reservations of the United States.

CHAPTER XXI

THE FREEDOM OF THE SEAS

THE forests of the Argonne are far away. In spite of the fact that in the last war we made that wilderness our battlefield, nevertheless, to the average American mind, great distances still separate us from it, and there is a deep-seated purpose not to let those distances be diminished. But, while the scene of war on land recedes in the perspective of both memory and imagination, the potential battlefields of the Sea Powers of the world reach to our very doors.

The open seas, which are to navies what the terrain of mountain, plain and river is to armies, are on the flank of every coast. A half hour's sail from any ocean port and we are in the "no man's land" of naval strategy; the thin stretch of territorial water which forms the protective glacis for the shore land behind is less than a cannon shot in width. When, therefore, the Sea Powers begin to talk about renouncing war there is something much more real in the proposition for us than in the pursuance of some far-away ideal in another part of the world. Our own navy is involved; and on the seaways that lead to peace we meet at once our more immediate and still unsolved problem of naval disarmament.

Above all, "the renunciation of war as an instrument of national policy" means to the Sea Powers a reformulation in terms suitable for our day of the old, historic doctrines of the "freedom of the seas." Originally, when the high seas were not the secure pathways of commerce that they are today, that doctrine was applied to times of peace as well as of war. But for more than a hundred years the peace-time aspects of the

227

problem have practically disappeared and the only question that remains is that of the rights of belligerents and neutrals upon the high seas. It is a question of war-time conditions.

Now the Briand-Kellogg negotiations proposed to eliminate war itself "as an instrument of national policy." If this were really accepted and applied throughout the civilized world, it would at the very least so change the problem of sea power as practically to eliminate those nationalist elements which have made belligerency a menace to peaceful commerce. It is a new era that is envisaged, which calls upon arbitrary power for a much greater renunciation than that involved in merely recognizing the rights of war-time trade at sea. The greater reform carries the lesser along with it; the elimination of national wars implies the freedom of the seas.

This fact has not been clearly seen as yet on this side of the Atlantic. But the British have begun to see it, coming to it the other way on, from the standpoint of a discussion of the freedom of the seas and through it reaching to the further and wider proposal of the elimination of national war. There is no more striking fact in the international debate now going on than that British statesmen and publicists are coming out in favor of the whole revolutionary proposal, fully aware that it would mean a reversal of the entire history of British naval strategy.

There is no soft streak in this discussion of a problem so vital to Britain, but a frank acceptance of the consequences, which are that the British fleet should never again be used as the instrument of a purely British blockade in a war waged by and for exclusively British aims and interests, but only in case its services were called into action by the community of nations which registers its will to peace in a great anti-war treaty, the Covenant of the League, or other similar commitment. The days of Great Britain's empire of the sea are recognized as over at last, if in its place can be erected the coöperation of sovereign states equally set upon the maintenance of freedom for commerce upon the high seas.

It is not necessary here to review the whole past history of this doctrine of the freedom of the seas, one of the oldest and most consistent doctrines of American foreign policy, older than the Constitution itself. Benjamin Franklin attempted to insert it in the treaty of peace with Great Britain in 1783, urging the adoption of a clause in that treaty that "all merchants or traders with their unarmed vessels, employed in commerce, exchanging the products of different nations, and thereby rendering the necessary conveniences and comforts of human life more easy to obtain and more general, shall be allowed to pass freely unmolested."

Although Britain did not grant this right, Franklin actually got the principle inserted into a treaty with Prussia two years later. The War of 1812 was largely due to the unsolved problem,—which it left still unsolved.

Throughout the nineteenth century the United States continued to urge the case of neutral rights at sea, and when in 1856 the Conference of Paris reformed the law of the sea, the United States brought up again its insistent proposal that not only should privateering be abolished but that private property, when not contraband of war, should not be subject to seizure upon the high seas.

The question came to the fore again at the Hague Conference through the insistence of the American delegation, and no more eloquent and convincing statement of America's case has ever been made than that of Mr. Choate in the Hague Conference of 1907, based not only upon Secretary Root's instructions and President Roosevelt's earnest insistence, but also upon a Resolution of Congress of April 28, 1904, which had called upon the President of the United States to secure the "incorporation into the permanent law of civilized nations of the principles of exemption of all private property at sea, not con-

traband of war, from capture or destruction by belligerents."
Mr. Choate quoted, on behalf of the American proposal, not
only the precedent of his own country but the opinions of
statesmen and eminent publicists in almost every civilized land.

The American proposal, however, met with the opposition
of the British delegation at the Hague Conference, because it
seemed to them to be somewhat self-contradictory, or at least
incomplete. While denying the right of belligerents to seize
the private property of the signatory Powers at sea, the proposal made an exception of contraband of war and the right of
commercial blockade. These two exceptions seemed to the British delegation to make the proposal itself an "equivocation
capable of misleading ill-informed public opinion." They
claimed that the abolition of the right of capture necessarily
involved the abolition of commercial blockade, for the object
of both measures is the same; and that as long as the term
"contraband of war" is not confined to articles that can be
used immediately for military purposes, but may include food-
stuffs and raw materials as well, the exceptions to the rule
might be as large as the rule itself.

Lord Reay described at length the widening field of contraband attendant upon the discoveries of modern science, showing remarkable prevision of the situation which was to develop
in the early days of the World War. He pointed out, as well,
the complications that would still exist in determining the character of articles of conditional contraband, and of making sure
of the ultimate destination of innocent-looking shipments. The
British solution for this complicated program was to propose
that "contraband be abolished so that neutral commerce should
regain the freedom it requires."

There is little more than historical interest now in this debate
between the British and the American delegations at The
Hague, for President Roosevelt refused to accept the British

proposal as the British had refused the American formula. But, looking back over it, it seems to bear a fatal resemblance to the recent Disarmament Conference at Geneva; for in both cases there was a desire upon the part of the Governments of Great Britain and the United States to reach the solution of a common problem, and each produced a formula suited to its needs. What prevented agreement in both cases was an underlying, fundamental difference in naval strategy, employed on the one hand by an island Power dependent upon the outside world for its sustenance, and on the other hand to maintain the external interests of a continent, self-contained and self-sustaining.

This is the Gordian knot; and so far the attempt to disentangle it by playing with both ends of the complicated skein has only added to the complications. The solution is now seen to lie in eliminating the knot altogether by the denial of the right of "private," that is, "national," warfare at sea under the terms of the Briand-Kellogg proposal.

The further history of this problem but emphasizes the points that have been made already. The Conference of London in 1908 left the law of the sea unreformed, and the World War revealed the danger which lay in this situation, a danger so real that it was only the existence of still more vital facts which prevented the involvement of the United States in the effort to make headway against the steady inroads of sea power upon neutral rights.

It was in the heart of this most serious phase of the war that Colonel House, at that time President Wilson's representative in Europe, attempted to revive the principle of the freedom of the seas and to use it as a formula of possible agreement between Germany and Great Britain. But his proposal found little response in England, owing both to the German diplomatic blunders of the hour and to the sinking of the *Lusitania*, and also to the fact that Great Britain was at that moment develop-

ing the blockade of the Central Powers as one of its other
weapons of the war. A reform of this far-reaching nature
needed peace-time conditions for its fulfillment—or else the
overwhelming conviction on the part of the belligerents that
in it lay the means of ending their tragic struggle. This conviction was lacking at the time, and the effort failed. Colonel
House's insistence was not without effect when President Wilson made the principle of the freedom of the seas the second
of his Fourteen Points, but in Paris the President dropped it
from his program in the later days of the Peace Conference.
With all the world organized in a league of nations, there
would be no neutrals in the wars to come, and, therefore, the
protection of neutral rights would no longer be a valid claim.

Although President Wilson's dream of a universal League
of Nations was not realized and the greatest neutral claimant
to the freedom of the seas still remained neutral, nevertheless
the project has been little discussed in these post-war years,
either here or abroad. In England only a few pacifist journals
or radical thinkers have referred to it from time to time and
their advocacy has not counted for much with Britain as a
whole.

The dependence of Great Britain upon the protection of its
fleet is a conception more deeply rooted in the British mind
than any other single fact. Convictions as well as conditions are
facts of history; and any proposal, therefore, which seems to
hamper or restrict naval strategy is regarded by the average
British citizen as a direct attack upon the security of the British Empire, the independence or even the very existence of
the British nation.

The battle fleet of Britain, to which it entrusts its safety,
was built for free use, under its own command, on those Seven
Seas which bind the Empire together. A doctrine which proposes to deny henceforth the legitimacy of the strategy which

has prevailed from the days of Drake and Frobisher to that of Jellicoe and Beatty—the heritage of Nelson—can only win its way to serious consideration by sheer weight of inescapable realities. Nevertheless, that is just what is happening at the present time.

The failure of the Geneva Conference on Naval Disarmament was a great shock to British opinion, especially to those, in all parties, of a liberal trend of opinion; all the more so as it was felt that one of the chief underlying causes·of that failure, so far as Britain was concerned, lay in the new obligations it has assumed under the Covenant of the League and the Treaty of Locarno to guarantee the peace of the world against violation, even when the war was not its own.

A new and serious reëxamination of the whole problem of the security of the British Empire is now under way, and in the forefront of the discussion lies this question of the rights of neutrals (meaning American) on the very seas which are both the nexus of the Empire and the field of strategy in case of League action.

It is recognized now that the conditions of the last war, the alignment of the Powers, at least, might not be repeated in a possible conflict in the future, and that if Great Britain had to maintain its food supply in the face of an attack by submarines with wide cruising radius and vastly increased sea coasts for refuge along neighboring countries, it might go hard with a nation dependent upon those supplies for its very life.

Then there is the question of hostile airplanes hunting the cargo boats as they near the ports but are still on the high seas.

The prospect of warfare is rapidly changing for those who look out of European windows; and, whatever the Admiralty may have in mind, the questions which are arising in the field of the technical expert are being taken over into that of poli-

tics by those who claim that the only settlement lies in eliminating the cause of the danger and not in attempting to out-
top the world in armaments.

So far, most of this political discussion has originated in
Labor or Liberal circles, and its thesis is frankly and fully developed in a volume by Commander Kenworthy and Mr.
George Young. Another interested group is that which has
given most attention to the League of Nations.

But if any color of political partisanship is discoverable in
these circles, this can hardly be said of a document prepared
as a draft treaty between the United States and Great Britain
by specialists in international law, which states the whole case
for freedom of the seas in terms consonant with the Kellogg
proposal. One of the proponents of this draft is a jurist of
world-wide fame, whose name is already attached to documents of lasting historical importance. The text itself, a copy
of which lies before me, has not yet been published, but has
been somewhat widely circulated in England and referred to
in discussions.

But more significant from the standpoint of practical politics
is the fact that the *Round Table* for March, 1928, devotes a
major article to this subject and comes to the conclusion that
Great Britain should not merely accept the theory of the freedom of the seas, but should do so without delay, and if necessary take the initiative.

The *Round Table* is a forum of outstanding importance for
the discussion of imperial politics and is conducted by a group
of men of long and distinguished service in the upbuilding of
the British Commonwealth of Nations, men who have had
much to do with the constitutional development of India and
South Africa and the negotiations which brought the Irish Free
State into existence, and who have had experience as well in
the conduct of imperial politics at home.

The fact that the *Round Table* publishes this article does not by any means imply that the British Government, let alone the Sea Lords at the Admiralty, have been won over to the new proposition. There are no signs yet from that direction.[1] But it does mean that the question is now seriously before the liberal section of those most concerned with the policies of the Empire—or Commonwealth—as a whole.

The article in question begins with a frank discussion of the reasons for the failure of the Geneva Disarmament Conference and finds them in the fact that America, Britain and Japan have each a different problem in sea strategy and, therefore, different needs in naval armament; the result being inevitable disagreement so long as the debate continues in its present terms. There is no likelihood of future conferences succeeding if they are to be held along the line of the Geneva attempt.

The solution of the problem, says the writer, "lies in the acceptance of the new principles of naval warfare, and the chief of these would be the proposition that Great Britain should not use its fleet in the future for any purely British blockade; that its control of the high seas should never be exercised for itself alone; but only in fulfillment of an international obligation to which the United States and Japan would be co-signatories.

"For Great Britain the issue is comparatively simple. The days of her imperial temptations are over. She is no longer the only Sea Power in the world. The choice before her is whether she will be prepared, not to relinquish her naval strength or her right to protect her vital communications against improper attack, but to recognize that she must only use it to interfere with the trade of other nations in accordance with international

---

[1] The later signs have been quite the contrary. The ill-omened secret negotiations with France show what continuing obstacles there are in the path of general pacification. The reader is reminded of Ambassador Houghton's comment quoted above (Chapter XIII) as to the reactionary tendencies of governments. But there is no reason for discouragement; the public outcry in Great Britain was as great as that in the United States six months earlier over the Navy Bill. Some damage has been done, in reviving the remains of that program, but it could be undone by a renewed British movement for "freedom of the seas."

law and in support of peace through arbitration. That may seem difficult. But the long view shows that it is by limitation not of her rights as a belligerent, but of her right to become a belligerent that her trade and that peace which is her greatest interest are secured. If she refuses she will simply impose competition on the United States under conditions which will justify such competition, and in such a contest the greater purse will prevail."

In another place the writer of this article states the issue still more clearly: "It is whether any nation shall have the right to interfere with the trade of neutral nations when it goes to war on its own initiative alone, or whether the title to exercise belligerent rights is in the future to be exercised only in wars undertaken under some kind of international sanction." This, as was stated above, is the direct application to naval policy of the proposal of the Briand-Kellogg negotiations, that nations should "renounce war as an instrument for the purpose of carrying out their own spontaneous, independent policy." But these words of M. Briand are at the same time the substance of the second of President Wilson's Fourteen Points:

"Absolute freedom of navigation upon the seas, outside territorial waters, alike in peace and in war, except as the seas may be closed in whole or in part by international action for the enforcement of international covenants."

It is a strange turn in history that now the British who opposed this doctrine at Paris are making it their own, and beginning to inquire if we will hold to it and apply it as a part of our contribution to the elimination of war from the free action of sovereign states.

But there is a still stranger element in this debate. It is that the very obstacle which the British have hitherto found in Geneva to the whole-hearted acceptance of League obligations —the danger of a League blockade involving Great Britain in hostilities with the United States—is now seen to be the possible means for overcoming those other obstacles which it advanced at the Hague Conference of 1907. When the American proposal of freedom of the seas reserved both contraband and the right of blockade the British saw no end of trouble in defining the exceptions. The shore blockade was no longer effective and there was no way of delimiting the permitted acts of an intercepting fleet from the violation of the freedom of the high seas, since most of the blockades of the future must be directed from the high seas themselves. The absence of geographical or other visible limit of the field of blockade rendered the whole proposition illusory.

But now there is a different kind of frontier possible, consisting of a juristic line drawn between the "private" warfare of a state for its own ends and the "public" warfare, in defense of the community of nations and waged only against a violator of the peace covenant itself. This juristic distinction means the prohibition of all war at sea but that of legitimate defense; not merely self-defense—for that would bring back the old vicious circle of private or national warfare and national armaments—but defense of the peace of the world against that Power which revives the lawless right of "war as the instrument of its national policy."

Moreover, the historic question of contraband assumes a new form. The problem shifts to a discussion of what acts of coercion should be permitted against a Power that runs amuck in the world. Once more we are brought back to the old question of Article XVI of the Covenant of the League with its obligations upon League members to coöperate against the covenant-breaker and in defense of the victim.

Great Britain's guarantee of peace in the Treaty of Locarno is but a more specific application of this principle. But in both these cases the underlying justification is the same as that which legitimizes force in any society, namely, defense against violence.

The principle of the freedom of the seas does not mean keeping them open for the highwayman or bandit. It would be maintaining anarchy at sea, in the name of freedom, if we insisted upon the right to make ourselves the accomplice of an aggressor nation by the free shipment of our supplies to it, under the support and protection of our navy. That kind of freedom is the very antithesis of our ideals and our interests; for where anarchy exists, violence is sure to follow.

Only by the development of an ordered community of nations, conscious of their interdependence in war as in peace, can there be any permanent reality in this most far-reaching revolution in international relations. The cost of freedom is its maintenance. In some form or other, therefore, we must recognize the second as well as the first part of President Wilson's formulation. The seas shall be open "except for the enforcement of international covenants"; for upon those covenants depends the freedom itself.

Thus it may yet be found that the very one of the Fourteen Points which was surrendered in Paris—under the belief that it was no longer valid with the United States in a League of Nations—will prove to be a means for reconciling our historic claims to be a nation apart from others—a neutral by tradition and conviction—with the obligations of a member of the community of nations. Isolation passes as the oceans narrow; and freedom upon them makes them narrower still, by the removal of those barriers which keep nations further apart than mere distance—distrust, suspicion and misunderstanding.

There is, finally, one other consideration in the application of the renunciation of war as an instrument of national policy to the strategy of the sea. If the doctrine of the freedom of the seas can be interpreted in the way indicated in this chapter, it should prove a help rather than a hindrance to the maintenance of the Monroe Doctrine, and indeed might reassure those states which have recently been openly questioning

American policy under that doctrine. The new law of the sea would not prevent American action against the state which violated the renunciation treaty itself, for provision is made for liberty of action in such cases. It would, on the other hand, call special attention to the fact of a violation when it occurred and place the presumption of aggression upon the violating Power. Moreover, if external, forceful interference in American affairs is, as the message of Monroe stated, "dangerous to our peace and safety," we should be doubly free to intervene to prevent action by a non-American Government both on the basis of defense and upon that of the still higher claims of protection of the rights of the community of nations, a protection which would be exercised in the limitation of the operations of war as well as the elimination of war itself. The freedom of the seas is merely the expression of the renunciation of war under the same conditions as those which are being worked out for wars on land. A reservation of the Monroe Doctrine from the operation of the Pact of Paris would be contrary to the spirit of both because they are in harmony.

CHAPTER XXII

JAPAN'S RENUNCIATION

IT is very strange how little attention has been paid in this country to the reaction in Japan to the proposal to renounce war as an instrument of national policy. One might have expected that this phase of the discussion would have attracted instant and widespread attention, and the fact that this has not been the case is, in itself, both significant and reassuring.

Not so very long ago any American traveler who was privileged to hear the political gossip of European capitals found there a widespread conviction that a war between the United States and Japan was almost inevitable, if not, indeed, within measurable distance. That this external judgment of Japanese-American relations was fundamentally wrong is now clearly established, even to the conviction of the European onlookers. That it never had any basis in reality, however serious may have been some of the political misunderstandings between the two countries, was apparent all the time to the sober observer in both the United States and Japan.

But, at the same time, we must admit that the acceptance of a formal pledge to eliminate the very idea of war as an instrument of national policy in American-Japanese relations is a matter of much greater significance to us than in the case of most other signatories of the multilateral treaty. For it ought definitely to mark the passing of the old régime in the area of the Pacific, the régime which has looked rather to the weight of armaments than to the discovery of mutual interests, which has encouraged distrust rather than confidence in friendly and peaceful intercourse. The Kellogg notes leave much still to be done, as the following points will show; but it is at least an outstanding milestone on the pathway of peace. And the Japanese have not only seen this clearly, but are acting upon it.

It may be that the relatively slight attention given to Japan's adherence to the Pact may be explained partly by the fact that the Western nations—we are not alone in this—have not yet learned to appreciate at its full value the sincere and genuine quality of Japanese foreign policy. Nowhere has the tried wisdom of the elder statesmen of Japan been more in evidence than in their dealings with these nations. The greatest of all assets which a nation can possess is that of the confidence and trust of the world at large. And in its dealings with the Western world, which have been so many and so important in these post-war years, the Japanese Government has consistently shown the most scrupulous regard for its honor and the fulfillments of its commitments.

This spirit has always animated it at Geneva and in the fulfillment of the political provisions agreed to at the Washington Conference. On that occasion Japan accepted with good grace a readjustment of its foreign policy, which in less experienced hands might merely have opened the doors to misunderstanding instead of to possible settlement. In short, Japan has established a record which should win something more than the official confidence of governments; it should have universal recognition of the high ideals and sincerity of its international dealings with the Western world.

This maintenance of an ideal standard is all the more notable when one turns to view the problems of Japan; for it is face to face with a situation which is far more critical than that of any of the Western Powers. There is one major fact which dominates all others, and that is that the Japanese people are increasing at the rate of about 800,000 a year, and are already rapidly nearing, and apparently bound soon to outrun, the limits of their means of subsistence.

There is no solution for such a vast increase of population by way of emigration, for even if there were a country ready to accept these millions, Japan could not find the means to export them, at least overseas. To transport an army of 800,000 emigrants yearly across the distances of the Pacific would be a vaster task than the miracle of the American transport service in the World War, which was only rendered possible by the shortness of the time taken for each trip, the coördination of other services and the swiftness with which marching soldiers can embark or disembark. All the passenger tonnage of Japan, requisitioned for the purpose, would not begin to meet the requirements of such a migration. The moment one stops to consider facts like this, the more clearly one sees that the population problem for Japan cannot be solved by emigration. The few thousands who might reach our shores, if they were freer of access, or the inhabitable areas of Australasia, would not materially change the condition of the mother country. The solution lies in moral and social checks upon the growth of population itself; the problem is not an international but a national one in its fundamentals.

Added to these problems of population and food supply, there are others temporary in character but for the present more pressing and serious. No other country has suffered from earthquake and its attendant disasters as Japan has; and its trade and commerce, upon which its industrial life depends, are affected by the unstable equilibrium of the neighboring lands of Asia. Compared with these grave problems, the politics of the United States seem almost care-free. In spite of the responsibilities inherent in wealth and power, there are no such cares of state in a country which is still the land of opportunity as those which confront the statesmen of Japan.

None of these problems, however, grave as they have been and are, seemed likely to prevent the steady upbuilding of pacific relations with us. It was an act of our own, which from the Japanese standpoint was utterly uncalled for and distinctly unfriendly, which stung the deepest of all national sentiments in Japan—that of national pride. No responsible statesman or publicist in Japan has ever questioned the right of the United States to determine its own residents and treat as a national problem its control of immigration, but the way in which our Congress asserted that right and the language used in connection with the Japanese Exclusion Bill seemed to the Japanese to have been pointed at them with something of the nature of a national slight. The incident continues to resound in the consciousness of the Japanese, while most Americans have now either forgotten it or recall it but confusedly to their memory.

The point at issue was not so much what we did as how we did it. Japan is a country schooled in courtesy and in the traditions of formal politeness; and it combines with these qualities a tenacity of purpose which has shown itself consistently throughout history. One, therefore, might expect that, with that very firmness which is the sign manual of national honor, they would tend to keep in mind any casual or wanton disregard of national sentiment.

It is only when these facts are recalled that one fully realizes the significance of the Japanese acceptance of an invitation from the Government of the United States to renounce war with it, and with all other civilized nations, as an instrument of national policy. It was not entirely easy for a nation suffering a sense of grievance unredressed to give instant and cordial acceptance to the enunciation of universal peace when the nation proposing these high ideals seemed unwilling to take any practical steps to lessen existing misunderstandings. Just as there were many honest Germans who felt in 1925 that the settlement of French occupation of the Rhineland should precede any such agreement as that made at Locarno, so there were those in Japan who felt that a proposal for permanent peace on the part of the United States should first undo what they all felt to be an injustice and a wrong inflicted upon them by the Congress of the United States.

This is not the place to discuss the merits of that other issue, one which so far as the United States is concerned has already practically passed into history; but if we have forgotten, Japan has not, and we can only repeat that this fact makes all the more significant the Japanese acceptance of the principles of the renunciation of war; for, although at first these memories might seem to present difficulties in the way of Japanese adherence to the American proposal, nevertheless such obstacles as these did not ultimately block the path of complete agreement.

When Mr. Kellogg first approached the Japanese Government, in his note of April 13, the Japanese Government replied (on May 26) in two short paragraphs. In the first it stated that as it understood the offer there could be nothing in it contrary to the right of self-defense or "the obligations of agreements guaranteeing the public peace, such as are embodied in the Covenant of the League of Nations and the Treaties of Locarno." The second paragraph was the important one. While accepting the American proposition in principle, it took it for granted that the text would have to be worked out between the six great Powers by free discussion. The text of this paragraph ran as follows:

The Imperial Government firmly believes that unanimous agreement on a mutually acceptable text for such a treaty as is here contemplated is well capable of realization by discussion between the six Powers referred to, and they would be happy to collaborate with cordial good will in the discussions, with the purpose of securing what they are persuaded is the common desire of all the peoples of the world—namely, the cessation of wars and the definite establishment among the nations of an era of permanent and universal peace.

Although in the meantime a good deal of water has run under the bridge and more is flowing every day, we must begin with this short but important statement of the Japanese Government if we are to get a clear understanding of the whole situation created by the Kellogg proposal as applied to the problems of the Pacific; for the Japanese answer contains more than is apparent at first glance. In the first place, the reference to the League of Nations and the Treaties of Locarno may seem to those who have not been following the trend of Japanese foreign policy to be merely formal statements without much reality behind them. Geneva is far away from Tokio and, as for the Treaty of Locarno, Japan is not even a party to it.

Why, then, this careful mention of the existing "obligations of agreements guaranteeing the public peace"? Was Japan merely playing up a friendly understanding with Britain, France and the other signatories of the League, to use the same language as they in the reply to the United States? The answer is a decided "No!" as will be clear to any student of the history of Japanese foreign policy during the last seven years. During these years it has been a member of the League of Nations and that membership has been a center of its interest in a way that has largely escaped notice in this country.

In spite of its distance from Europe, Japan has been a major figure in the concerns of Geneva. It has taken its membership in the League very seriously indeed. This membership, it should not be forgotten, has given its statesmen a share in most of the important problems of the post-war adjustments, in which Japan could never have had any say or even expressed any interest had it not been for its League membership. It has not only been a member of the Council of the League as one of the Great Powers, but it has had an important share in the membership of the Secretariat at Geneva.

At the present time the director of the political section of the Secretariat is a distinguished and experienced Japanese expert who is also Under-secretary General of the League. Throughout the formative period of the work at Geneva the Director of the Division of Intellectual Coöperation was a Japanese scholar, known and loved throughout the whole world of scholarship, Dr. Inazo Nitobe. The fact that Dr. Nitobe's chief contribution in the past to Japanese thought had been in the interpretation of American literature did not prevent his devoting himself with equal enthusiasm to the upbuilding of an international mind through the agencies of Geneva.

From the very beginning of the discussions in the Peace Conference in Paris it was evident that Japan was studying the new world order, that seemed then to be taking shape, in a more detached way than was the case with the European powers. For a nation which had just emerged from feudalism and had in a single lifetime passed from the Middle Ages to the scientific era of today the conceptions of a new world order were not so revolutionary as they were to the established and deeply rooted state system of the older Western world. For in the history of politics Europe is much older than even the oldest people of the Orient. Japan had already made a readjustment of its internal structure which was at least as revolutionary as any called for in the acceptance of the League of Nations. The result was that the League of Nations acquired a reality in Japanese foreign policy which must be reckoned with in all our dealings with it.

This was evident in the earliest of all experiments at international legislation. In the very first year after the Treaty of Versailles the International Labor Office held its first international conference at Washington. The American political world being at that time in the midst of its great fight over the Covenant of the League, did not know quite what to do with this body and officially gave it no recognition whatever. Japan, however, sent a delegation of its most notable representatives of both capital and labor, as well as of its Government, and many observers and experts as well, for it was taking seriously the proposed reform which was to prohibit the exploitation of children in industry, safeguard the conditions of labor of women and secure the uniform acceptance of the eight-hour day.

When the conference was over the Japanese Government was the first to take seriously its recommendations; and if the resolutions which it drafted are not yet fully in force in the laws of Japan, it is chiefly because the European nations have failed to keep step with that very country which in 1919 seemed most behind the rest in the laws and conditions of labor. In short, in both internal and external policy, Japan has been deeply affected by its membership in the League of Nations.

If we had only the single sentence in the reply to Mr. Kellogg, the mention of the Covenant of the League would hardly call for any of this general discussion of the place of the League in Japanese policy; but the Japanese discussions of the proposal "to renounce war as an instrument of national policy" began to appear in the Japanese press some time before the Kellogg offer was made, and a survey of that discussion shows very clearly how the League is a constant preoccupation of Japan.

The articles in the Japanese press go back to M. Briand's original proposal of April, 1927; but there was no intensive discussion of this proposal in the public press until the Draft Treaty in reply to it was published in the early summer of last year by Professor Chamberlain and myself. This Draft Treaty was discussed in the month of August at the Honolulu Conference of the Institute of Pacific Relations. The news of this discussion received wide comment in the Japanese press. Incidentally, some of those present at Honolulu, who were most experienced in Japanese politics, were rather disturbed at a publicity which they regarded as premature, for it was a distinctly new thing to have a major question of foreign policy initiated in unofficial conferences and in the press instead of waiting for the initiative to come from the government.

It is a further sign of the new day which is dawning in the

Orient that the publicity did not prove to be premature and the public discussion apparently merely prepared the way for governmental action. Already by the month of December last there were whole columns of editorials in the greatest papers of Japan and articles in the popular as well as the technical reviews discussing the informal proposals made known to them through the Pacific Conference; and the outstanding fact in this discussion was the practically unanimous approval of the general principle which had been set forth by M. Briand. There were, however, divergent opinions as to the ways and means for realizing it and applying it in definite treaty form.

When the Kellogg offer of the multilateral treaty appeared, Japan was therefore by no means taken by surprise. It accepted the general principle of the renunciation of war as an instrument of national policy, but suggested that the application of this principle should be studied in an international conference. This suggestion of a conference had been made before, especially by the British, and has been discussed in that connection. But Washington stated clearly that it was not in favor of meetings by either experts or diplomats in whose minds the original purity and simplicity of the great principle of war renunciation might be lost in the confusion of practical politics. The State Department held to the opinion that the application of the principle is secondary to the acceptance of the general formula, and should follow it. The negotiations were to be carried on as they had been begun by the exchange of notes and the continued discussion in the public press. Japan, therefore, yielded as Great Britain had done, but instead of stating its case more fully in a public way, it followed rather the precedent of Germany than of Great Britain in its reply, and accepted the proposal without the detailed analysis of the way in which the renunciation of war would affect its policies, or how they in turn might react upon it.

It is of the utmost importance to note that Japan was silent concerning any special reservations of its own. It is well known that it, too, had in the past drawn an analogy with the Monroe Doctrine for its special interests in the Orient, a parallel which has even been in substance recognized by the United States, itself, in one chapter of its diplomatic history. The Japanese reply said nothing of this; and the significance of that silence is all the more notable in view of the problem with which Japan is confronted. The very existence of Japan depends upon its relations with the continent of Asia, and some of its most vital interests lie in territories outside its own political boundaries, especially in Manchuria. It will help us to appreciate Japanese policy and interpret any declarations it may yet feel called upon to make if we turn for a moment to examine this situation.

If the student of politics were to search the world over for that area which presents the greatest menace to international peace, he would probably select Manchuria. I do not wish to imply even for a moment that a great Oriental war over this disputed territory is really either planned or immediately probable. But among the menacing possibilities of conflict in the world today, there are, perhaps, no others so definitely presenting danger and inviting cautious statesmanship as the problem of Manchuria.

It is Chinese territory, and Chinese sovereignty over it is freely acknowledged by Japan. Nevertheless, Japan has claims within it and rights and privileges established by treaty which open the gravest of international problems. While they seem to the Chinese, and especially to the nationalist Chinese, to be of the nature of that kind of inadmissible concession due to intervention from which China is engaged in freeing herself elsewhere at the present time, from the standpoint of Japan the situation is one not only of acquired rights, but of the deepest springs of sentiment.

For those railroad lines which are the heart of the Japanese concession run through a territory that is sacred to Japan by reason of some of the most heroic exploits in her military annals. Japan is not the nation to forget, even if other nations do, how heavy was her loss in 1904-1905 in what was at that time reckoned to be the greatest of all battles in the world's history. The armies of Marshal Oyama and those of Kuropatkin seem now, in the perspective of the World War, to have been hardly more than a few armed corps in comparison with the great *levée en masse* of the World War.

In the Orient, however, the struggle for Manchuria or for Japan's rights against those of Russia on that foreign soil remains the one outstanding fact of recent military history. The slopes of Verdun are not so real as the hillsides of Port Arthur.

There is, therefore, ardent sentiment as well as vital economic interest in the claims of Japan within this section of Chinese territory. But equally the sentiment of nationalist China and the rights of its citizens, who have moved into Manchuria in the last few years in a greater wave of migration than any other in modern history—these are as strong forces of national assertion as any of the claims of Japan, if not stronger. Judging this situation in the light of all past history, one would be led to only one conclusion, that of an inevitable conflict in the not distant future. And then, moving dimly in the background at present, but potentially of portentous significance, is the vast might of Russia; some day bound to support its claims or to revive them.

In view of this most serious situation in the Far East and especially because of its proximity to that nation which is at once the oldest and the youngest as well as the most populous in the whole world—China—there are problems for Japan of the most definite reality in any proposal to renounce war as an instrument of its national policy. The uncharted future is obscure enough, even if statecraft were permitted all the instruments which history supplies; it surely calls for the highest quality of leadership in those responsible for the Government of Japan to accept, as they have done, the principle involved in the Kellogg treaty, which, if effectively applied, places such definite limitations upon the freedom of action of a sovereign state.

But there is still another difficulty in the situation; this time a historical one, but with vital effects in the world today. The peoples that are now called upon to renounce war as an instrument of their policies have all of them used it in the past in the process of the upbuilding of the national state. The Great Powers of the Western world, however, had substantially finished this process some time ago; and the World War is thought to have rounded it off for most of the smaller European nations in our own day.

But in the case of Japan, and more especially of China, statebuilding, in the Western sense of the word, lies almost entirely within recent and contemporaneous history. The use of war for national ends has therefore seemed not only legitimate, but symbolizes high ideals and great endeavors, the living memories of which are not yet lost by the present generation.

The result, to speak of Japan alone, is that no other country in the world, not even France, has such a religious sense of, or devotion to, *la patrie* as exists in the spirit of the Japanese people; nor is there any other nation where the sense of national honor penetrates more deeply through the entire body of its citizens.

Under conditions like these, the foreigner would be led at first to the conclusion that Japan might naturally tend to adhere to a gospel of militarism rather than to accept the renunciation of war. But a study of recent discussions in the Japanese press, as well as an analysis of Japanese policy, shows that in this regard, as in so many others, Japan offers a surprising capacity for adjustment to the new order of things.

Finally, to get back to Japanese-American relations, if the two nations renounce war as their instrument of national policy, what are the "specific means" which, according to Article 2 of the Pact of Paris, are to be the substitute for war? This constitutes a special question which may be considered apart from the more general problem discussed below; for there are precedents to build upon in the region of the Pacific which do not apply to European relations. At the meeting of the Institute of Pacific Relations in Honolulu, in August, 1927, a suggestion was made which has been developed since and may serve to solve the technical problem created by the fact that Japan's structural relations with other Powers are governed by its membership in the League of Nations, and that the United States is not within the circle of these obligations. This anomaly might be met by building upon the precedent established by the Four Power Pact of the Washington Conference and fusing into it the conciliation procedure of the Bryan treaties. It is true that Japan is not at present a signatory of a Bryan treaty, but there have been indications recently of a readiness to adhere. If these two treaties due to American initiative were fused together, we might have a relatively simple instrument for the peaceful settlement of Japanese-American questions. Following the Bryan treaty model, there would be a Commission of Inquiry composed of experts including neutrals; upon the presentation of their report the signatories would not, as in the present Bryan treaties, regain full liberty of action, but would follow the precedent of the Four Power Pact and go to conference instead, to discuss there freely and without prejudice the recommendations of the investigating commission. These two wheels of the machine of pacific settlement, when made to work together, would furnish a mechanism much more suitable for delicate and difficult problems, which are sure to arise in the adjustments of the Pacific area, than a court whose task it is to render judgments according to existing law, and might also deal with those other problems of national honor and vital interest which nations are always reluctant to arbitrate. The machinery of conference is the only practicable one for the kind of dispute which acquires that degree of momentum which may lead to war; it is fortunate that it can be set going in the Pacific by merely building upon precedents already established. The Four Power Pact calls for international conference in case of disputes concerning the island possessions of the Powers of the Pacific. The scope of that provision might be enlarged to cover all disputes and no reservation made as to national honor and vital interest; for while a conference leads toward a settlement, it does not necessarily impose one. Then, if this were combined with the great principle of the renunciation of war, we should, indeed, have established the framework of a new era in the Pacific.

CHAPTER XXIII

ALTERNATIVES FOR WAR

SEVERAL times in the course of our study we have emphasized the fact that mere renunciation of war is not enough to rid the world of it. There must be substitutes for it worked out beforehand in times of peace, so that when the crises come with their pressure for rapid action and their unescapable demand for decisive measures, there will be alternatives to which both parties already have agreed as being the suitable method for dealing with them. Without this provision, as has been said above more than once, the act of renunciation is incomplete. How then is it to be completed? This is not, strictly speaking, a part of the discussion of the Pact of Paris, since that document leaves this whole problem undefined, merely providing that the settlement of disputes "shall never be sought except by pacific means." [1] But while the treaty does not carry us forward into this area of constructive statesmanship, the way must yet be found by which we can reconcile the claims of national sovereignty with international obligations. Giving up war as an instrument of policy must mean either the strengthening of other instruments or, if they are not adequate, the invention or discovery of new ones. This is not a rapid process. We should not be discouraged if our experimentation in so vast a field goes slowly. There will be mistakes and disappointments; but where the need is so imperative, we can surely count upon that adequate measure of applied intelligence which will, in the long run, assure success.

[1] The negative wording also calls attention to the fact that peace may be preserved by leaving disputes unsettled.

This chapter, therefore, looks beyond the Pact of Paris to other problems which are before us in the future. They are before us just as definitely whether the Pact of Paris is accepted and ratified or not. Indeed, the point of view may be maintained with all sincerity that this question of finding the pertinent alternatives for war is a more fundamental chapter of the peace problem than the formal renunciation in the Pact of Paris. However that may be, the Pact has made this question once more a matter of present interest to the United States, as it has been a continuing problem for the old world throughout these post-war years.

The formal alternatives for war are at least four in number —Arbitration, the World Court, Conciliation, and Conference. Of these the first two are juristic in character. The Permanent Court of International Justice, as defined in the statute which established it, deals primarily with questions involving treaty rights and the interpretation of international law. This is also the proper field of Arbitration, although its scope is widened to include as well those miscellaneous cases which lie outside the categories of international law but are nevertheless reducible to an accepted formula, or *compromis,* embodying the agreed statement of the issue to come before the arbitration tribunal.

The procedure in both the Permanent Court of International Justice and an arbitration tribunal is juridical, culminating in a judgment or award; on the other hand, Conciliation and Conference are political institutions. Conciliation is a procedure which examines the substance of a dispute but does not present conclusions in terms of a decree. It investigates and may recommend, but it does not bind. Conference is much wider in scope. It also may investigate the issues; but since its members, unlike those of Commissions of Conciliation, include the plenipotentiaries of the disputant nations, it works toward an agreement which may be just as binding as the verdict of a court, differing from it only in the fact that the agreement is self-imposed.

In recent discussions the procedure of these various institutions of international settlement has been much confused. The word arbitration, for example, has been used by advocates of international peace to cover the whole field of political as well as judicial dispute; on the other hand, almost equally comprehensive claims have been made for the function and authority of the Permanent Court of International Justice. The misconception as to the nature of arbitration arises apparently from the fact that in the preparation of the case there must be political negotiation, and this preliminary action is more a matter of current interest and is much better news than the technical debate in the arbitration proper. As for the World Court, it seems to me an open question whether it has suffered more in this country from the reservations of a reactionary Senate or from the over-statement of its function by those who have been its most ardent protagonists. Neither arbitration nor the World Court is a pertinent instrument for the settlement of political disputes.

These distinctions are not mere legal quibbles. They are essential in the planning of an ordered world which is the fundamental aim of the peace movement. It is not progress to advocate the denaturing of institutions which can only function effectively within their proper sphere. The institutions of international justice have enough handicaps inherent in their pioneering nature without adding the difficulty of claiming too much for them. Their chief problem lies not in the realization of illimitable possibilities, but in making good within the narrow limits prescribed by the national states themselves. An international court, whether of law or of arbitration, must take its place in the existing system of jurisprudence. It is not a new invention, but the application of existing machinery to new needs. Any system of international justice must depend primarily upon those nations that have developed within themselves responsible systems of national justice; nations in which obligations assumed are understood and are likely to be fulfilled. But the prior existence of these national systems is also an obstacle to the growth of international jurisprudence, for nations which have realized for themselves all the implications of sovereignty are naturally reluctant to yield ground before the new and relatively untried experiment of an international tribunal. If, therefore, the instruments of international justice are to develop, we must find a way to harmonize two seemingly irreconcilable ideals: on the one hand, the demand that we maintain and strengthen the solid gains of past generations which have established the judicial institutions within each country and made provision for them in the law and constitution; and on the other hand, the demand that these developed systems of national justice make way, in part, for that international procedure in which each nation may participate but which no one controls.

In one way or another this antithesis between local interests and the interests of the Community of Nations shows itself in every proposal for the development of international arbitration. The formula of "vital interest and national honor" is giving way to that of "domestic jurisdiction," but in both cases the aim is the same; it is to safeguard that heritage of constitutional freedom which is the justification, in terms of history and of civilization, for the existence of the nations themselves. The maintenance and development of such a heritage is surely not less important than the establishment of the international judiciary.

The only one way of harmonizing the seeming conflict is through a study of procedure. This must include not merely the procedure of the tribunal itself, but also—and more especially —the attendant or ancillary institutions which are not strictly judicial but support the cause of international justice by providing for the initial stages of agreement and by furnishing the materials for the later formulation of law. This carries us over into the political institutions which we have referred to above, less binding than a court or arbitration tribunal. Viewed from the standpoint of arbitration and international law, they are ancillary to judicial procedure, but that is only the legal aspect of their work. They also furnish governments a medium for solving disputes that never reach the court, and cover that vast and miscellaneous field of non-justiciable dispute in which lie most of the causes of war.

Let us turn now to these two institutions of political settlement, Conciliation and Conference. Unfortunately, within this political field, there is as yet no program or agreed method of procedure such as already has been worked out for both arbitration and the Permanent Court of International Justice, a fact which has recently been called to our attention by the German Government in a memorandum to the League of Nations. There is even confusion between conferences and commissions, a confusion producing something worse than failure when one government sends plenipotentiaries and another mere agents bound by rigid instructions, as has happened more than once since the war. This matter should receive the attention of an international conference, similar to those Hague Conferences which preceded the erection of the Court of Arbitration. The fundamental contribution of those conferences has not yet been fully recognized, because it chiefly lay in the field of law and not of politics, and consequently was not effective in the dark days of 1914. But the Hague Conferences started plans for political organizations as well. The Commissions of Inquiry provided for in the Hague Conventions were ultimately given a definite form in the Bryan Treaties.

These Commissions of Inquiry are not tribunals of justice or arbitration. They have no power to register a decree, and even halt on the brink of offering a suggestion or a recommendation.

They simply investigate the facts at issue between nations and report their findings, leaving the disputants free to take such action as they may think best. The presence of neutrals on the Boards of Inquiry is counted upon to produce a statement of the case which may ultimately lead to an agreement through negotiation. The scheme of Commissions of Conciliation has recently been developed in the whole series of treaties which culminated in the central one of Locarno, and the network now includes nearly all of the civilized nations of the world. In these later treaties, however, the device has been carried a step further, in that the Commissions are definitely empowered to recommend terms of settlement. Recommendation is, of course, very different from the judgment of a court, but it is much more than mere fact-finding.

One weakness in these Commissions of Conciliation is that, in general, they have not been brought together by multilateral agreement; each separate treaty has called for the erection of a different Commission. The result is that few of the Commissions ever have any work to do; the machinery grows rusty; and when members of the Commission die, the governments forget to appoint their successors and even perhaps the very existence of the Commissions themselves. There has not been enough business before the ordinary Bryan Commission to keep it genuinely alive.

There is another weakness in the Bryan plan. If all the civilized nations were to make separate treaties of this kind between themselves the number of the resulting commissions would be absurdly great. There would be somewhere between two and three thousand commissions and about ten thousand commissioners. It is easy to see, therefore, that if the Bryan system of treaties were extended throughout the whole world it would become inoperative by its very intricacy and unwieldiness. If international Conciliation is to keep alive agencies capable of functioning effectively in emergencies, those agencies must be consolidated. Steps in this direction were taken in the Central American Treaty of 1923 and in the Santiago Convention of that year. But if the process is to be extended over the whole civilized world, it would necessarily involve the coöperation of the League of Nations. Conciliation is directly pertinent to the League's work. At the same time, there could be no surer way of wrecking the device of Conciliation than by over-stressing the centralizing machinery. The League has been careful not to interfere with the erection of these commissions of the Locarno type, recognizing that there is as great a need to keep local susceptibilities in mind as there is of speeding up effective action. When Conciliation has to be used, the nations involved are already so much on each other's nerves that they will not listen to advice from any but known friends, or those in whose impartiality they may repose confidence. The appointment of a Commission of Conciliation, therefore, comes back to a question of personalities. It was this question which originally blocked the organization of international justice. There was a fear of an unfair or packed court. But in the juristic field there has been steady progress, from the reluctance of the Hague Conference to accept the principle of a fixed bench down to the embodiment of that very principle in the World Court. A similar advance may ultimately take place in the sphere of Conciliation.

Alongside International Conciliation there is another institution which at first sight may seem to be so well understood as not to call for any detailed comment—that of Diplomatic Conference. This, like Conciliation, deals with all kinds of international issues in the field of policy, even those which may be of vital interest or involve national honor. Generally in the past such matters have rested in the hands of a diplomacy which has had the weight of armaments behind it. International Conference also cannot escape the realism of such arguments, and to a certain extent recognizes them in recognizing great and small Powers. Nevertheless a new procedure in diplomacy is developing with the evolution of the Conference method.

When the secrecy of diplomacy gives place to public discussion, questions must be argued on their merits rather than according to the dictates of a single will. To be sure, when a powerful nation speaks it may force its way in Conference against the opposition of the rest, but it is not likely to do so unless it can state its case in terms of a common interest. This was the characteristic of the Washington Conference. It was not a coöperative affair but followed the lead of the United States. The results may have been beneficent, but the method was not a perfect precedent for the development of the institution itself.

The method of Conference which is exemplified in the meetings of the Council of the League is perhaps the best example of the procedure of the new diplomacy; it is strictly political, offering the solvent for disputes in the field of national policy, withholding them from the arbitrament of either the sword or the law, and providing in their place the merely human give-and-take of a discussion on policy. In the early days of theorizing about the League of Nations, before the Covenant was signed, there were some who thought this method of Conference so fundamental that they would have created a League that provided little else. Such plans were discussed both in England and here. They were not adequate for a League containing all the European Powers, but they would have gone a long way toward meeting the needs of the United States and the British Empire. In any case, this method of Conference is still open to us without necessarily involving us in the rest of the League structure, in which it is being most effectively developed.

Now we come to the application of this discussion to the problems of today. The proposal "to renounce war as an instrument of policy" indicates in the very formula used that the chief

substitutes for the discarded instrument must be those which
function in the field of politics. The other current phrase, "outlawry of war," places the emphasis upon the legal alternatives.
This is perhaps why it has made so strong an appeal to the
pacifists whose slogan was "law not war," although the "outlawry" movement itself is not pacifist. It has seemed to offer
a way of settling all international disputes that was clear,
definite and final. The anarchy of a "society based upon war"
would end by common agreement, and a world court would be
the accepted arbiter. The more responsible leaders of the "outlawry" movement have escaped the fallacy of those who repose
all their hopes of permanent peace in such a judicial process,
but, while agreeing as to the importance of conferences, they
have put emphasis upon a code of international law, with war
excised from its text, and a court to whose judgment the public
opinion of the world would yield obedience. The apparent
finality of such an operation has had a wide appeal in a country
which does not have to think realistically in international matters. Yet it is this very rigidity in the procedure and judgment
of a court which is the chief obstacle to the submission to it of
just those issues over which wars are fought—issues of
"national honor and vital interest" under whatever name we
may disguise them; and no other country emphasizes quite so
strongly as we do these exceptions to international judicial
action. The result is a downright contradiction. On the one
hand we have the advocacy of peace policies based upon a court
or arbitration, on the other hand the insistence upon reserving
from these bodies the issues of war and peace. It is anomalies
like this which produce the sins of futility which the unsympathetic foreigner calls national hypocrisy. The only way
to escape it in this instance is to explore still further the alternatives to arbitration which lie in the field of politics. The practical proposal is "to renounce war as an instrument of policy,"

not, as some pro-Court proponents seem to imply, "to renounce war as an instrument of justice."

A political question differs from a purely "justiciable" question in that the interest shifts from the material issue to the way in which that issue affects the parties to it. Recently a political question arose between France and Germany over the number of military police needed for the protection of the Saar Valley. The French claimed that they needed eight hundred men; the Germans asserted that five hundred were sufficient to keep order. The material issue was merely whether three hundred men should be retained or not. But the political issue which arose from this was something of quite a different nature. The nationalist press of Berlin had as headlines, "Germany must not permit the continuance of a disguised French military occupation in the Saar Valley." The French nationalist press replied, "France must not yield to German threats the first time the German Foreign Minister presides over the Council of the League." The kernel of the dispute was only a detail of administration, a purely technical matter. What would the police have to do and how would the inhabitants of the Saar be affected? Then politics came in and it changed the nature of this local problem. The real issue ceased to be the government of the Saar Valley and became that of the good faith and "honor" of the two Powers. The local problem was enveloped in a new one and almost lost sight of.

That meeting of the Council of the League of Nations in March, 1927, was one of those historical events, the significance of which tends to escape the attention of a world which still judges events by the disturbance which they create. Catastrophe is news; had Germany and France failed to settle the problem of the Saar, the mutual recriminations growing from that incident would have intensified the mutual distrust which has corrupted so much of the post-war policy of Europe. Had there been nothing but the old diplomacy to fall back upon, with the Government in Berlin writing a secret but formal note to the Government in Paris, delivered with rigid etiquette by the Ambassador, in a strictly regulated formula supplied him by the Government at home; and had France replied in similar unreal terms, the whole intercourse dominated or influenced by a press whose suspicions would be fed by governments anxious to mobilize opinion for the winning of their case,—such an incident as this of the Saar Valley would have supplied the fuel for that kind of dispute which leads to war. Lesser incidents than this have caused war in the past. As the debate on the Saar Valley continued in the League Council, all morning and afternoon, and when at last settlement was reached and the grim consequences of a possible disagreement no longer menaced the work of European reconstruction, Herr Stresemann turned to M. Briand, the Foreign Minister of Germany to that of France, and said in a voice not unshaken by emotion, that if this instrument of reconciliation, which is the conference of responsible statesmen, had existed as a known and recognized instrument of policy in 1914, the World War would not have taken place.

This is not the place, however, to discuss the validity and growing strength of the international instrument at Geneva. We have been dealing rather with the distinction between justiciable and political issues, taking the Saar Valley question as an example of the political issue. The illustration points to at least one characteristic of these political questions which seems to have escaped notice. They are complex, while justiciable issues are simple or direct. They add to the substance of the claim a further question as to the attitude of the disputants. Indeed it is this second phase of the matter which more often contains the dangerous explosive of emotion. Court or arbitration tribunals are not likely to be accepted when matters get this far. When men and nations feel so keenly about some issue that they are prepared to sacrifice their lives for it, they do not readily accept a procedure which leads to a hard and fast judgment. In short, for political disputes there must be political institutions. I think, therefore, that in the treaties which propose to further the cause of international peace, the emphasis should be shifted from Court and Arbitration to Conciliation and Conference.

So far as the device of Conciliation goes, the Bryan Treaties, although they have not been taken very seriously, nevertheless furnish a precedent which may lead to real progress. In their most fully developed form, in the Treaties of Locarno, the Commissions of Conciliation really reconcile. What is more important still, the Treaty of Locarno leads to further settlement and does not leave the parties with that "liberty of action," which is provided in the Bryan text—by which is meant the right to go to war. By a very slight change in the Bryan text an entirely different setting could be given to those treaties. If, instead of granting freedom of action to the disputants at the close of the investigation, there was an engagement to carry over the findings of Conciliation into international conferences, the link could be forged between the two institutions of political settlement which really deal with matters of war and peace.

It seems to have escaped most observers that the technique of Conference has been steadily perfected in the course of these years since the war. It has been especially the work of the League of Nations to raise it from its amateur and casual aspects of the early days to an institution with a definite place in international polity. Our country has not yet learned the rather obvious lesson that international conferences dealing with matters so complicated and far-reaching as Disarmament cannot be improvised over-night, but that they must be provided with an apparatus capable of disentangling the two phases of the problem, the technical, which has to do with armaments proper, from that which has to do with national policy. While Europe has been perfecting this mechanism through some eight years of experimentation, we have made very little advance. International Conference has meant for us hardly more than an opportunity to express our views and ask the rest of the world to agree with us. In the Washington Conference this method more or less succeeded. The failure in the Disarmament Conference is known to all the world.

We come back to the point which has already been mentioned, that the chief instrument of international settlement in political questions, namely, international Conference, is an instrument which has not yet been defined for us by any document comparable to the statute which provided the World Court with its constitution or defined its powers, or even the earlier constitution of the so-called Court of Arbitration at The Hague. Lacking this, we are at a double disadvantage as a result of our absence from Geneva where the technique is taking shape.

There are many points of difference between the procedure of a conference and that of a court, but there is one which seems to have escaped notice in most of the all-too-serious discussions of these problems. There is a solvent which can be applied in Conference but which never is permitted in Court; it is a sense of humor. When great nations begin to talk in terms of national honor or of vital interest over issues which in themselves have never involved more than a few individuals—as, for instance, when the Saar Valley case was imagined to affect sixty million Germans and forty million French instead of three hundred soldiers—the solemn farce needs only some dispassionate or penetrating remark from a cool-headed member of the Conference to reduce it to realities. If, at such a time, there pierces through the tensity of the moment some humorous remark (as happened in this very instance), it gives a chance for common sense to take the place of over-wrought patriotic emotions. Business men are familiar with the way in which this purely human touch may solve the most involved situations. The business of nations calls for it equally.

The sense of humor is a sense of proportion; and proportion is the prime condition of justice. Some time, perhaps, in the far-off future, perhaps nearer our own time than we have dared to hope, the world of science and industry—applying to human affairs the intelligence it has devoted to its own techniques,—will definitely set about the realization as between nations of those principles of conduct which had already been applied to citizens by the jurists of the ancient world, from Hammurabi and Moses to Justinian. For nowhere else can we find a nobler expression of the meaning of the whole problem with which this inquiry deals than in the inspiring phrase which,—embodying Greek philosophy and Christian teaching,—opens that handbook of the Roman law known as Justinian's Institutes: "Justice is the fixed and constant purpose which gives to every man his due."

APPENDICES

APPENDIX I

DRAFT TREATY OF PERMANENT PEACE BETWEEN THE UNITED STATES OF AMERICA AND . . .[1]

For purposes of reference, the text of the Draft Treaty described in Chapter VI is given here, not on account of the interest which it stimulated in the proposal of M. Briand, but because the student will find in it an arrangement of the pertinent texts of those existing treaties, which furnish the background or starting point for the negotiations—the Treaty of Locarno and the Root and Bryan treaties. Comparison of this comprehensive and detailed text with the two simple articles of the Pact of Paris should not be made without recalling that the latter text was, at least in the case of France, supplemented by the Arbitration Treaty of February, 1928 (see Chapter XI). This latter treaty must be regarded as the parallel for all of Part II of the text below. Because of this existing treaty it was unnecessary for the Pact of Paris to go into detail in the matter of arbitration. Article 2 of the Pact of Paris refers to pacific procedure in the most general terms, merely providing that the settlement of disputes among the signatories "shall never be sought except by pacific means." It is clear that the unfinished negotiations on arbitration and conciliation with the other Powers should be completed in order to implement the Pact of Paris, for otherwise it is left incomplete on its constructive side, which is the all-important one of providing alternatives or substitutes for war.

PART I

RENUNCIATION OF WAR

Article 1. The United States of America and . . .[1] mutually undertake that they will in no case

RENUNCIATION OF WAR
(General Treaty of Locarno, Art. 2)

[1] Insert here the name of the other signatory. The Draft Treaty is drawn with especial reference to those Powers which are signatories to the General Treaty of Locarno but is also capable of extension to other Powers. The text of the stipulation providing for the renunciation of war is literally that of the Treaty of Locarno; with this the Monroe Doctrine as worked out historically in relation to non-European Powers is stated in parallel terms.

271

attack or invade each other or resort to war against each other.

Article 2. The stipulation in the above article shall not, however, apply in the case of—

LEGITIMATE
DEFENSE
PERMITTED
(Treaty of Locarno,
Art. 2)
AND DEFINED
(Treaty of Locarno,
Art. 5)

a. The exercise of the right of legitimate defense, that is to say, resistance to a violation of the undertaking contained in the previous article,

provided that the attacked party shall at once offer to submit the dispute to peaceful settlement or to comply with an arbitral or judicial decision;

MONROE
DOCTRINE

b. action by the United States of America in pursuance of its traditional policy with reference to the American continents,

provided that the United States will use its best endeavors to secure the submission to arbitration or conciliation of a dispute between an American and a non-American power.

GENERAL
PROVISIONS

Article 3. For the furtherance of universal peace among nations, the High Contracting Parties agree:

that in the event of a breach of a treaty or covenant for the compulsory peaceful settlement of international disputes other than this covenant, each of them undertakes that it will not aid or abet the treaty-breaking Power. In the event that the treaty-breaking Power is one of the High Contracting Parties, the other Party recovers full liberty of action with reference to it.

The measures to be taken in this regard shall be determined in the case of the United States of America by the action of its own Government, in the case of . . .[1] in accordance with its existing treaty obligations.

CODIFICATION
OF INTER-
NATIONAL LAW

Article 4. Recognizing the importance of accepted rules of law in the preservation of peace, the

[1] See footnote on preceding page.

High Contracting Parties agree that they will undertake to further a progressive codification of international law based upon the renunciation of war as an instrument of policy, as set forth in this treaty.

Article 5. In view of the greater degree of security provided by this treaty, the High Contracting Parties undertake to coöperate with one another in furthering the progressive reduction of armaments and to that end to study the appropriate ways and means in international conferences on disarmament which shall meet at regular intervals.

DISARMAMENT

PART II

ARBITRATION AND CONCILIATION

Article 6. The High Contracting Parties agree to submit disputes arising between them to arbitration, judicial settlement, or conciliation as set forth in the following articles of this treaty,

provided that the dispute does not concern a matter which under international law is solely within the domestic jurisdiction of one of the High Contracting Parties;

nevertheless in every case the provisions of Part I shall apply.

ARBITRATION

Article 7.[1] Differences which may arise of a legal nature, or relating to the interpretation of treaties existing between the two Contracting Parties, and which it may not have been possible to settle by diplomacy, shall be referred to the Permanent Court of Arbitration *or to the Permanent Court of International Justice,* established at The Hague,

(Adapted from the existing Arbitration Treaty between the United States of America and France, expiring February 27, 1928. The similar treaty with Great Britain will expire June 4, 1928, that with Japan August 24)

[1] The text is identical with that of the existing treaty except for the possible reference to the Court of International Justice as an alternative to the Court of Arbitration. The inserted text is given in italics.

provided, nevertheless, that they do not affect the vital interests, the independence, or the honor of the two Contracting States, and do not concern the interests of third Parties.

Article 8. In each individual case the High Contracting Parties, before appealing to the Permanent Court of Arbitration *or to the Permanent Court of International Justice* shall conclude a special agreement defining clearly the matter in dispute. If the matter is referred to the Permanent Court of Arbitration, the special agreement shall also define the scope of the powers of the Arbitrators and the periods to be fixed for the formation of the Arbitral Tribunal and the several stages of the procedure.

It is understood that on the part of the United States such special agreements will be made by the President of the United States, by and with the advice and consent of the Senate.

CONCILIATION

(Adapted from the (Bryan) Treaty between the United States of America and France for the Advancement of General Peace: Articles 1, 2, 3, 4, 5)

Article 9.[1] *Subject to the conditions of Article 6,* any disputes arising between the Government of the United States of America and the Government of . . .[2] of whatever nature they may be, shall, when ordinary diplomatic proceedings have failed

---

[1] The text of this section follows literally that of the Bryan treaties except where indicated by italics. Four changes have been made. (1) The Bryan treaties covered "any disputes of whatever nature they may be"; this section applies only to those which lie outside of the field of domestic law. (2) The Bryan treaties provided only for inquiry as to the facts; this section provides for "recommendations for settlement," which may enable the parties to adjust their difficulties but do not bind them to do so. (3) In the last article of the section the Bryan treaties allowed the parties to recover full liberty of action, but here (under Article 13) the provisions of Part I still apply, so that they do not recover liberty to go to war. They may not agree as to the settlement, but in that case they simply leave matters unsettled awaiting some more favorable basis of future agreement. (4) The provision in the second section of Article I of the Bryan treaties, that neither Party "shall resort to any act of force" during the period of investigation, has been here transferred to a separate article (Art. 14), so as to apply as well to arbitration procedure.

[2] Insert here the name of the other signatory.

and the High Contracting Parties do not have recourse to arbitration, be submitted for investigation and report *and recommendations for settlement* to a Permanent International *Conciliation* Commission constituted in the manner prescribed in the following article.

Article 10. The International *Conciliation* Commission shall be composed of five members appointed as follows: Each Government shall designate two members, only one of whom shall be of its own nationality; the fifth member shall be designated by common consent and shall not belong to any of the nationalities already represented on the Commission; he shall perform the duties of President.

In case the two Governments should be unable to agree on the choice of the fifth commissioner, the other four shall be called upon to designate him, and failing an understanding between them, the provisions of Article 45 of The Hague Convention of 1907 shall be applied.

The Commission shall be organized within six months from the exchange of ratifications of the present convention.

The members shall be appointed for one year and their appointment may be renewed. They shall remain in office until superseded or reappointed, or until the work on which they are engaged at the time their office expires is completed.

Any vacancies which may arise (from death, resignation, or cases of physical or moral incapacity) shall be filled within the shortest possible period in the manner followed for the original appointment.

The High Contracting Parties shall, before designating the Commissioners, reach an understanding in regard to their compensation. They shall bear by halves the expenses incident to the meeting of the Commission.

Article 11. In case a dispute should arise between the High Contracting Parties which is not settled by the ordinary methods, each Party shall have a right to ask that the investigation thereof be entrusted to the International Commission charged with making a report. Notice shall be given to the President of the International Commission, who shall at once communicate with his colleagues.

In the same case the President may, after consulting his colleagues and upon receiving the consent of a majority of the members of the Commission, offer the services of the latter to each of the Contracting Parties. Acceptance of that offer declared by one of the two Governments shall be sufficient to give jurisdiction of the case to the Commission in accordance with the foregoing paragraph.

The place of meeting shall be determined by the Commission itself.

Article 12. The High Contracting Parties shall have a right, each on its own part, to state to the President of the Commission what is the subject-matter of the controversy. No difference in these statements, which shall be furnished by way of suggestion, shall arrest the action of the Commission.

In case the cause of the dispute should consist of certain acts already committed or about to be committed, the Commission shall as soon as possible indicate what measures to preserve the rights of each Party ought in its opinion to be taken provisionally and pending the delivery of its report.

Article 13. As regards the procedure which it is to follow, the Commission shall as far as possible be guided by the provisions contained in Articles 10 to 34 and Article 36 of Convention 1 of The Hague of 1907.[1]

The High Contracting Parties agree to afford the Commission all means and all necessary facilities for its investigation and report.

The work of the Commission shall be completed within one year from the date on which it has taken jurisdiction of the case, unless the High Contracting Parties should agree to set a different period.

The conclusion of the Commission and the terms of its report shall be adopted by a majority. The report signed only by the President acting by virtue of his office, shall be transmitted by him to each of the Contracting Parties.

Subject to the provisions of Part I, the High Contracting Parties reserve full liberty as to the action to be taken on the report *and recommendations for settlement* of the Commission.

INTERIM MEASURES [2]

Article 14. During the procedure of conciliation or arbitration or judicial procedure, the High Contracting Parties agree—

a. not to resort with respect to each other, to any act of force, and in general to abstain from any sort of action whatsoever which may aggravate or extend the dispute.

(Adapted from the Bryan Treaty, Art. 1, Sect. 2

and

b. to abstain from all measures likely to have a repercussion prejudicial to the execution of the de-

the Locarno Arbitration Treaties Art. 19)

---

[1] There is a slight change here from the Bryan treaties. In the Bryan treaties the reference is to Articles 9-36. This has been changed so as to exclude Articles 9 and 35 of the Hague Convention which limited the scope of the Commission to fact finding, so that these two articles were not applicable to a Conciliation Commission with power to recommend terms of settlement.

[2] The provision of the Bryan treaties preventing measures of force during the period of investigation is here extended to apply to the cases of arbitration or judicial procedure, using the text of the Locarno treaties literally.

cision or to the arrangement proposed by the Conciliation Commission or Court.

PART III

RATIFICATION

(Adapted from the (Bryan) Treaty between the United States of America and France for the Advancement of General Peace: Article 6)

Article 15. The present treaty shall be ratified by the President of the United States of America, with the advice and consent of the Senate of the United States, and by the . . .[1] in accordance with the constitutional laws of . . .[1]

It shall go in force immediately after the exchange of ratifications, and shall remain in force until the expiration of a period of twelve months after either Party shall have notified the other of the intention to terminate it.

In witness whereof the respective plenipotentiaries have signed the present treaty and have affixed thereunto their seals.

Done at Washington this   day of   , the year nineteen hundred and   .

[1] Insert here the name of the other signatory.

APPENDIX II

THE AMERICAN CONSTITUTION AND THE RIGHT
TO DECLARE WAR

THE two sections of the Constitution which have reference to the war power invested in the American Government are those which enumerate on the one hand the powers of Congress and on the other those of the Executive. For purposes of reference, these two sections are quoted below.

A survey of American constitutional history, and especially of the debates in the Constitutional Convention itself, will fully support the view maintained here, that the real point in the attribution to Congress of the right to declare war was not the assertion of the right itself but its location in the Government. From the very first, the Republic was safeguarding itself against autocratic possibilities in the Presidency, and that was the preoccupation which gives meaning to this clause. At the same time, the right or power to declare war was held to be inherent in the very nature of sovereignty but even this theory would not prevent the possible limitation upon its use to the point of an agreed renunciation.

This is not the place for a detailed legal argument, but it should not be forgotten that the use of war by sovereign states has been definitely limited and curtailed in various ways and by a large number of agreements in which the United States has participated. As many as eight distinct modes of restriction have been pointed out and analyzed by Dr. David Jayne Hill.[1] These are:

1. The laws of neutrality, which necessarily limit the free right of the belligerent.

2. The reduction of armament, which is in effect a weakening of the possibility of the use of war as an instrument of policy.

3. The restriction of belligerents themselves by conventions concerning the laws of war.

4. The renunciation of inhuman and barbarous practices in war itself.

[1] *Saturday Evening Post*, April 18, 1925.

5. The delay imposed by such treaties as those of the Bryan type which call for the renunciation of war for a limited period of time.

6. The prohibition of conquest, as in Article 10 of the League of Nations Covenant. While the United States was opposed to the acceptance of this provision, the statement was made and reiterated and unanimously accepted as embodying the American policy, that the United States itself, so far as it was concerned, did not go to war for conquest.

7. Members of the League of Nations have in Article 11 admitted the principle that "any war or threat of war . . . is a matter of concern to the whole League, and the League shall take any action that it may deem wise and effectual to safeguard the peace of nations." This means that a League member is not free to go to war without regard to the "concern" of other nations, and implies that there is already a voluntary acceptance of a restriction upon its freedom of action.

8. The implication from the foregoing is that international law may, by the agreement of the society of Sovereign States, "fix the conditions under which military action may be legally initiated—and this without invalidating or imperilling the sovereignty of States."

In addition to these eight points, Dr. Hill recalls the fact that the second Convention of the Hague Conference of 1907 forbade the use of armed force for the collection of contract debts, a Convention signed and ratified by all the great Powers including the United States. This Convention "clearly discriminates between a just and unjust resort to military action."

The partial renunciation of war or of its practice is therefore provided for already in international law and is in unquestioned operation under the Constitution of the United States. The question of the complete renunciation of war is equally adjustable under the Constitution if the Constitution continues to be adjustable to the growing pacific tendencies of which these facts just cited are convincing evidence. The United States can give effect to a national purpose not to use war as the instrument of its policy just as it may limit the use of war in certain ways. The action of the Government lies within the sphere of policy even if the statement is in the form of a general doctrine. It is not likely that the question here debated will ever seriously arise, but it could be effectively met by joint action of both branches of the Government, Congress and the State Department, if Congress were to pass a joint resolution such as that suggested by Senator Capper, declaring it to be the established policy of the United States to make treaties of the kind suggested by M. Briand, renouncing war as an instrument of public policy and proposing to settle its international disputes by pacific means. It would still be possible for the theorist to claim that the right to resort to war remained within the concept of sovereignty, although the Government had renounced its use. This, however, would be no more than a metaphysical quibble, for the real question in fact and in history is the exercise of the right and not its theoretic possession.

UNITED STATES CONSTITUTION

ARTICLE I

SECTION 8.—POWERS GRANTED TO CONGRESS

The Congress shall have power:

To lay and collect taxes, duties, imposts, and excises, to pay the debts and provide for the common defense and general welfare of the United States; but all duties, imposts, and excises shall be uniform throughout the United States;

To borrow money on the credit of the United States;

To regulate commerce with foreign nations, and among the several States, and with the Indian tribes;

To establish a uniform rule of naturalization, and uniform laws on the subject of bankruptcies throughout the United States;

To coin money, regulate the value thereof, and of foreign coin, and fix the standard of weights and measures;

To provide for the punishment of counterfeiting the securities and current coin of the United States;

To establish post-offices and post-roads;

To promote the progress of science and useful arts, by securing, for limited times, to authors and inventors the exclusive right to their respective writings and discoveries;

To constitute tribunals inferior to the Supreme Court;

To define and punish piracies and felonies committed on the high seas, and offenses against the law of nations;

To declare war, grant letters of marque and reprisal,[1] and make rules concerning captures on land and water;

[1] Letters granted by the government to private citizens in time of war, authorizing them, under certain conditions, to capture the ships of the enemy.

To raise and support armies, but no appropriation of money to that use shall be for a longer term than two years;

To provide and maintain a navy;

To make rules for the government and regulation of the land and naval forces;

To provide for calling forth the militia to execute the laws of the Union, suppress insurrections and repel invasions;

To provide for organizing, arming, and disciplining the militia, and for governing such part of them as may be employed in the service of the United States, reserving to the States respectively the appointment of officers, and the authority of training the militia according to the discipline prescribed by Congress;

To exercise exclusive legislation in all cases whatsoever over such district (not exceeding ten miles square) as may, by cession of particular States, and the acceptance of Congress, become the seat of the government of the United States,[1] and to exercise like authority over all places purchased by the consent of the Legislature of the State in which the same shall be, for the erection of forts, magazines, arsenals, dockyards and other needful buildings;—And

To make all laws which shall be necessary and proper for carrying into execution the foregoing powers, and all other powers vested by this Constitution in the government of the United States, or in any department or officer thereof.

SECTION 2.—POWERS OF THE PRESIDENT

The President shall be commander-in-chief of the army and navy of the United States, and of the militia of the several States, when called into the actual service of the United States; he may require the opinion, in writing, of the principal officer in each of the executive departments, upon any subject relating to the duties of their respective offices; and he shall have power to grant reprieves and pardons for offenses against the United States, except in cases of impeachment.

He shall have power, by and with the advice and consent of the Senate, to make treaties, provided two-thirds of the senators present concur; and he shall nominate, and by and with the advice and consent of the Senate shall appoint ambassadors, other public ministers and consuls, judges of the Supreme Court, and all other officers of the United States, whose appointments are not herein otherwise provided for, and which shall be established by law; but the Congress may by

---

[1] The District of Columbia.

law vest the appointment of such inferior officers, as they think proper, in the President alone, in the courts of law, or in the heads of departments.

The President shall have power to fill up all vacancies that may happen during the recess of the Senate, by granting commissions which shall expire at the end of their next session.

APPENDIX III

THE ARBITRATION TREATY
SIGNED FEB. 6, 1928 [1]

The President of the United States of America and the President of the French Republic

Determined to prevent so far as in their power lies any interruption in the peaceful relations that have happily existed between the two nations for more than a century;

Desirous of reaffirming their adherence to the policy of submitting to impartial decision all justiciable controversies that may arise between them;

Eager by their example not only to demonstrate their condemnation of war as an instrument of national policy in their mutual relations, but also to hasten the time when the perfection of international arrangements for the pacific settlement of international disputes shall have eliminated forever the possibility of war among any of the Powers of the world;

Having in mind the treaty signed at Washington on September 15, 1914, to facilitate the settlement of disputes between the United States of America and France;

Have decided to conclude a new treaty of arbitration enlarging the scope of the arbitration convention signed at Washington on February 10, 1908, which expires by limitation on February 27, 1928, and promoting the cause of arbitration and for that purpose they have appointed as their respective Plenipotentiaries:

The President of the United States of America:

Mr. Robert E. Olds, Acting Secretary of State, and

The President of the French Republic:

His Excellency Mr. Paul Claudel, Ambassador Extraordinary and Plenipotentiary of the French Republic to the United States, who, having communicated to one another their full powers found in good and due form, have agreed upon the following articles:

[1] Text taken from Vol. 69 *Congressional Record* (Feb. 8, 1928), p. 2810. Cf. Chapter XI above for discussion.

ARTICLE I

Any disputes arising between the Government of the United States of America and the Government of the French Republic of whatever nature they may be, shall, when ordinary diplomatic proceedings have failed and the High Contracting Parties do not have recourse to adjudication by a competent tribunal, be submitted for investigation and report, as prescribed in the treaty signed at Washington, September 15, 1914, to the Permanent International Commission constituted pursuant thereto.

ARTICLE 2

All differences relating to international matters in which the High Contracting Parties are concerned by virtue of a claim of right made by one against the other under treaty or otherwise, which it has not been possible to adjust by diplomacy, which have not been adjusted as a result of reference to the above-mentioned Permanent International Commission, and which are justiciable in the [their] nature by reason of being susceptible of decision by the application of the principles of law or equity, shall be submitted to the Permanent Court of Arbitration established at The Hague by the Convention of October 18, 1907, or to some other competent tribunal, as shall be decided in each case by special agreement, which special agreement shall provide for the organization of such tribunal if necessary, define its powers, state the question or questions at issue, and settle the terms of reference.

The special agreement in each case shall be made on the part of the United States of America by the President of the United States of America by and with the advice and consent of the Senate thereof, and on the part of France in accordance with the constitutional laws of France.

ARTICLE 3

The provisions of this treaty shall not be invoked in respect of any dispute the subject matter of which

(a) is within the domestic jurisdiction of either of the High Contracting Parties,

(b) involves the interests of third parties,

(c) depends upon or involves the maintenance of the traditional attitude of the United States concerning American questions, commonly described as the Monroe Doctrine,

(d) depends upon or involves the observance of the obligations of France in accordance with the covenant of the League of Nations.

ARTICLE 4

The present treaty shall be ratified by the President of the United States of America by and with the advice and consent of the Senate thereof and by the President of the French Republic in accordance with the constitutional laws of the French Republic.

The ratifications shall be exchanged at Washington as soon as possible, and the treaty shall take effect on the date of the exchange of the ratifications. It shall thereafter remain in force continuously unless and until terminated by one year's written notice given by either High Contracting Party to the other.

In faith thereof the respective Plenipotentiaries have signed this treaty in duplicate in the English and French languages, both texts having equal force, and hereunto affix their seals.

Done at Washington the sixth day of February in the year of our Lord one thousand nine hundred and twenty-eight.

ROBERT E. OLDS [SEAL]

CLAUDEL   [SEAL]

EXTRACTS FROM THE TEXT OF THE ROOT ARBITRATION TREATY SIGNED WITH FRANCE, FEBRUARY 10, 1908 [1]

[For purposes of reference and more especially for a comparative study of the two texts, the pertinent sections of the Root Arbitration Treaty, of 1908, which the 1928 Treaty replaced, is given below.]

The Government of the United States of America and the Government of the French Republic, signatories of the Convention for the pacific settlement of international disputes, concluded at The Hague on the 29th July, 1899;

Taking into consideration that by Article XIX of that Convention the High Contracting Parties have reserved to themselves the right of concluding Agreements, with a view to referring to arbitration all questions which they shall consider possible to submit to such treatment,

Have authorized the Undersigned to conclude the following arrangement:—

[1] I *Malloy's Treaties*, p. 549.

ARTICLE I

Differences which may arise of a legal nature, or relating to the interpretation of treaties existing between the two Contracting Parties, and which it may not have been possible to settle by diplomacy, shall be referred to the Permanent Court of Arbitration established at The Hague by the Convention of the 29th July, 1899, provided, nevertheless, that they do not affect the vital interests, the independence, or the honor of the two Contracting States, and do not concern the interests of third Parties.

ARTICLE 2

In each individual case the High Contracting Parties, before appealing to the Permanent Court of Arbitration, shall conclude a special Agreement defining clearly the matter in dispute, the scope of the powers of the Arbitrators, and the periods to be fixed for the formation of the Arbitral Tribunal and the several stages of the procedure. It is understood that on the part of the United States such special agreements will be made by the President of the United States, by and with the advice and consent of the Senate, and on the part of France they will be subject to the procedure required by the constitutional laws of France.

APPENDIX IV

THE ALTERNATIVE FRENCH DRAFT TREATY OF APRIL 20, 1928 [1]

Draft of proposed treaty submitted by the Government of France to the Governments of Great Britain, Germany, Italy, Japan, and the United States on April 20, 1928

[*Translation*]

The President of the German Empire, the President of the United States of America, the President of the French Republic, His Majesty the King of England, Ireland and the British Dominions, Emperor of India, His Majesty the King of Italy, His Majesty the Emperor of Japan:

Equally desirous not only of perpetuating the happy relations of peace and friendship now existing among their peoples, but also of avoiding the danger of war between all other nations of the world,

Having agreed to consecrate in a solemn act their most formal and most definite resolution to condemn war as an instrument of national policy and to renounce it in favor of a peaceful settlement of international conflicts,

Expressing, finally, the hope that all the other nations of the world will be willing to join in this humane effort to bring about the association of the civilized peoples in a common renunciation of war as an instrument of national policy, have decided to conclude a treaty and to that end have designated as their respective plenipotentiaries:

The President of the German Empire: ....
The President of the United States of America: ....
The President of the French Republic: ....
His Majesty the King of Great Britain, Ireland and the British Dominions, Emperor of India: ....
His Majesty the King of Italy: ....
His Majesty the Emperor of Japan: ....

Who, after exchanging their full powers found to be in good and due form, have agreed on the following provisions:

[1] *Cf.* above, p. 142.

288

ARTICLE 1

The high contracting parties without any intention to infringe upon the exercise of their rights of legitimate self-defense within the framework of existing treaties, particularly when the violation of certain of the provisions of such treaties constitutes a hostile act, solemnly declare that they condemn recourse to war and renounce it as an instrument of national policy; that is to say, as an instrument of individual, spontaneous and independent political action taken on their own initiative and not action in respect of which they might become involved through the obligation of a treaty such as the Covenant of the League of Nations or any other treaty registered with the League of Nations. They undertake on these conditions not to attack or invade one another.

ARTICLE 2

The settlement or solution of all disputes or conflicts, of whatever nature or origin, which might arise among the high contracting parties or between any two of them, shall never be sought on either side except by pacific methods.

ARTICLE 3

In case one of the high contracting parties should contravene this treaty, the other contracting powers would *ipso facto* be released with respect to that party from their obligations under this treaty.

ARTICLE 4

The provisions of this treaty in no wise affect the rights and obligations of the contracting parties resulting from prior international agreements to which they are parties.

ARTICLE 5

The present treaty will be offered for the accession of all powers and will have no binding force until it has been generally accepted unless the signatory powers in accord with those that may accede hereto shall agree to decide that it shall come into effect regardless of certain abstentions.

ARTICLE 6

The present treaty shall be ratified.

The ratifications shall be deposited at . . . .; within three months from the date of the deposit of the ratifications it shall be communicated by the Government of . . . . to all the powers with an invitation to accede.

The Government of . . . . will transmit to each of the signatory powers and the powers that have acceded a duly certified copy of the instruments of accession as they are received.

One year after the expiration of the three months' period provided in Article 5, the Government of . . . . will send out a statement of the signatories and accessions to all the powers that have signed or acceded.

In witness whereof the above-named plenipotentiaries have signed this treaty and sealed it with their seal.

Done at . . . . in . . . . copies, drawn up in French and English and having equal force.

. . . ., 1928.

APPENDIX V

THE BRITISH NOTE OF MAY 19, 1928

The British Secretary of State for Foreign Affairs (Chamberlain) to the American Ambassador (Houghton)

LONDON, *May 19, 1928.*

YOUR EXCELLENCY: Your note of the 13th April, containing the text of a draft treaty for the renunciation of war, together with copies of correspondence between the United States and French Governments on the subject of this treaty, has been receiving sympathetic consideration at the hands of His Majesty's Government in Great Britain. A note has also been received from the French Government, containing certain suggestions for discussion in connexion with the proposed treaty, and the German Government were good enough to send me a copy of the reply which has been made by them to the proposals of the United States Government.

2. The suggestion for the conclusion of a treaty for the renunciation of war as an instrument of national policy has evoked widespread interest in this country, and His Majesty's Government will support the movement to the utmost of their power.

3. After making a careful study of the text contained in your excellency's note and of the amended text suggested in the French note, His Majesty's Government feel convinced that there is no serious divergence between the effect of these two drafts. This impression is confirmed by a study of the text of the speech by the Secretary of State of the United States to which your excellency drew my attention, and which he delivered before the American Society of International Law on the 28th April. The aim of the United States Government, as I understand it, is to embody in a treaty a broad statement of principle, to proclaim without restriction or qualification that war shall not be used as an instrument of policy. With this aim His Majesty's Government are wholly in accord. The French proposals, equally imbued with the same purpose, have merely added an indication of certain exceptional circumstances in which the violation of that principle by one party may oblige the others to take action seeming at first sight to

291

be inconsistent with the terms of the proposed pact. His Majesty's Government appreciate the scruples which have prompted these suggestions by the French Government. The exact fulfilment of treaty engagements is a matter which affects the national honour; precision as to the scope of such engagements is, therefore, of importance. Each of the suggestions made by the French Government has been carefully considered from this point of view.

4. After studying the wording of Article 1 of the United States draft, His Majesty's Government do not think that its terms exclude action which a state may be forced to take in self-defense. Mr. Kellogg has made it clear in the speech to which I have referred above that he regards the right of self-defence as inalienable, and His Majesty's Government are disposed to think that on this question no addition to the text is necessary.

5. As regards the text of Article 2 no appreciable difference is found between the American and French proposals. His Majesty's Government are, therefore, content to accept the former if, as they understand to be the case, a dispute "among the high contracting parties" is a phrase wide enough to cover a dispute between any two of them.

6. The French note suggests the addition of an article providing that violation of the treaty by one of the parties should release the remainder from their obligations under the treaty towards that party. His Majesty's Government are not satisfied that, if the treaty stood alone, the addition of some such provision would not be necessary. Mr. Kellogg's speech, however, shows that he put forward for acceptance the text of the proposed treaty upon the understanding that violation of the undertaking by one party would free the remaining parties from the obligation to observe its terms in respect of the treaty-breaking state.

7. If it is agreed that this is the principle which will apply in the case of this particular treaty, His Majesty's Government are satisfied and will not ask for the insertion of any amendment. Means can no doubt be found without difficulty of placing this understanding on record in some appropriate manner so that it may have equal value with the terms of the treaty itself.

8. The point is one of importance because of its bearing on the treaty engagements by which His Majesty's Government are already bound. The preservation of peace has been the chief concern of His Majesty's Government and the prime object of all their endeavours.

It is the reason why they have given ungrudging support to the League of Nations and why they have undertaken the burden of the guarantee embodied in the Locarno treaty. The sole object of all these engagements is the elimination of war as an instrument of national policy, just as it is the purpose of the peace pact now proposed. It is because the object of both is the same that there is no real antagonism between the treaty engagements which His Majesty's Government have already accepted and the pact which is now proposed. The machinery of the covenant and of the treaty of Locarno, however, go somewhat further than a renunciation of war as a policy, in that they provide certain sanctions for a breach of their obligations. A clash might thus conceivably arise between the existing treaties and the proposed pact unless it is understood that the obligations of the new engagement will cease to operate in respect of a party which breaks its pledges and adopts hostile measures against one of its co-contractants.

9. For the Government of this country respect for the obligations arising out of the Covenant of the League of Nations and out of the Locarno treaties is fundamental. Our position in this regard is identical with that of the German Government as indicated in their note of the 27th April. His Majesty's Government could not agree to any new treaty which would weaken or undermine these engagements on which the peace of Europe rests. Indeed, public interest in this country in the scrupulous fulfilment of these engagements is so great that His Majesty's Government would for their part prefer to see some such provision as Article 4 of the French draft embodied in the text of the treaty. To this we understand there will be no objection. Mr. Kellogg has made it clear in the speech to which I have drawn attention that he had no intention by the terms of the new treaty of preventing the parties to the Covenant of the League or to the Locarno treaty from fulfilling their obligations.

10. The language of Article 1, as to the renunciation of war as an instrument of national policy, renders it desirable that I should remind your excellency that there are certain regions of the world the welfare and integrity of which constitute a special and vital interest for our peace and safety. His Majesty's Government have been at pains to make it clear in the past that interference with these regions cannot be suffered. Their protection against attack is to the British Empire a measure of self-defence. It must be clearly understood that His Majesty's Government in Great Britain accept the new treaty upon the distinct understanding that it does not prejudice their freedom of

action in this respect. The Government of the United States have comparable interests any disregard of which by a foreign power they have declared that they would regard as an unfriendly act. His Majesty's Government believe, therefore, that in defining their position they are expressing the intention and meaning of the United States Government.

11. As regards the measure of participation in the new treaty before it would come into force, His Majesty's Government agree that it is not necessary to wait until all the nations of the world have signified their willingness to become parties. On the other hand, it would be embarrassing if certain States in Europe with whom the proposed participants are already in close treaty relations were not included among the parties. His Majesty's Government see no reason, however, to doubt that these states will gladly accept its terms. Universality would, in any case, be difficult of attainment, and might even be inconvenient, for there are some states whose governments have not yet been universally recognized, and some which are scarcely in a position to ensure the maintenance of good order and security within their territories. The conditions for the inclusion of such states among the parties to the new treaty is a question to which further attention may perhaps be devoted with advantage. It is, however, a minor question as compared with the attainment of the more important purpose in view.

12. After this examination of the terms of the proposed treaty and of the points to which it gives rise, your excellency will realise that His Majesty's Government find nothing in their existing commitments which prevents their hearty cooperation in this movement for strengthening the foundations of peace. They will gladly cooperate in the conclusion of such a pact as is proposed and are ready to engage with the interested Governments in the negotiations which are necessary for the purpose.

13. Your excellency will observe that the detailed arguments in the foregoing paragraphs are expressed on behalf of His Majesty's Government in Great Britain. It will, however, be appreciated that the proposed treaty, from its very nature, is not one which concerns His Majesty's Government in Great Britain alone, but is one in which they could not undertake to participate otherwise than jointly and simultaneously with His Majesty's Governments in the Dominions and the Government of India. They have, therefore, been in communication with those Governments, and I am happy to be able to inform

your excellency that as a result of the communications which have passed it has been ascertained that they are all in cordial agreement with the general principle of the proposed treaty. I feel confident, therefore, that on receipt of an invitation to participate in the conclusion of such a treaty, they, no less than His Majesty's Government in Great Britain, will be prepared to accept the invitation.

I have [etc.]

AUSTEN CHAMBERLAIN

APPENDIX VI

MR. KELLOGG'S NOTE OF JUNE 23, 1928

Note of the Government of the United States to the Governments of Australia, Belgium, Canada, Czechoslovakia, France, Germany, Great Britain, India, Irish Free State, Italy, Japan, New Zealand, Poland, and South Africa, June 23, 1928

It will be recalled that, pursuant to the understanding reached between the Government of France and the Government of the United States, the American Ambassadors at London, Berlin, Rome and Tokyo transmitted on April 13, 1928, to the Governments to which they were respectively accredited the text of M. Briand's original proposal of June 20, 1927, together with copies of the notes subsequently exchanged by France and the United States on the subject of a multilateral treaty for the renunciation of war. At the same time the Government of the United States also submitted for consideration a preliminary draft of a treaty representing in a general way the form of treaty which it was prepared to sign, and inquired whether the Governments thus addressed were in a position to give favorable consideration thereto. The text of the identic notes of April 13, 1928, and a copy of the draft treaty transmitted therewith, were also brought to the attention of the Government of France by the American Ambassador at Paris.

It will likewise be recalled that on April 20, 1928, the Government of the French Republic circulated among the other interested governments, including the Government of the United States, an alternative draft treaty, and that in an address which he delivered on April 28, 1928, before the American Society of International Law, the Secretary of State of the United States explained fully the construction placed by my Government upon the treaty proposed by it, referring as follows to the six major considerations emphasized by France in its alternative draft treaty and prior diplomatic correspondence with my Government:

(*1*) *Self-defense.* There is nothing in the American draft of an antiwar treaty which restricts or impairs in any way the right of self-defense. That right is inherent in every sovereign state and is implicit in every treaty. Every nation is free at all times and regardless of treaty provisions to defend its territory from attack or invasion and it alone is competent to decide whether circumstances require recourse to war in self-defense. If it has a good case, the world will applaud and not condemn its action. Express recognition by treaty of this inalienable right, however, gives rise to the same difficulty encountered in any effort to define aggression. It is the identical question approached from the other side. Inasmuch as no treaty provision can add to the natural right of self-defense, it is not in the interest of peace that a treaty should stipulate a juristic conception of self-defense since it is far too easy for the unscrupulous to mold events to accord with an agreed definition.

(*2*) *The League Covenant.* The Covenant imposes no affirmative primary obligation to go to war. The obligation, if any, is secondary and attaches only when deliberately accepted by a state. Article 10 of the Covenant has, for example, been interpreted by a resolution submitted to the Fourth Assembly but not formally adopted owing to one adverse vote to mean that "it is for the constitutional authorities of each member to decide, in reference to the obligation of preserving the independence and the integrity of the territory of members, in what degree the member is bound to assure the execution of this obligation by employment of its military forces." There is, in my opinion, no necessary inconsistency between the Covenant and the idea of an unqualified renunciation of war. The Covenant can, it is true, be construed as authorizing war in certain circumstances but it is an authorization and not a positive requirement.

(*3*) *The treaties of Locarno.* If the parties to the treaties of Locarno are under any positive obligation to go to war, such obligation certainly would not attach until one of the parties "has resorted to war in violation of its solemn pledges thereunder." It is therefore obvious that if all the parties to the Locarno treaties become parties to the multilateral antiwar treaty proposed by the United States, there would be a double assurance that the Locarno treaties would not be violated by recourse to arms. In such event it would follow that resort to war by any state in violation of the Locarno treaties would also be a breach of the multilateral antiwar treaty and the other parties to the antiwar treaty would thus as a matter of law be automatically released from their obligations thereunder and free to fulfil their Locarno commitments. The United States is entirely willing that all parties to the Locarno treaties should become parties to its proposed antiwar treaty either through signature in the first instance or by immediate accession to the treaty as soon as it comes into force in the manner provided in Article 3 of the American draft, and it will offer no objection when and if such a suggestion is made.

(*4*) *Treaties of neutrality.* The United States is not informed as to the precise treaties which France has in mind and cannot therefore discuss their provisions. It is not unreasonable to suppose, however, that the relations between France and the states whose neutrality she has guaranteed are sufficiently close and intimate to make it possible for France to persuade such states to adhere seasonably to the antiwar treaty proposed by the United States. If this were done no party to the antiwar treaty could attack the neutralized states without violating the treaty and thereby automatically freeing France and the other powers in respect of the treaty-breaking state from the obligations of the antiwar treaty. If the neutralized states were attacked by a state not a party to the antiwar treaty, the latter treaty would of course have no bearing and France would be as free to act under the treaties guaranteeing neutrality as if she were not a party to the antiwar treaty. It is difficult to perceive, therefore, how treaties guaranteeing neutrality can be regarded as necessarily preventing the conclusion by France or any other power of a multilateral treaty for the renunciation of war.

(5) *Relations with a treaty-breaking state.* As I have already pointed out, there can be no question as a matter of law that violation of a multilateral antiwar treaty through resort to war by one party thereto would automatically release the other parties from their obligations to the treaty-breaking state. Any express recognition of this principle of law is wholly unnecessary.

(6) *Universality.* From the beginning it has been the hope of the United States that its proposed multilateral antiwar treaty should be world-wide in its application, and appropriate provision therefor was made in the draft submitted to the other governments on April 13. From a practical standpoint it is clearly preferable, however, not to postpone the coming into force of an antiwar treaty until all the nations of the world can agree upon the text of such a treaty and cause it to be ratified. For one reason or another a state so situated as to be no menace to the peace of the world might obstruct agreement or delay ratification in such manner as to render abortive the efforts of all the other powers. It is highly improbable, moreover, that a form of treaty acceptable to the British, French, German, Italian and Japanese Governments, as well as to the United States, would not be equally acceptable to most, if not all, of the other powers of the world. Even were this not the case, however, the coming into force among the above-named six powers of an effective antiwar treaty and their observance thereof would be a practical guaranty against a second world war. This in itself would be a tremendous service to humanity and the United States is not willing to jeopardize the practical success of the proposal which it has made by conditioning the coming into force of the treaty upon prior universal or almost universal acceptance.

The British, German, Italian and Japanese Governments have now replied to my Government's notes of April 13, 1928, and the Governments of the British Dominions and of India have likewise replied to the invitations addressed to them on May 22, 1928, by my Government pursuant to the suggestion conveyed in the note of May 19, 1928, from His Majesty's Government in Great Britain. None of these Governments has expressed any dissent from the above-quoted construction, and none has voiced the least disapproval of the principle underlying the proposal of the United States for the promotion of world peace. Neither has any of the replies received by the Government of the United States suggested any specific modification of the text of the draft treaty proposed by it on April 13, 1928, and my Government, for its part, remains convinced that no modification of the text of its proposal for a multilateral treaty for the renunciation of war is necessary to safeguard the legitimate interests of any nation. It believes that the right of self-defense is inherent in every sovereign state and implicit in every treaty. No specific reference to that inalienable attribute of sovereignty is therefore necessary or desirable. It is no less evident that resort to war in violation of the proposed treaty by one of the parties thereto would release the other parties from their obligations under the treaty towards the belligerent state. This principle is well recognized. So far as the Locarno treaties are concerned, my Government has felt from the very first that participation in the antiwar treaty by the powers which signed the Locarno agreements, either through signature in the first instance or thereafter, would meet every practical requirement of the situation, since in such event no state could resort to war in violation of the Locarno treaties without simultaneously violating the antiwar treaty, thus leaving the other parties thereto free, so far as the treaty-breaking state is concerned. As your excellency knows, the Government of the United States has welcomed the idea that all parties to the treaties of Locarno should be among the original signatories of the proposed treaty for the renunciation of war and provision therefore has been made in the draft treaty which I have the honor to transmit herewith. The same procedure would cover the treaties guaranteeing neutrality to which the Government of France has referred. Adherence to the proposed treaty by all parties to these other treaties would completely safeguard their rights since subsequent resort to war by any of them or by any party to the antiwar treaty would violate the latter treaty as well as the neutrality treaty, and thus leave the other parties to the antiwar treaty free, so far as the treaty-breaking state is concerned. My Government would be entirely willing, however, to agree that the parties to such neutrality treaties should be original signatories of the multilateral antiwar treaty, and it has no reason to believe that such an arrangement would meet with any objection on the part of the other Governments now concerned in the present negotiations.

While my Government is satisfied that the draft treaty proposed by it on April 13, 1928, could be properly accepted by the powers of the world without change except for including among the original signatories the British Dominions, India, all parties to the treaties of Locarno and, it may be, all parties to the neutrality treaties mentioned by the Government of France, it has no desire to delay or complicate the present negotiations by rigidly adhering to the precise phraseology of that draft, particularly since it appears that by modifying the draft in form though not in substance, the points raised by other Governments can be satisfactorily met and general agreement upon the text of the treaty to be signed be promptly reached. The Government of the United States has therefore decided to submit to the fourteen other Governments now concerned in these negotiations a revised draft of a multilateral treaty for the renunciation of war. The text of this revised draft is identical with that of the draft proposed by the United States on April 13, 1928, except that the preamble now provides that the British Dominions, India, and all parties to the treaties of Locarno are to be included among the powers called upon to sign the treaty in the first instance, and except that the first three paragraphs of the preamble have been changed to read as follows:

Deeply sensible of their solemn duty to promote the welfare of mankind;
Persuaded that the time has come when a frank renunciation of war as an instrument of national policy should be made to the end that the peaceful and friendly relations now existing between their peoples may be perpetuated;
Convinced that all changes in their relations with one another should be sought only by pacific means and be the result of a peaceful and orderly process, and that any signatory power which shall hereafter seek to promote its national interests by resort to war should be denied the benefits furnished by this treaty;

The revised preamble thus gives express recognition to the principle that if a state resorts to war in violation of the treaty, the other contracting parties are released from their obligations under the treaty to that state; it also provides for participation in the treaty by all parties to the treaties of Locarno, thus making it certain that resort to war in violation of the Locarno treaties would also violate the present treaty and release not only the other signatories of the Locarno treaties

but also the other signatories to the antiwar treaty from their obligations to the treaty-breaking state. Moreover, as stated above, my Government would be willing to have included among the original signatories the parties to the neutrality treaties referred to by the Government of the French Republic, although it believes that the interests of
those states would be adequately safeguarded if, instead of signing in
the first instance, they should choose to adhere to the treaty.

In these circumstances I have the honor to transmit herewith for the
consideration of your excellency's Government a draft of a multilateral treaty for the renunciation of war containing the changes out-
lined above. I have been instructed to state in this connection that the
Government of the United States is ready to sign at once a treaty in
the form herein proposed, and to express the fervent hope that the
Government of . . . . will be able promptly to indicate its
readiness to accept, without qualification or reservation, the form of
treaty now suggested by the United States. If the Governments of
Australia, Belgium, Canada, Czechoslovakia, France, Germany, Great
Britain, India, the Irish Free State, Italy, Japan, New Zealand,
Poland, South Africa and the United States can now agree to conclude
this antiwar treaty among themselves, my Government is confident
that the other nations of the world will, as soon as the treaty comes
into force, gladly adhere thereto, and that this simple procedure will
bring mankind's age-long aspirations for universal peace nearer to
practical fulfilment than ever before in the history of the world.

I have the honor to state in conclusion that the Government of the
United States would be pleased to be informed at as early a date as
may be convenient whether your excellency's Government is willing
to join with the United States and other similarly disposed Governments in signing a definitive treaty for the renunciation of war in the
form transmitted herewith.

[Enclosure]

Text of draft treaty [1]

The President of the United States of America, the President of the
French Republic, His Majesty the King of the Belgians, the President of
the Czechoslovak Republic, His Majesty the King of Great Britain, Ireland and the British Dominions beyond the Seas, Emperor of India, the
President of the German Reich, His Majesty the King of Italy, His Majesty the Emperor of Japan, the President of the Republic of Poland;

[1] As this text was accepted by the other Powers, it is the final text of the Pact
of Paris.

Deeply sensible of their solemn duty to promote the welfare of mankind;

Persuaded that the time has come when a frank renunciation of war as an instrument of national policy should be made to the end that the peaceful and friendly relations now existing between their peoples may be perpetuated;

Convinced that all changes in their relations with one another should be sought only by pacific means and be the result of a peaceful and orderly process, and that any signatory power which shall hereafter seek to promote its national interests by resort to war should be denied the benefits furnished by this treaty;

Hopeful that, encouraged by their example, all the other nations of the world will join in this humane endeavor and by adhering to the present treaty as soon as it comes into force bring their peoples within the scope of its beneficent provisions, thus uniting the civilized nations of the world in a common renunciation of war as an instrument of their national policy;

Have decided to conclude a treaty and for that purpose have appointed as their respective plenipotentiaries:

The President of the United States of America:.....................

The President of the French Republic:...........................

His Majesty the King of the Belgians:............................

The President of the Czechoslovak Republic:......................

His Majesty the King of Great Britain, Ireland and the British Dominions beyond the Seas, Emperor of India:

For Great Britain and Northern Ireland and all parts of the British Empire which are not separate members of the League of Nations:........

For the Dominion of Canada:..................................

For the Commonwealth of Australia:............................

For the Dominion of New Zealand:.............................

For the Union of South Africa:................................

For the Irish Free State:......................................

For India:...

The President of the German Reich:.............................

His Majesty the King of Italy:.................................

His Majesty the Emperor of Japan:.............................

The President of the Republic of Poland:........................

Who, having communicated to one another their full powers found in good and due form have agreed upon the following articles:

ARTICLE I

The high contracting parties solemnly declare in the names of their respective peoples that they condemn recourse to war for the solution of international controversies, and renounce it as an instrument of national policy in their relations with one another.

ARTICLE 2

The high contracting parties agree that the settlement or solution of all disputes or conflicts of whatever nature or of whatever origin they may be, which may arise among them, shall never be sought except by pacific means.

ARTICLE 3

The present treaty shall be ratified by the high contracting parties named in the preamble in accordance with their respective constitutional requirements, and shall take effect as between them as soon as all their several instruments of ratification shall have been deposited at . . . .

This treaty shall, when it has come into effect as prescribed in the preceding paragraph, remain open as long as may be necessary for adherence by all the other powers of the world. Every instrument evidencing the adherence of a power shall be deposited at . . . . and the treaty shall immediately upon such deposit become effective as between the power thus adhering and the other powers parties hereto.

It shall be the duty of the Government of . . . . to furnish each Government named in the preamble and every Government subsequently adhering to this treaty with a certified copy of the treaty and of every instrument of ratification or adherence. It shall also be the duty of the Government of . . . . telegraphically to notify such Governments immediately upon the deposit with it of each instrument of ratification or adherence.

In faith whereof the respective plenipotentiaries have signed this treaty in the French and English languages, both texts having equal force, and hereunto affix their seals.

Done at . . . . the . . . . day of . . . . in the year of our Lord one thousand nine hundred and twenty . . . .

INDEX

Aggression, definition of, 58, 97, 99, 132, 138-140, 209, 212, 213, 216, 225
American Committee, 225
American Foundation, 53
American-Japanese relations, 240
"American Locarno," 68, 120
American Society of International Law, 157, 291, 296
Anglo-French Society, 161
Arbitration, 52, 99, 120, 123, 124, 126, 127, 137, 236, 255; *see also* Treaties
Aristotle, 20, 28
Arms, export of, 101, 223
Arsenals, 223
Artisans' charters, 12
Associated Press, 41, 180
Australia, 56, 170, 296
Australasia, 242

Baldwin, Stanley, 48
Beatty, Lord, 233
Belgium, 18, 56, 296
Bethlehem Steel Works, 223
Bethmann Hollweg, 214
Bismarck, 159, 210
Blockade, 230, 232, 236
Borah, Senator W. E., 140, 191, 209, 218; Resolution in Congress *December 12, 1927* on outlawry of war, 93 *sqq.;* first public explanation, *February 5, 1928,* 136, 158; interview New York *Times, March 25, 1928,* 224
Briand, Aristide, *see* Pact of Paris
British Labor Party, suggestion of Anglo-American treaty outlawing war, 97
British Monroe Doctrine, 193, 200 *sqq.,* 213
Bryce, Lord, 73
Bulgaria, 211
Burton, Congressman Theodore E., Resolution, 62, 93, 101, 223
Butler, Nicholas Murray, Letter to New York *Times, April 25, 1927,* 42, 44, 54, 104; comment on Draft Treaty of Permanent Peace, 60; in support of Capper Resolution, 116

Caesars, the, 19, 37
Canada, 56, 161, 170, 296
Capper, Senator Arthur, Resolution in the Senate, *December 8, 1927,* 62, 93 *sqq.,* 116, 209, 212, 280; comment on the Resolution, 96
Carlyle's essay on Voltaire, 23
Carnegie Endowment for International Peace, 34
Cecil, Lord, 97, 164
Chamberlain, Sir Austen, 90, 143, 161-164, 169, 200, 204, 217
Chamberlain, Professor J. P., *see* Draft Treaty of Permanent Peace
Chamberlain, Joseph, 162
Chemical warfare, 37
Chile, 27
China, export of arms to, 101; British interests, 161, 201; problem of Manchuria, 249
Choate, William, 229
Church Fathers, 19
Citizenship, right of nation to determine its own, 61
Clark, Professor John Bates, 33
Claudel, M., 113, 122, 140
Clausewitz, 131
Commerce, beginnings of, 13; an exchange of necessities, 27; predatory conception, 30
Committee on Foreign Relations, United States Senate, 93, 97, 101, 108, 116, 124, 125, 136
Community of nations, 5, 27, 80
Conciliation, 99, 120, 122, 126, 127, 137, 255, 274
Condé, 178
Conference as a substitute for war, 64, 255, 260, 266
Conference of experts on treaty, suggested, 152, 153, 156, 248
Conference of London, *1908,* 231
Conference of Paris, *1856,* 229
Congress, power to declare war, 77, 279; Resolution, *1888-1890,* calling for arbitration in the settlement of disputes with all other countries, 124; Resolution, *April 28, 1904,* ex-